VINCENT VAN GOGH:
A LIFE

VINCENT VAN GOGH: A LIFE

Philip Callow

ALLISON & BUSBY

An Allison & Busby book
Published in 1991 by
W. H. Allen & Co. Plc
26 Grand Union Centre
338 Ladbroke Grove
London W10 5AH

Copyright © 1990 by Philip Callow

Phototypeset by Input Typesetting Ltd., London

Printed in Great Britain by
Butler & Tanner Ltd, Frome and London

ISBN 0 74900 021 X

To Jim Morgan

From childhood's hour I have not been
As others were; I have not seen
As others saw; I could not bring
My passions from a common spring.
From the same source I have not taken
My sorrow; I could not awaken
My heart to joy in the same tone;
And all I loved, I loved alone.

Edgar Allan Poe

Ethos anthropou daimon (A man's character is his fate)

Heraclitus

How am I to tell you half of what these paintings
said to me? . . . Here suddenly I was in front of
something, a mere glimpse of which had previously,
in my state of torpor, been too much for me. I
had been haunted by that glimpse. Now a total
stranger was offering me – with incredible
authority – a reply – an entire world in the form of
a reply.

Hugo von Hoffmannsthal

CONTENTS

ACKNOWLEDGEMENTS

Youthful enthusiasm first plunged me into the world of van Gogh, when I came on a selection of letters entitled *Dear Theo*, and was astonished by the words of a man who seemed to withhold nothing and who spoke so entrancingly from the heart. An understanding of his work came much later, and is still far from complete. Two fairly recent van Gogh studies, by Albert J Lubin and A M and Renilde Hammacher, have provided much illumination. I am indebted to them for this, and for being instrumental in convincing me that the biography I had had in mind for so long was possible, and that there was a need for it.

Grateful acknowledgement is also made for the use of an excerpt from 'The Trap' by Isaac Bashevis Singer, a short story in his collection *The Death of Methuselah*, published by Jonathan Cape.

LIST OF ILLUSTRATIONS

The author and publisher gratefully acknowledge permission to reproduce these illustrations, by courtesy of the Vincent van Gogh Foundation/National Museum Vincent van Gogh, Amsterdam.

CHRONOLOGY

1853	Zundert	30 March: Birth of Vincent in the parsonage at Groot Zundert in North Brabant, the eldest child of Reverend Theodorus van Gogh and Anna Carbentus van Gogh.
1857		1 May: Birth of Theo.
1869	The Hague	Starts apprenticeship at Goupil & Co.
1872		August: Correspondence with Theo begins.
1873	London	June: Transferred to local branch of Goupil & Co. Rejected by Eugenia Loyer.
1874	Paris	October: Sent to Goupil & Co's main office.
1875	London/Paris	January: Returns to London branch. May: Sent once more to Paris office. Turns to religion.
1876	England	April: Dismissed by the firm. Returns to Ramsgate as assistant teacher. June: Assistant teacher and curate at Isleworth. Delivers sermon at Richmond. December: Leaves to visit Holland and remains there.
1877	Dordrecht/ Amsterdam	Takes job as clerk in bookshop. May: Studies for university entrance examination.
1878	Etten/Brussels	July: Gives up studies and enters missionary school. Leaves after three months.
1879	The Borinage	January: Evangelist in coalfields. Dismissed in July.
1880	Brussels	September: Finds vocation, goes to Royal Academy of Fine Arts. Meets van Rappard.
1881	Etten	April: Returns to live with parents. In love with his cousin, Kee Vos, and rejected by her. December: leaves parsonage after argument with father.

1882	The Hague	Studies with Mauve and falls out with him. Lives with Sien. June: Enters hospital. Sien's child born.
1883	Drenthe	Parts from Sien and roams moorland regions in north-east. December: Rejoins his parents at Nuenen.
1884	Nuenen	July/August: Relationship with Margot Begemann. Tutors three students. Reaches agreement on collaboration with Theo.
1885		27 March: Death of his father. April/May: Paints *The Potato Eaters*.
1886	Antwerp	January: Enters the Academy of Art.
	Paris	February: Leaves for Paris and moves in with Theo. Joins the Atelier Cormon. Associates with Lautrec, Pissarro, Signac, Degas, Seurat, Bernard, and Gauguin.
1888	Arles	20 February: Leaves for Provence. September: Moves into Yellow House. October: Gauguin joins him. December: Theo announces engagement to Johanna Bonger. 23 December: Mental collapse. Gauguin leaves on 27th. Two weeks in hospital.
1889		7 January: Returns to Yellow House. 9 February: Returns to hospital after second collapse. Stays till April. 17 April: Theo marries.
	Saint-Rémy	8 May: Admitted to the asylum. Periods of lucidity between two violent attacks.
1890		January: Article by Albert Aurier in praise of Vincent's work. March: Sells *The Red Vineyard*.
	Paris	17 May: Visits Theo and meets Johanna. Stays three days.
	Auvers	21 May: Meets Dr Gachet. 1 July: Visits Theo and Lautrec in Paris. 27 July: Shoots himself, dies on the 29th. 30 July: Buried in cemetery at Auvers.
1891		25 January: Theo dies.

FOREWORD

We call him Vincent because he wished it, and because in millions
of homes his painted sunflowers befriend us, clumsy and yet
regal, bold-breasted and full of seeds. In the scene in which he is
depicted dying he is a modern saint. No mess, no agony, no
death rattle. He smokes a last pipe and talks gently. Theo, his
brother and spiritual twin, attends him. This beatific picture
perfectly encapsulates the myth of van Gogh – great, sad, humble,
and defeated – with which we are now familiar. Indeed, so
immediate is it that we no longer remember where we read it,
or whether it has been passed on by word of mouth. Or is it
perhaps a dream in which we have all participated.

Heinrich Heine's definition of Romanticism as 'a red rose
sprung from the blood of Christ' conjures up at once a van Gogh
who was at the same time a Christ-lover and Christ-identifier, as
well as a lifelong admirer of Monticelli, the Romantic painter
whose fate he imagined as very like his own. But it is his
Expressionistic fervour which has helped to inspire the popular
image of that virile heart-sore savage presented by Irving Stone
in his famous novel, who moves through life to his death so
energetically and vividly, in a rush of breathless scenes. Like a
movie this kaleidoscopic whirl of scenes never rests, and the
writing between the lusty pouring of lives is left out. For all the
fierce ranting passion, somehow we remain skin-deep.

Why is this? Sentimentality is hard to define. Applied to people,
it could be said negatively to involve the sheering away of a whole
dimension, namely the psyche, so that what is left is not a real

human being but a simulacrum, substituted as a preferred ideal. In the case of van Gogh, an acceptably healthy 'lust for life' tends to shove into near oblivion the darker evidence of a growing craving for death. This frontal approach achieves little, genuine though the intention may be. A very different portrait emerges as soon as the viewpoint shifts and recognition becomes oblique rather than full face.

Many factors must have contributed to Vincent's wish to die. His suicide, seen as the last word in a story of immense pathos, could be regarded from one standpoint as a goal triumphantly reached, after the paroxysms of mad activity convulsing his Arles years. Certainly he was fully aware that, as he himself puts it, 'killing oneself turns one's friends into murderers.' Yet it must have been there as a temptation he found increasingly hard to resist. It is as though each act of painting is a consummation which flings him forward on to the next and then the next work, yet always denying him that vertical movement from the earth into the heavens that his most explosive pictures seem to promise, bursting up into the blue. Out of the strange brutality of this struggle come the love and sorrow of a man wistfully contemplating his own extinction. Finally, one day at Auvers, his chained spirit makes its escape. The perplexing nature of his actual death is left to trouble us with its unanswered questions.

VINCENT VAN GOGH:
A LIFE

1

THE FLAT OF THE LAND

Despite everything, something in us always wants to go back. An old desire rises up and convinces us, against all the odds, that our birthplace matters. The most unpromising countryside becomes eternal. 'During my illness I saw again every room in the house at Zundert, every plant in the garden, the views of the fields outside, the neighbours, the graveyard, the church, our kitchen garden at the back – as far as the magpie's nest in a tall acacia in the graveyard.'[1] In a letter from Isleworth, full of the homesick hankering after past Christmases of a young man of twenty-three, we read: 'How beautiful Bois-le-Duc looked, the market square and the streets covered with snow and the dark houses with snow on the roofs. Brabant is ever Brabant, and one's native country is ever one's native country.'[2]

Without some appreciation of van Gogh's background and his land at the time of his birth, the man is well nigh incomprehensible to us. What was the weather like, the terrain, how did Dutch people live, and what moulded their temperaments? The national image of a dour, docile people comes across as a joke, almost a cliché of stolidity in Dutch literature. Yet the strong sense of realism prevalent in this bit of Europe yielded up something quite magical and extraordinary. It was in Flanders after all that the method of painting with the oil medium was discovered and then exploited. Indeed, the very words 'landscape' and 'still-life' have entered the English language from the Dutch. As a modern historian tells us, 'they were substantially Dutch inventions, just as

1

genre painting is associated in most people's minds with the Netherlands.'[3]

Like so many Dutchmen, van Gogh was a hard worker, self-critical, and taciturn. Attention directed at himself was disliked. A quiet pride in his country was contradicted by a strain of stubborn independence and a liking for seclusion. The geographical vulnerability of the Netherlands has meant that perseverance and cooperative effort, essential for national survival, have been valued above personal achievement. Self-glorification in a country where maintaining the land came first was distasteful, and so was demonstrative and frivolous behaviour. Van Gogh embodied all these traits and prejudices. Growing up, he found them endorsed by the religion of his father and grandfather, a faith he gladly accepted. It was only when he broke with his father and became an artist that he said of his fellow countrymen: 'they have something gloomy, dull, stale, so much so that it makes me sick'.[4]

What must Holland (literally Hollow Land) have been like in the mid nineteenth century for a growing, physically robust, impressionable boy who was often left to his own devices? A glance at the map shows a tiny country, about the size of Wales, and more sea-dominated then than now, its coast fretted with waterways leading to lakes and marshes. People kept watch on the rising tides, always a menace. The Netherlands, consisting mainly of a delta formed by the flowing of the Rhine, the Maas, and the Schelde into the North Sea, was more or less a drained swamp, largely man-made, its system of dykes, canals, locks, polders, and reservoirs as complicated as were the local regulations governing daily life. Around Amsterdam and the Zuider Zee (a huge tongue of water now converted to 'polderland') the landscape had a liquid quality. Rain falling every other day and the large amount of water lying everywhere meant that the mornings emerged out of the ground rather than the sky. The atmosphere was humid. Light came off the sea, hard and cold, whereas meres and rivers helped to create a relaxed, patient, if stolid character. Fortitude was combined with tolerance. The Dutch have a saying: 'The making of Holland is never ended.'

The United Provinces of the Netherlands – which had arisen out of the War of the Spanish Succession, concluded with the Treaty of Utrecht – was a state as paradoxical as the Dutch character. 'It was a Republic,' our historian informs us, 'but contained one family of princes who took their name from the South of France (Orange) and married into the royal House of Stuart. Its society included brokers who frequented the Exchange in Amsterdam and sailors and adventurers who travelled to the ends of the earth. It produced freebooters who preyed on enemy shipping, and it cultivated the domestic virtues – sometimes in the same person. There is something characteristic in the career of Klaas Compaan, 'the terror of the sea', who ended his days living peacefully with his wife in their small brick house in Oostzan. It officially recognised only Calvinist worship, but in practice it indulged Catholics, Jews, and a variety of sectaries. Its rulers were relatively tolerant and liberal, but based their enlightenment on no general principles.'[5]

England's proximity to Holland made for obvious links, but many factors were contributing to the growing importance of this country with a population no more than twice that of London. To say that Dutch greatness was founded on water sounds strange, until one remembers that their fleets of merchantmen and men-of-war sailed in all the oceans. Navigational charts were generally Dutch. Dutch place-names, the legacies of their sailors, are scattered throughout the world.

And England is connected with Holland geologically, joined by the water of the North Sea. The Fens, inland from the Wash, are eastern England's Netherlands. People living on this great plain of fertile and featureless peat, carved up in grids by drains and artificial rivers, have been preoccupied in just the same way for centuries by the ceaseless battle against flooding. Go in any direction and you seem to wallow, get nowhere. The horizon mocks. An unbroken monotony creates a sailor's eye. Van Gogh's ancestors were a water people, and so are the natives of these Fens. Myths tagged to them are not pleasant: inbreeding, violence, drowning; in fact all the fatalism that seems sucked up out of waterlogged soil.

The Dutch came to the Fens, says novelist Graham Swift; they were hired first by King Charles and then by the Earl of Bedford. One of their most illustrious engineers, Cornelius Vermyden, arrived to oversee the cutting of drains, lodes, dykes, eas, and ditches, and the building of sluices and bridges. 'Practical and forward-looking people, the Dutch.'[6]

'And perhaps,' says Swift, speculating imaginatively, 'the Fen people became amphibians. . . . Every Fenman suffers now and then the illusion that the land he walks over is *not there*, is floating.'[7]

As well as their expertise, no doubt the Dutch brought their pumps, the black-sailed windmills, until there were 700 of them whirring away day and night on the rain-swept land sunk below water-level between Lincoln and Cambridge. An environmental determinism held sway. Glueing you to flatness it generated duty, even a kind of humour: the black laughter of need and fixity. This scouring and pumping and embanking made people into watchdogs. And so with the Dutch.

In the early nineteenth century, John Clare, son of a thresher, wrote his curiously intent, pure verses – and went mad – on the edge of the Fens. To the north-east, out of sight, Boston stump broke the skyline of the flooded wind-swept land. When the sun did come, and the spring, it was lovely and magical. From it came the hand-clapping delight of Clare's happiest poems. Mainly though the weather was fitful:

> The fitful weather changes every hour
> And many a footstep hurries from the shower
> The men at plough the shepherd on the lea
> Look up and scamper to the nearest tree. . . .

Drainage and 'improvement' brought the affliction of isolation to his native parish, always endemic but made worse by the remorseless levelling:

> The dreary fen a waste of water goes
> With nothing to be seen but royston crows
> The traveller journeying on the road for hours
> Sees nothing but the dyke and water flowers . . .

Closer to the home of the van Goghs, Emile Verhaeren, a Belgian poet born two years after Vincent in 1855, fifteen miles from Antwerp, grew up in a similar water-dominated world. He was a child of the Schelde; the approaches to the North Sea were his consecration. It is probable that the Verhaerens were of Dutch origin. Verhaeren himself has been described as the poet of internal energy, of the struggle against oneself. Reflections in water,

4

especially the stagnant water of meres and marshes, are an obsession throughout his writings. The images of mud, damp, melancholia, and empty spaces cast a spell. At any moment, one feels, this denial of any tonic or elevation, this awful flat reality, could turn into a place where intimate secrets are laid bare:

> Villages and hamlets moan in the north wind;
> The damp blights the walls with green patches . . .
> The snow falls and lies, and heavily puts to sleep
> Black hovels humping their inert backs side by side.[8]

The Reverend Theodorus van Gogh and his wife Anna Cornelia, married in 1851, and had their first child, Vincent, in 1852. This was not our Vincent, however. The first Vincent died at birth. A year later to the day, the still-grieving mother was delivered of Vincent Willem. Following him came Anna in 1855, Theo in 1857, Elizabeth in 1859, Wilhelmina in 1862, and finally Cornelius in 1867.

Pastor van Gogh had been called to the living in Zundert two years before his marriage. He was twenty-seven, and poor. The household was an austere one. Unlike his father, Theodorus remained obscure, his sermons delivered in a tentative, halting manner. Modest in the extreme, he accepted one insignificant parish of Brabant after another.

Prosperity in the Netherlands in the middle of the century was in the developing north, where the large towns and cities thrived. North Brabant, the country's cheap labour market, had always known a lower standard of living. At the time of Vincent's birth it was still deprived, as were all the basically rural territories. In Zundert, a large village only five miles from the Belgian border, the majority of the inhabitants were linked in one way or another with the land and the locality.

For historical reasons North Brabant, as distinct from the rest of Holland, was mainly Catholic. Vincent's father was a minister of the Dutch Reformed Church, his church a tiny, simple structure like a barn, with a ridge roof and central belfry tower. It would only have held a handful. Others attended the imposing Roman Catholic church which dominated the village. Thus van Gogh belonged to a minority, and would have been distrusted because of it, according to one biographer, who adds that Vincent must have suffered the jibes and humiliations a child experiences in these circumstances. But this is guesswork. Next to nothing is known of the boy's childhood and youth. The gaunt house where he was born stood directly opposite the old town hall in the village square (it was pulled down in 1903). From the manse to the little church and its graveyard was only a short distance.

The marshy border land of Brabant was a region of small farms, of unworkable tracts of moor, of pine forests. Farmers grew potatoes, rye, buckwheat. The peasants existed on meagre rations, like peasants everywhere. The country was similar in atmosphere to the Somerset Levels, a stranded terrain of peat marsh and heath intersected by canals dug straight as a ruler, where the fields oozed and bled water, the horizontal land meeting the sky in a damp blur. With no facts to go on, we have to try to imagine how it would have been for a small boy, with two sisters and a baby brother by the age of six, growing up in a world of grey grass and lichen, pollard willows, and stands of pine, its two centres the house of many windows where he lived and the tiny church where his father preached. Summer would come, the water in the ruts of the road would wake and reflect blue, the heather rosy on the moors.

These same half-flooded moors around the settlement of a thousand or so souls would darken swiftly under low skies at the approach of winter, snow soon blotting out the sounds, lying in great flat expanses under a perpetual gloom. Peasants with ruddy bright faces peered from their hovels, muffled in rough clothes, shod in cumbersome clogs. These labourers of the district were a dark, ever present, silent people, only coming boisterously and frighteningly alive at festivals, then guttering back into dumbness.

Christmas in this devout van Gogh household would be solemn, with bursts of joyousness flaring briefly and dying out. Anticipation would be intense, as the pine branches were brought in, the yule log, and the chilly church interior decorated with holly and fir. On walks with his father and mother, treading the creaking snow, a strange pallor everywhere and the ragged tree branches luxuriantly upholstered, was Vincent's nascent eye already hungry for detail? If so he would have spotted the footsteps of birds, their starry footprints in pretty patterns, and the hopping marks left by rabbits. In the garden he would have laughed to see the cat, forced out and disliking it, shaking its paw fastidiously and skipping back, leaving round plops of holes.

His mother, still tragic and heavy-souled, half absent, was a bookish woman, a strong, plain female, clever at drawing and watercolours, who sewed as perseveringly as she wrote her letters. Her father was a bookbinder, and she had married late, the last of three sisters to leave home.

So we have this house of powerful concentration, growing ever more tense as Christmas approached, with most of the Christian year an epic of suffering and death and stern application to right deeds, on the path to salvation. Suddenly, by a curious shift, hearts were fierce with joy and expectation. Ecstasy was at hand. The boy running in and out would have been excited by the change of atmosphere, as it dawned on him that they were moving into a happiness full of light, the source of which he was unable to detect. And what a colourless world next day, after such a wonderful morning. Death was re-established, and the march towards crucifixion. It had all been a moment, a mistake. Not that the rightness of this rather remote and withheld man, his father, with his staunch faith, could ever be doubted. But there was a snag, which Vincent had yet to discover. Though his father asked for nothing, expected nothing for himself, he expected and hoped for much in the way of achievement from his sons.

A new year began, in this remote sunken world which was truly a nether region, not leading anywhere and of no real account. Its uneasily divided populace puts one in mind of a present-day Irish border town.

From this unlovely material Vincent would one day fashion his Eden, as any sensitive boy does, wherever he finds himself and whatever his fate is to be. Northern artists observe more slowly than their southern counterparts, suggests E R Meijer of the Rijksmuseum, Amsterdam, by which he means more closely, more intently. Along with this tendency goes a respect for details and a refusal to neglect them for the sake of the monumental. Vincent's fascination with looking was soon noticed and remarked on, and we can be sure that it began in childhood. In his own description of a portrait of his god, Millet, he drew attention to 'the intense look of a painter – how beautiful it is – also that piercing gleam like a cock's eye.'[9] A photograph of Vincent at thirteen – one of only two photographs existing – was shown soon after it was discovered to Picasso, who exclaimed at once: 'What a striking resemblance to the young Rimbaud, especially the keen and penetrating eyes!'[10] Rimbaud was a near exact contemporary, born the year after van Gogh and dying a year later than him, in 1891.

Vincent Willem van Gogh was born into an extraordinary epoch. Nothing remotely like it had been known before, or could conceivably happen again. Rapidly becoming an advance of global proportions, the industrial revolution – from its roots in the final third of the eighteenth century – exploded suddenly into unstoppable growth. Iron was sent 'pouring in millions of tons over the world, snaking in ribbons of railways across continents, submarine cables crossing the Atlantic', soon to be followed by the building of the Suez Canal. Huge armies of migrants were on the move. 'History from now on became world history.'[11]

Five years before van Gogh's birth, the famous 'springtime of peoples' had come and gone, no sooner born than vanquished. Within eighteen months this wave of connected European revolutions was spent. Only one new regime, the French Republic, survived, and this in a form far from revolutionary. However, long before these astonishing and widespread insurrections, the proletarian revolution was being heralded – and feared – almost daily. The eminent Frenchman Alexis de Tocqueville warned the Chamber of Deputies early in 1848, 'We are sleeping on a volcano . . . the storm is on the horizon.' At about the same time the poet George Weerth was writing to urge his mother, 'Please read the newspapers very carefully – now they are worth reading . . . . This revolution will change the face of the earth – and so it should and must!'[12] An anonymously published first Manifesto of the Communist Party appeared in London in February 1848, drafted by two German exiles, Karl Marx and Friedrich Engels. Dostoevsky had published his first novel, *Poor Folk*, in 1848, and Dickens' *Hard Times*, his novel of industry and the cash-nexus, appeared in 1854. In England an Act of 1847 had laid down a ten-hour day and a fifty-eight-hour week for all women and young persons, though it took longer to end the use of children for work in Great Britain.[13]

In fact the one enduring revolution continued to be industrial and economic, and its victors 'the conquering bourgeois'. Its progress, continuing as it does to this day, was confidently expected to create an ebullient world full of hitherto undreamed of opportunities, advancing human knowledge in every field – in short an entirely new society. But the nineteenth century was also a haunted time, famous for prophets with strangely frightening visions, who seemed capable of catching glimpses of the modern times ahead, waiting with its twentieth-century horrors. Called variously The Age of Optimism, of Laissez-faire, of Expansion, the nineteenth century by the end of the 1870s was no longer a march of unqualified triumph. The massive boom spanning twenty-five years had by then turned into a slump, called by contemporaries the 'Great Depression'. Subterranean disturbances were still undermining the age's self-confidence with dangerous fissures in 1890, the year of van Gogh's death.

2

THE INTIMATE ENEMY

At the age of twenty-three, Vincent applied for a job in Isle-worth as a teacher's assistant. On his application he wrote: 'My father is a clergyman in a village in Holland.'

Vincent's forebears belonged in the main to two professions: either they were ministers of religion or art dealers. His great-grandfather was a lay preacher in his native city, The Hague. Vincent van Gogh, the painter's paternal grandfather, was a pastor by profession. By all accounts he was an impressive character, zealous and distinguished, a man of intellect. Soon he became prominent in Breda, Zundert's nearest town. One of his wealth-iest and most influential sons would also make his home there: this was yet another Vincent – we had better call him 'Cent', as did his family, or Uncle Vincent.

Reverend Vincent van Gogh had six sons. Only one, Theo-dorus, followed him into the ministry. The others soon over-shadowed with their accomplishments the quiet young priest, who at first even failed to find a position as substitute preacher in North Brabant, regarded as the most godforsaken corner of Holland. Three of his brothers became successful art dealers; one of these was 'Cent'. Johannes, the fourth, was eventually an admiral, and Willem a civil servant. Adding to this aura of achievement were two sisters, both of whom married generals. Young Vincent must have grown up in some awe of these elegant and forceful northern relatives.

His father envied no one, being without ambition himself. Eminence was not for him. In his gentle and diffident way he

11

was of a mystical nature, and seems to have rejoiced at finding his post in the wilderness, with a congregation of no more than fifty Protestant faithful. A small man, austerely handsome, of indifferent health, he had fallen seriously ill while at university, and once collapsed after coming in from an immensely long walk to visit his brother.

Vincent's mother, Anna Carbentus, was made of sterner stuff. After her childhood in The Hague, a bustling merchant city, the open country and its wild moors must have come as something of a shock. As must these raw country folk, not citizens at all but looming presences, brushing against her on sick visits like disorderly beasts, tied to the land and graceless, with no civilized inhibitions. The rigour of the Calvinist north had yet to reach them. There was crime here, violent fights, debauchery. Her husband, installed at twenty-seven, was still not at ease in the place after two years. No one knows what his wife felt. She must have shrank, known fear, revulsion. And she was not so young. But this was a determined woman.

At thirty-two, she was three years older than Theodorus at the time of their marriage. Half resigned by then to spinsterhood, she was the last of three sisters to marry. The eldest was the wife of Pastor Stricker, an eminent Amsterdam clergyman. The youngest was in fact married to Theodorus' brother, the above mentioned Vincent. This Uncle Cent, a favourite relative of both the future painter and his brother Theo, would later, in 1858, join forces with a much bigger dealer, Goupil and Company, soon to develop into the largest chain of art dealers in Europe. His country nephews were often taken to visit him in his well-appointed suburb of Princenhage, to a house which actually boasted a private art gallery.

Although far from robust, the Protestant minister of Zundert enjoyed walking. Just as well, for his parish covered a wide area. It took him two hours to walk from one end of it to the other. Vincent, too, as we shall see, was a tremendous (and solitary) walker. But the father was a man of the light. His son as a young man would plunge into the darkness, tramping mile after mile in all weathers, sometimes walking the whole night long and into the dawn to complete a journey.

Vincent's first biographer, Theo's widow, tells us that Anna Carbentus had a deep abiding love of nature and was in fact a devoted botanist, knowledgeable about flowers and plants. In temperament she was neither passive nor inclined – as was her husband – to be aloof. On the contrary she was outgoing, positive, a fluent talker and letter-writer, eager to embrace her new life, crude though its externals were. Above all she was passionate to succeed as a good wife and mother. We are told she was gifted artistically, and the proof has come down to us. A family album, only discovered in 1956, has pages covered with her sketches. A watercolour of hers which has survived, of violets, myosotis, sweet peas, and lily of the valley spilling from a basket, shows her to be a painter of some accomplishment. She knitted away at a ferocious speed, and she went with Theodorus when he visited the sick, determined to do her duty. Donations of food for the poor were prepared and dispensed by her, regardless of whether they were Catholic or Protestant.

All at once tragedy struck. Eleven months after her marriage, a son, Vincent Willem, was born. The infant was stillborn. Anna was thirty-three, about to have her deepest wishes fulfilled. The crib, carefully and lovingly prepared, stood in a corner and mocked them. A pale silent Christ on a cross looked down, in a church cold and clammy like a tomb. The dead child was buried in the church graveyard. This 'perfect' Vincent's gravestone had for an inscription the legend:

Vincent van Gogh
1852
Let the Little Children
Come to Me
For of Such Is
the Kingdom of God
Luke 18, vs 16

A year later to the day, on 30 March, 1853, the sad father went to the town hall opposite the vicarage and registered the birth of another child, also called Vincent Willem. Biographers have pounced on this dead namesake with avidity, and on the parents' lack of foresight in choosing to name the new son identically. Psychoanalytical opinion makes out a convincing case for the influence this would probably have had on Vincent's formative years. Let us look at the facts. In the margin of the birth register

13

at Zundert the registrar has written 'lifeless' against the first son's name. And because of some unexplained error the two Vincents, live and dead, appear disconcertingly under the same serial number, 29.

With both the parents suffering trauma and grief, there is every reason to suppose that the second child was conceived in sorrow. Current theory holds that an unborn child is bound to be affected by the physical and mental state of the mother who bears it. The father, too, is believed to exert an influence. Humberto Nagera, in his psychological study of van Gogh, maintains that Vincent's attacks of morbid anxiety during the course of his life, and especially after leaving home, were the probable result of these unhappy circumstances. This seems to me reductive and simpli-fied, as does any theorem which fails to take into account the more nebulous workings of a modern anguish, or *angst:* that is to say, something which gnaws away invisibly, and is essentially nameless.

Be that as it may, the pain of loss endured by Anna and her husband would, one would think, have been replaced, as the new pregnancy advanced, by many conflicting emotions. Was the same thing about to happen again, and all the torment and recrimination have to be gone through a second time? There may even have been unconscious resentment at the prospect of this vigorously growing foetus blotting out with its demands the enshrined memory of the lost child. Nagera favours this view.

Vincent nowhere mentions the dead brother and has nothing to say on the question of his mother's reaction to the death. It is as if the whole subject became a matter of secrecy as far as the family was concerned. Every Sunday he was taken to the church and was able to see, in the little graveyard, his own name on the tombstone. His birthday was also a death-day. His parents would tend the tiny grave, among grey wintry grass and a few prim-roses. Dr Albert Lubin suggests strongly that 'the first Vincent influenced the psychological development of the second, and the latter's life was dominated by the idea that he was unloved and ignored by a mother who continued to grieve for her beloved dead son.'[1] Nor was this idea necessarily unfounded. Some mothers, unable to help themselves, have been found to equate a firm attachment to the live child with abandoning the memory of the dead one.

If we go along with the theory, then we have to speculate further and ask whether Vincent saw himself as the unwanted live 'twin', with his mother's apparent reluctance to show him physical affection a symptom of her resentment. Leaving aside for a moment the possibility that his mother's guilt about the death was displaced to him, so that he became the guilty one, it is worth remembering that Vincent was familiar from childhood with the biblical twins Cain and Abel, and Jacob and Esau. 'Father used to ponder over the story of Jacob and Esau with regard to you and me,' Vincent wrote to Theo, 'but fortunately there is less discord.'[2] Theo was to be the perfect live twin, as Vincent's glorified namesake was the dead one. How could one be the same, to gain the love and praise of parents, and at the same time strive for difference and for recognition of oneself? One way out was to create a spiritual double in the form of work, something beautiful beyond death and made in one's own image.

As the boy grew up, and was joined by his sisters and brother Theo – Cornelius, the younger brother, arrived fourteen years later – the word 'strange' began to crop up in descriptions of him. Relatives, schoolmates, teachers, and acquaintances were at a loss to know how else to account for this child who puzzled everyone with his curious aloofness. A widow who had worked as a serving maid in the vicarage said when she was questioned in old age that there was something *odd* about him. He didn't seem like a child. He had queer manners, his hair was fiery red, his face a mask of freckles. He resembled his mother, this witness said, without elaborating further, adding only that she couldn't remember him being at school for very long.[3]

The few personal accounts there are all agree that he was intensely serious, earnest, unsmiling, his lips as a rule clamped obstinately shut, his eyes narrowed. In his sister Elizabeth's memory he was 'broad rather than slender, his back slightly bent from the bad habit of hanging his head, his red hair cropped short', and with a face 'not the face of a young man. His forehead was already a little wrinkled.' This was in adolescence. Of his behaviour earlier, she commented: 'Not only were his little sisters and brother like strangers to him, but he was a stranger to himself.'[4]

A picture emerges of a somewhat moody problem child, who did nothing wrong exactly but was guilty at times of a kind of dumb insolence. The worst that could be said of him was that he was 'born old', as adults are inclined to say of difficult children who oppress and irritate by their refusal to behave typically, that is to say openly and playfully. A man who had once been the sexton at the Catholic church in Zundert and was in the same school classroom as Vincent has described him as an ugly red-headed boy who liked to go slouching off across the fields on his own. He had a knack of disappearing, going missing, now and then for hours at a time, sometimes venturing quite a distance from the village. Johanna Bonger relates an incident from this shadowy childhood which brings him vividly into focus for us. Vincent's grandmother had come from Breda, and while she was in the house the self-willed little boy threw one of his tantrums. The old lady, having had twelve children of her own, promptly boxed Vincent's ears and ordered him from the room. Anna, described here as 'the tender-hearted mother', was so upset by this action that she didn't speak to her mother-in-law for the rest of the day. It took the peace-loving father some time to bring about a reconciliation.[5]

We know that Theo as a child spread harmony and his brother did not, provoking Vincent to define his brother as one 'who comforts his mother and is worthy to be comforted by his mother.'[6] He on the other hand, he said in self-castigation – in which there was usually a buried protest – only brought sorrow and loss and should be thought of as a leper. Many years afterwards he remembered his earliest years as 'gloomy and cold and sterile', and went on to complain, 'The germinating seed must not be exposed to a frosty wind – that was the case with me in the beginning.'[7]

Whose fault it was is another matter. From an early age he seemed intent on making himself inaccessible, rejecting rather than accepting, manifesting only the negative signs of a dormant force waiting inside him for release. The juvenile drawings attributed to him – one is of a cat climbing a bare apple tree – pleased his mother. Viewed in the light of his subsequent development they are unremarkable. There was no precocious mastery, and he exhibited none of the self-confidence characteristic of the gifted child. A M and Renilde Hammacher have commented: 'Perhaps

16

the most extraordinary thing about van Gogh's life is the fact that he did not discover his artistic vocation until his twenty-eighth year.'[8]

He wasn't a Mozart, or a Picasso. No one was being dazzled. He was merely tiresome, an enigma: probably not even the worry to his initially fond mother and father that he later became. One wonders what he did with his time. He was, it seems, a budding naturalist. His sister Elizabeth wrote in her memoirs in 1910: 'Without a greeting he passed us by, out of the garden gate, through the meadows along the path that led to the stream.' He was carrying a bottle for specimens and a fishnet, so there was no need to guess what he was up to. But no invitations. The other children didn't bother to ask. Yet he would show them what he'd caught when he got back. What were those horrible things? Water beetles! 'There were broad beetles with their glossy backs, and others with great round eyes and crooked legs that nervously wriggled . . .'.[9]

These creatures, which the little girl found so fearsome, had formidably long names to go with their long legs, and her secretive brother knew them all. He knew too how to prepare them, pinning them carefully in a small box lined with white paper, the Latin names pasted neatly over each insect.

As well as insect-catching he collected empty birds' nests, and went hunting for wild flowers. From an early age his parents had taken him for long walks, so his love of nature was kindled at least partly by them. But naturalists are essentially solitaries, and so are walkers, so are readers. Reading can be a very anti-social activity. Starting very young he read all the time, indiscriminately, voraciously, anything he could lay his hands on, beginning, needless to say, with the Bible. None of it could have done much for his morose temperament, his fits of bad temper, his habit of day-dreaming. The negative emotions he did display only served to engender silence, and would lead in time to an avoidance of his fellow man whenever possible. Methods used to bring this about would include a cultivated boorishness and a natural eccentricity that he was quick to nourish. For the moment he went about passively enough, unless forced into a corner and made to respond, to explain himself. Then he would react rudely.

Estranged, perhaps. No one suggests he was maladjusted. He had found out how to dodge the demands made on him by others, and that was by escaping. He could lose himself in the land. Before long he was drawn more and more to its near silent people, the peasants who asked nothing of him, rough outsiders who in a sense resembled him. Or so he liked to think. To identify with them was to drop social ambition, sterile cleanliness, and his middle-class privileges. If only he could be 'a peasant of Zundert', as he once dubbed himself, his painful selfconsciousness nullified by the need to eat and to keep warm. Tolstoy in far-off Russia was similarly inspired. When Vincent came to declare his ambition to be a peasant painter he meant it literally, and wrote: 'I am ploughing on my canvases as they do on their fields.'

In years to come, in England, Belgium, in the Midi, he would remember the flat countryside of his childhood and its immense skies. Whenever he did it would be tenderly, caressingly. All his life he carried the sights and sounds of home around inside him like an ache. In London he read a book on Cromwell that seemed to speak for him too, and he quoted it to Theo: 'The soul of a land seems to enter into that of a man. Often a lively, ardent and profound faith seemed to emanate from a poor and dismal country; like country, like man.'[10] On seeing the face of a dead friend of his father, he exclaimed, 'Oh, it was so beautiful, to me it was characteristic of the peculiar charm of the country and the life of the Brabant people.'[11]

Even the miserable aspects of the landscape pleased him in retrospect. A painting done in the last year of his life called *Memory of the North* depicts a red winter sun dropping behind heaps of murky cloud. The sky itself is composed of dingy, torn bits of cloud, sun-tinted. Small, mean-looking houses litter the foreground. The picture is bathed in a greenish light. Nothing could be less attractive, but it was not a shop window that he saw. His spirit had come into being there, and he was painting its workshop.

There remains the mystery of his education, which seems scrappy to say the least. At the age of twelve he was taken out of the village school. For one thing, the master was often drunk, and for another, the rough village lads were turning Vincent into a bit of a ruffian, or so his parents feared. They found a small boarding school run by a Protestant, at Zevenberg, nineteen miles from Zundert. The man there, Jan Provily, was authorised to teach French, English, German, maths, and social sciences.

Vincent stayed there for two years, causing so little stir that afterwards no one remembered anything about him, except as an absence. He was 'silent'. From there he was transferred to a similar establishment at Tilburg, where he stayed for eighteen months. He was back home again in March, 1868.

Why did his formal education stop so abruptly at fifteen? It could be that his parents were unable to afford any more board and tuition – after all, their means were extremely limited. Why he was brought home in the middle of March is another mystery. His proficiency in languages, evident in the letters, could only have been gained at Zevenberg and Tilburg. Then back he came, and was at a loose end again at Zundert for the next fifteen months – an enormous stretch of time. On 30 July, 1869, he set off to begin his first job. It was at The Hague. There had been a family discussion; the socially important relatives were consulted and their help sought. Something had to be decided about young Vincent's future, and it was. Theodorus and Anna had done their best for the boy; now it was up to him. He went off dutifully to learn the art dealing trade at Goupil and Company.

3

FIRST LOVE

The journey is the artery of the story, from the *Aeneid* on, wrote Sylvia Townsend Warner in a letter. She is right. Vincent lived in over twenty places during his short life. Always on the move, he was sometimes hunted and sometimes the hunter, on a quest. Would he have stopped, if he had survived into old age? Vincent as a sedentary old man is a picture very hard to imagine.

His journey proper starts here, in 1869. Presumably he had some say in the choice of a profession, though probably not much. Here again, as with his schooldays, we are faced with a yawning gap. The details of his daily life are hard to establish. The great correspondence with Theo, teeming with word-pictures, itineries, budgets, and all his intimate and confessional outpourings, hasn't yet begun. All we have are the noncommittal notes: 'I missed you in the first few days; it was strange not to find you when I came home in the evening.'[1] In effect we lose sight of him for three whole years. Then on 1 January, 1873, Theo left college and entered the same firm of Goupil in Brussels. Vincent hastened to tell Theo how happy this news made him. 'I am glad that we shall be in the same profession and the same firm. We must be sure to write to each other regularly.' Here is the first real letter, to be followed in due course by hundreds more during the next seventeen years, some of enormous length, some heartbreaking, nearly all of them ardent, a composite autobiography that is called by Meyer Shapiro 'a vast work of self-revelation, which may be set beside the works of the great Russian writers.' Gradually the correspondence with his brother opened up, until by the mid 1880s it had acquired a driving visceral rhythm that nothing could stop.

In The Hague he had to find lodgings. His mother was from The Hague, so she had connections. He was given a home with the Roos family, comfortably middle-class and kind, if dull. There were also friends of his mother in the city to visit, and an aunt.

A stubborn, seemingly ungrateful boy, he always responded warmly to kindness shown him by strangers. Later on, when Theo came to lodge there in his place, he didn't forget to ask Theo to pass on his regards to the straightforward Roos folk.

So he was free of paternal restrictions at last. How it suited him we don't know. For all his stubborn insistence on keeping his own company, there was perhaps a half conscious sense of some impending fate which told him to make the most of the experience, whatever it was. It seems he did. The head of the business was very young, only twenty-four. Vincent was now the youngest member of the Dutch branch of Goupil, thanks to the recommendation of Uncle Cent. Vincent and his young employer, Tersteeg, hit it off. At the end of his apprenticeship, Tersteeg wrote to the van Goghs and said how well his pupil had done and how promising his future was. When he was transferred to London, Vincent was handed a glowing testimonial to take with him.

He had won a measure of freedom, and we can assume he was glad. He existed in his own right, apart from his parents. He was a member of the working community. The homesickness and loneliness he felt was the cost of this other self and its independence. For all his strangeness he was intensely attached to his family, to his home and its surroundings, and to the secret world he had created for himself there. Torn out of this, he would have suffered. Only sixteen, he was unformed. He went through the motions expected of him, and, if his London experience is any indication, sank back into himself, not knowing how to behave spontaneously because he *had* no real self – it had not yet been revealed to him. Strung up tight, this was how you were supposed to act in the adult world of responsibilities if you were to get on. It was impressed on him that he had a great opportunity, and was not to waste it. This was where people came, to establishments of this kind, high-ceilinged, spacious, hung with velvet, the paintings in gilt frames, in order to succeed. His childhood world of secret dens and birds' nests and long-legged beetles had been exchanged for this, so that he could prosper. He worked away dullishly and gave satisfaction. At his lodgings he struck up a friendship with the Rooses' nephew, Willem. They would go boating together on Sundays if the weather was fine.

The works of art he saw affected him, if confusedly, and in the flood of impressions he overheard conversations with artists, customers, and dealers, and the language of art and commerce which he had to master. The knowledge of painting he absorbed during this intense early period was extensive, and would influence him for the rest of his life. So far as he was aware he had no talent for drawing or painting himself, so he persevered in the acquisition of knowledge, and in the process was introduced willy-nilly to a whole variety of people caught up in the arts and in buying and selling. It was a chaos in which he kept his feet purely by instinct, outwardly fairly efficient but not understanding all of it. He wanted to please his parents and his uncle and to do well, to make up for the disappointment he had so far caused them. This was seen as diligence. Inwardly he was neutral, dazed, and passive.

It was a curious and unlikely period of worldly success, made possible, we suppose, because he was living only from the superficial part of himself, experiencing each moment as it came, without reference to his as yet undiscovered real nature. His development, chilled and bulb-like, lay dormant underground, nonexistent as far as he was concerned. Rather he was anxious to absorb whatever happened to impinge on him in the way of experience. We can assume some process of assimilation taking place, to be evaluated and used one day and meanwhile stored – a process going on continually and steadily in spite of himself.

After three years at The Hague he had a visit from Theo, then a submissive, shy boy of fifteen, red-haired, with the refined handsome features of his father. If Vincent could be called unruly, Theo was the model son. Theo stayed at the Rooses' with Vincent for two days. They walked out happily together to a mill in the suburbs, where they sat down outside a cafe and drank milk to refresh themselves. Out of this simple meeting came a vow of friendship. They would stay true to each other for ever, they promised. It was a vow Vincent would remember often, in good

23

times and bad, adding once: 'That Rijswijk road holds memories for me which are perhaps the most beautiful I have.'[2]

We are now exactly one hundred years away from van Gogh's death. Psychological considerations, in particular the analyses of conflicts within the psyche, are inseparable from our approach to the man. In his own time, psychological scrutiny by writers and philosophers was in the air, and there was widespread questioning of religious belief and dogma. Darwin's *Origin of Species* was published in 1859, Dostoevsky's *Crime and Punishment* (dealing with a Godless hero) in 1866. Nietzsche, whose father, like Vincent's, was a Protestant clergyman, was soon to announce that God was dead. Karl von Hartman's *Philosophy of the Unconscious* appeared in 1872, Bakunin's *God and the State* in 1874. In the following year Mary Baker Eddy founded a new sect, Christian Science. While at university Nietzsche had read Schopenhauer and been captivated by his gloomy observation that 'Life is a sorry affair, and I am determined to spend it on reflecting on it.' Before all this, Rembrandt in the seventeenth century – 'the first heretic of painting' – had stripped the masks from his subjects and given us the first truly psychological portrait. His self-portraits are a series of devastating confessions from deep within, flowing from a total privacy that had never before been breached.

Psychoanalysis has inevitably been brought to bear on the twists and turns of van Gogh's history. Some of it is rewarding, some foolish. One has to tread warily. A predetermined goal can result in studies which are at their best approximate, at their worst absurd. Work done by the Dutch psychoanalyst Westerman Holstijn avoids these hazards to a certain extent, and Dr Albert Lubin's compassionate study from America, far and away the best to date, is clearly aware of them.

Strange to say, none of this concentrated scrutiny seems to have focused on the burden placed on the eldest child by a large family, especially if that child is by nature solitary. Before taking leave of Vincent's childhood it might help if we looked again at the situation he had seemingly outgrown.

Anyone who has been the eldest child in a large expanding family knows what it can be like. The eldest soon comes to feel ejected, passed over. His place in the house seems no longer important. Resentment, jealousy only bring punishment or ridicule down on his head. The baby is always the darling, to be doted on; and the next baby, and the next. The one who is eldest can soon feel out in the cold.

An eldest girl is liable to become a nursemaid, whether she wants to or not. A boy has no obvious role. He is the onlooker, the little embryo adult. Later on he will gain playmates. In Vincent's case this didn't seem to happen. For whatever reason, he discouraged it. He preferred not to join in. Being on his own was apparently the one reliable source of satisfaction.

In his case, too, there was also the dead, immortalised infant in the church graveyard casting its longer and longer shadow, never to be forgotten because it bore his name. The whole thrust of his growth was in a sense entangled with this image, which could be seen as the corpse of his hope. For the rest of his life he would find a fascination in burial grounds, and this obsession would extend to include mines and miners, digging workers on the roads, peasants ploughing and sowing the earth, peat cutters, as well as trenches and ditches, and objects such as potatoes and dead branches which had been buried in the ground.

There followed the years of being a hanger-on, seeking attention from the doubly preoccupied mother who faced both ways, looking back to the grave and forward to yet another pregnancy. Neither parent seems to have been very personal or intimate with him. Between the breeding mother and the praying father, the one haunted by a catastrophic death, the other bound up with the death of a saviour, the boy with so much time on his hands was left to indulge his own wild nature. Away from the close suffocation of domesticity he was able to find his own paths to comfort. Slowly, however, he was being made conscious of the ignominy of his 'hanging about'. It was as if the whole family, together with his well-to-do relatives looking on from a distance, had in the end joined together to direct one stare of curiosity and bafflement at him. Instead of easing things as he grew older by sly compromise, acting a cheerfulness he could not feel, Vincent's answer was to dig himself in and seek to disappear, like an animal burrowing its way to safety underground. It was almost comic. But of course not to him. Like it or not he was the elected front runner in a family of six, that should, but for the will of God, have been seven.

Working at The Hague, though it meant living away from home, allowed him to stay in touch with relatives and friends of his mother, as a kind of lifeline to home. And it was Holland still. Zundert never seemed far away. Now he was off to London, a huge metropolis, to exist for the first time as a quite separate social being. The transfer, seen as a promotion, made him proud and eager. All the same, there was an undercurrent of dread. Somehow he had to find the courage to live away from home if he was going to prove himself: and he would.

Armed with his testimonial from Tersteeg, Vincent travelled to Zeebrugge in Belgium and took the boat train to Harwich. So began a fateful year, probably the happiest, most carefree of his entire life.

The future looked bright. His troublesome years at home lay behind him, and now seemed about nothing at all. *This* was reality, this busy country which energised him. No sooner was he in contact with it than he felt sharp and keen with resolve. He saw good omens everywhere in this leafy England he was experiencing with such excitement.

He lodged first in a boarding house kept by two ladies who owned a couple of parrots. The place was nice but expensive, and really too far out. Goupil's, miles away, was off the Strand. The other lodgers were three noisy young Germans who loved music, thumping away on the piano and singing lustily. Vincent liked it at first – he found it jolly. He told Theo that his evenings were very pleasant, but 'my boarding house costs me 18 shillings a week, washing excepted,' and in addition he had to buy dinner in town. Like any hard-working Dutchman he remarked on the easier working hours compared with those at The Hague: 'only from nine to six, and on Saturdays we close at four.'[3]

Vincent at twenty was ungainly, deep-chested, of medium height. He had small narrowed eyes which gazed out piercingly, disconcertingly. One is reminded of Tolstoy at the same age, giving no indication of anything special to come, similarly a prey to inner tension, who described himself in a diary entry as 'ugly, awkward, untidy, and socially uneducated.' Another entry announces: 'I wish to believe in the religion of my fathers and to respect it.'

Vincent's uncouth air, like someone thwarted and dark, was nevertheless not without its appeal. Before women he could sometimes lose the power of speech, convinced of his own ugliness. And perhaps they, for their part, recognised a humble solitary in need of love, a young man who had learned to take pleasure in his pain.

Vincent believed that he was 'bad', the obverse of his gentle brother, and could only become like him by applying the Calvinist doctrine of vigilance and effort. This continual self-scrutiny made him doubly bashful in company. His half buried light blue eyes seemed to darken and he would hang back in a corner, blackly miserable, craggy brows beetling, hands thrust out of sight. He blushed furiously, was ashamed of his coarse hairy red eyebrows, and either talked in a blind rush if he was cornered or else hung his head like a country bumpkin. Backing out of a room he was quite likely to fall over his feet.

Goupil and Company was now a rapidly expanding firm. It had three branches in Paris alone – Theo would one day take charge of the one in the Boulevard Montmartre – as well as those in The Hague, London, and New York. Supplying an increasing demand, it not only sold paintings but manufactured and distributed photogravure art reproductions. The historian E J Hobsbawm sums up the period as follows:

> There is no understanding the arts of the later nineteenth century without a sense of this social demand that they should act as all-purpose suppliers of spiritual contents to the most materialist of civilisations. One might almost say that they took the place of traditional religion among the educated and emancipated, that is the successful middle classes, supplemented of course by the inspiring spectacles of 'nature', ie landscape. . . . Creative artists were sages, prophets, teachers, moralists, sources of *truth*.

However, there were snags. Realism had to be edited for it to be palatable.

> The image of itself which (society) desired could not represent *all* reality in so far as that reality was one of poverty, exploitation, and squalor, of materialism, of passions and aspirations whose existence threatened a stability which was felt to be precarious. . . . At best the bourgeois

version of 'realism' was a socially suitable selection, as in the famous Angelus of J-F Millet, where poverty and hard labour seemed to be made acceptable by the obedient piety of the poor.[4]

Vincent, naively eager to please and succeed in this difficult business of making a living, and encouraged by his favourite uncle, was to a large extent unaware of these compromises. The subject of art intrigued him as a sensuous world denied by his father's religion, a strict creed purged of the images, rituals, and mystical leanings of the Roman Catholic Church. The contamination of art by usury was something he would confront later in his own way, when personal humiliation had opened his eyes to it. For the present he lived in a state of dreamy excitement from day to day, simply happy to be alive. He counted himself fortunate, but he was unfulfilled, yearning to overflow, to love and be loved.

Homesick though he was in spasms, he prided himself now on being 'a cosmopolite'. 'I live a rich life here, "having nothing yet possessing all".' Instead of feeling Dutch, he had an urge to throw off national restrictions and be 'simply a *man*. And as a homeland the whole world.' This was now his ideal, he said triumphantly, sealing the aspiration with Anton Mauve's catchphrase: 'That's it! (Dat is het).'[5] Mauve, an established Hague painter, was married to his maternal aunt, Jet.

Vincent's own words provide touching glimpses of this rough-hewn, awkward youth, brought up in the country, as he made his way in the big city. Lonely and homesick when dusk fell, he loved to stand on the Embankment, consoled by his nearness to water and fascinated by the city's lights. Light arising from darkness would be one of his major themes. Glowing lights of house windows spoke of intimacy, the family, a warmth and happiness cupped within four walls that would silence and overcome him, perhaps because it was to be denied him. Perversely, he learned to derive pleasure from its denial. Standing by the Thames at night inspired him to attempt one or two drawings. He attached no importance to them.

Tiring of the jolly pandemonium at his lodgings, he said good-bye to his kindly landladies with their parrots and the loud Germans crazy about music, and found a room to rent in Kennington. His salary, £90 a year, was just about sufficient for his needs, but he hoped to economise so that he could send part of it home. His parents' financial straits preyed on his mind. The Kennington house, at 87 Hackford Street, belonged to a Mrs Loyer. She was a curate's widow and came from Provence. This delightful woman took to him at once, and he to her.

The first thing Vincent did on settling into a new place was to put up some cheap prints to adorn his walls. The sensitive Theo, guessing that his brother would be suffering the anguish of exile, sent a bunch of Brabantine grass and a wreath of oak leaves from Vincent's beloved woods for him to sniff at whenever he missed Holland.

Mrs Loyer ran a kindergarten for boys in another small house in her back garden, helped by her daughter Eugenia (until recently thought to be Ursula – the mother's name). The girl was nineteen, small-boned and slender, with large smiling eyes in a piquant sort of face. In the mornings when it was time for breakfast she called up sweetly to Vincent. When he came down she served him at table. He was soon dumbly in love with her, and in a sense with the mother too. He wrote to one of his sisters, 'I never saw or dreamed of anything like the love between her and her mother,' adding fervently, 'Love her for my sake.'[6]

Family closeness and affection always impressed him deeply. He often implied in his letters that Theo inspired motherliness and he did not. His parents' attitude towards him, he said once, could be likened to the way they would feel about a dog dirtying up the room. Theo was welcome in the house and he wasn't, because 'he barks so loud'. Whether Theo ever did receive preferential treatment is unclear, although Johanna Bonger draws attention in her memoir to the peculiar fact that Theo's correspondence with the family was 'preserved in full', and Vincent's was 'unfortunately destroyed'.

He liked Kennington, he liked the house, he loved the family, and he was delighted with his room. 'Oh boy, I should like to have you here to show you my new lodgings, of which you will certainly have heard. I now have a room such as I have always longed for, without a slanting ceiling and without blue paper and a green border.'[7]

After breakfasting with the Loyers he would step out into the fresh suburban streets with their flowering chestnuts, the fine gardens full of lilacs and laburnums in bloom, and stride off towards the heart of London. He walked like a savage, swift and tireless, covering the distance to Southampton Street and the gallery in forty-five minutes. As he got near, the big stone buildings rising higher around him were like his spirit lifting upwards, taking flight with every stride. The morning traffic, the parks, the tower at Westminster Cathedral, everything exhilarated him.

Showers of rain fell lightly and stopped again, like in Holland. But here everything was different, more vital, more important. Accepting this transfer had been right. He felt poised for a new start, an adventure. The roads gleamed wetly as if new-born, like his aspirations; on his head was the glossy top hat he had bought for himself – 'you cannot be in London without one'. And he'd bought himself some gloves. Now he looked and felt every inch the young up-and-coming businessman. What a thing it was to go marching past others, important people like himself, to feel accepted, part of this vibrant new world, and to be secretly in love into the bargain! That other, interred Vincent, his double or ghostly replica, seemed far behind. Or it had changed character and become beneficial, rejuvenating.

Reading avidly now, he often completed a book in a single night. With his 'irresistible passion for books' he would race through a favourite book many times. Among these were *Uncle Tom's Cabin*, the Bible, and Dickens' Christmas stories, such as *A Christmas Carol* and *The Haunted Man*. The Dickens tales were old childhood reading, 'and they are new to me again every time.' Both Marley's ghost and the ghost who appeared to Redlow in *The Haunted Man* were beneficent doubles, and in both cases the ghosts helped to resurrect dejected characters.

One of the gains of Vincent's transfer to London was the opportunity it gave him to improve his English. Another was his discovery of English illustrated magazines, the weeklies in particular. During this first stay in England he went each week to *The Graphic* and the *London News* to feast his eyes on the new issues. He was fascinated by popular art, the most looked-at, the topical. The English art noticed by critics he found mostly 'bad and uninteresting. . . . Some time ago I saw one which represented a kind of fish or dragon, six yards long. It was awful. And then a little man, who came to kill the aforementioned dragon.'[8] The picture was called *The Archangel Michael Killing Satan*.

The note of ridicule is significant: so is the confidence. He knows what he likes, and why. Contemporary English art might be abysmal, but the graphic art of draughtsmen who supplied the magazines was another matter. Their stark realism made a direct appeal to him. He set about decorating his room with cuttings. Illustrations with titles like *Men Shovelling Snow, People Waiting for Ration Tickets, The Mineshaft, Sunday at Chelsea Hospital,* moved him deeply with their depiction of the way ordinary people lived, worked, and endured. Scenes of deprivation woke an instinct for morbid self-punishment in him, which he experienced as a shudder of recognition but refrained from acting out. It was rather a thrill of relief he perhaps felt, surging through him to blot out obscure personal guilts. 'At night,' he confided, 'when I cannot sleep, which often happens, I look at the wood engravings with renewed pleasure.'[9] These images kept him company, as they would often do in the future, soothing him when he was distressed, in whatever lonely room he happened to be.

Already, under that shiny top hat and prosperous exterior, ideals were forming in him which owed something to his Calvinist heritage but more to the image he was beginning to have of himself as a 'rough dog with wet paws'. But for the moment everyone was well pleased with him. His mollified parents were delighted by the good reports they were getting from Uncle Cent. And in January, Vincent had a raise in salary. His mood buoyant, he kept Eugenia safely secret in his heart, telling friends in The Hague: 'These days I have greatly enjoyed reading the poems of John Keats. . . . He is the favourite of all the painters here. . . . Here is something by him' – and he copied out 'The Eve of St Mark' and 'Autumn'.[10]

In another letter he assumes the role of the big brother who knows what's what, urging Theo to 'Admire as much as you can; most people do not admire enough.' Then a spate of advice follows: 'Try to take as many walks as you can and keep your love of nature, for that is the true way to learn to understand art', and a stupefying roll-call of painters to look out for: 'Scheffer, Delaroche, Hebert, Hamon, Leys, Tissot, Lagye, Boughton, Millais, Maris, De Groux, De Baekeleer, Millet, Jules Breton, Feven-Perrin, Eugene Feyen, Jundt, George Saal, Israels, Anker . . .'.

The list went on and on. Nor did he neglect the writers: 'I am glad you read that book by Burger; read as much about art as you can, especially the *Gazette de Beaux-Arts*, etc'[11] and even weighed in with worldly caution on the fraught subject of the opposite sex. 'As I already let you know, you are quite right about those priggish girls. I also agree with you about Bertha Hannebeek; but watch your heart, boy.'[12]

Watch your heart, boy! Here was a warning that the big brother, living bravely abroad in a rosy glow of anticipated love, should have addressed to himself.

At Goupil's he was serious and hard-working, submitting politely to the whims and objections of customers. The customer in this business was always right. It was all one to him: he dwelt within the bubble of his lovely infatuation, where nothing could harm him. Looking forward to his rapid advancement and to marriage, he dreamed and fantasised. 'I never saw or dreamed of anything like the love between her and her mother.' Their close relationship enchanted him like a long-imagined ideal, something forever beyond his reach. He was in love, but with the whole of womanhood, its difference, its mystery and untouchableness.

A new influence set him on fire – and no wonder. Jules Michelet, the French philosopher and historian, was a champion of the poor and oppressed, a critic of clergy and Church. Michelet's *L'Amour* was a book that Vincent fastened on obsessively. His awakening feelings for women were fed by this romantic, a self-styled authority on woman and how to deal with her. Bewitched daily as he was by real-life images of two women he adored, Michelet's language affected him like music. *Pilgrim's Progress* was another book that thrilled him, especially the vampish Temptress encountered on the pilgrimage. His imagination was morbidly engaged by fantasies of strong females overcoming difficulties (like his mother), and by the dark linking of love with death, Eros and Thanatos, roots of the romantic agony.

Two emblematic pictures appeared on the walls of his room, of two women whom he admired and loved to contemplate. They would accompany him to Paris, then to Dordrecht and Amsterdam. These creatures of his imagination were the portrait in the Louvre of the *Woman in Mourning* by Philippe de Champaigne which had inspired Michelet's 'woman in black', and a drawing from the tomb effigy of Anne of Brittany, called by

Vincent 'a real king's daughter'. This woman, twice Queen of France, defended the lost Breton cause, and died at thirty-seven – Vincent's age when he died. 'The expression on her face is noble, and reminds one of the sea and rocky coasts,' he wrote in 1877 when he was in Dordrecht, recalling her on the wall of his London room.[13]

In London in the autumn of 1873 he copied out these passages from the chapter 'Aspirations of Autumn' in Michelet's *L'Amour*:

> From here I see a lady, I see her walk pensively in a not very large garden, bereft of its flowers early in the season, but sheltered, as you see them behind our cliffs in France or the dunes of Holland . . . . The fallen leaves reveal a number of statues. An artistic luxury which contrasts a little with the lady's very simple, modest, dignified dress, of which the black silk is almost imperceptibly brightened by a lilac ribbon.
>
> But haven't I seen her already in the museums of Amsterdam or The Hague? She reminds me of a lady by Philippe de Champaigne who took my heart, so candid, so honest, sufficiently intelligent, yet simple, without the cunning to extricate herself from the ruses of the world. This woman has remained in my mind for thirty years, persistently coming back to me, making me say: 'But what was she called? What happened to her? Did she know some happiness? And how did she cope with life?'[14]

A modern critic, George Poulet, deals summarily with these cloying sentiments, and with the spurious spontaneity of a Michelet. 'He does violence to himself because there is violence in his temperament.' Sentimentalists invariably force and exploit, but for someone as solitary and introspective as Vincent, romances were simply there to be devoured. Nothing would have been easier – or more of a temptation – than to split Michelet's virginal lady in two and have them move among the autumn leaves of a pretty Kennington garden, to be watched in secret and dreamed about. Eight years later he was out of sympathy with the kind of frustrated passion which yearns to pour out love and kneel in adoration, but never dares to touch, or want, and he said brutally that in love it was necessary to take as well as give. We can guess what he meant.

Christmas at the Loyers' was all his blazing heart could have desired. Mrs Loyer threw a party, inviting him. In the new year he sent drawings home to his mother – sketches of the house, the street, the interior of his room. Afterwards he confessed to Theo how often he had tried to draw, on the Thames Embankment going home in the evenings, and how his ignorance of perspective had made him miserable.

Towards the end of July, 1874, about to go home for his summer holidays, he made a move that must have seemed violent, petrified as he was by the audacity of his love. Its consequences shattered him for months to come, stayed with him for years, and changed the course of his life.

All at once he came to the end of his fantasising. Dutch tradition and his own upbringing had taught him to fear and distrust imaginings and prefer the real thing. Worshipping Eugenia from a distance was an indulgence, a sin. Vincent blundered up to her and declared himself. Perhaps the glorious weather had incited him. They were alone in the garden. No one knows how she reacted, whether she frowned, looked contemptuous, was astounded, or simply horrified. What she told him made him recoil in shocked disbelief. She was secretly engaged to the man who had boarded with them before Vincent arrived.

The paralysing fear of rejection which had kept him in check for nearly a year now became an absolute refusal to accept what his pain was telling him. Desperately this future devotee of suffering begged to be let off. He demanded to know why he hadn't been told, when it was obvious to anyone how he felt about her. It was apparently not evident at all, but how could he be expected to believe that, when the very skin of his face proclaimed it to the world, as her presence poured enriching rays straight into his veins? Where was this fiancé? Had he visited her since Vincent had taken over his room? If she hadn't seen him for over a year, what kind of love was that? How could it be compared with his burning passion, seething now to anguish and falling back shamed in his blood. We can reconstruct the scene in the light of a later, better documented agony.

Eugenia was the first of his *mater dolorosa*s – apart, that is, from his mother. Asexual in his eyes, she was to have a number of successors, before he finally gave up and turned to sexual Magdalenes, prostitutes and ailing women, who did at least have a use for him. At twenty, steeped in the romanticism of the age, sex and a God-fearing mother spiritualised by sorrow were opposing forces he could only contend with in the recesses of his imagination. Tolstoy, in England for sixteen days in 1861, commented dryly on the army of prostitutes and the double standards of the English: 'Imagine London without its eighty thousand Magdalenes! What would become of families?'

Vincent was distraught. He 'tried everything' to make her break off her engagement, but in vain. At the gallery he lost interest in his work, hardly spoke – except to argue with his employers – and was brusque to the point of rudeness with customers. If someone chose to buy bad rather than good art he could hardly contain his disgust. Even worse, he objected to the practise of selling worthless pictures to uninformed buyers. In his rage and despair he took up religion, endlessly reading and studying the Bible. If he had been 'strange' in his childhood, now he was seen as eccentric rather than just wilful. Eccentricity is a permanent condition, something helplessly exhibited before conventional society. Vincent was now a person whose unpredictable responses had to be steered around, a man to be handled gingerly. Soon he would be classed as a liability.

In the house, Eugenia went out of her way to avoid him. His last few days there dragged by. Vincent had lost all his illusions. When he went home in defeat, the mysterious fiancé from Wales, the rival he had done his best to supplant, took over his room. His disgrace was total. 'He was thin, silent, dejected – a different being,' a sister said.[15] His mother took note of his bitter humour and drew her own conclusions. His father said nothing either. Perhaps to him it was no surprise: Vincent's moods came and went like changes in the weather.

This time it was different. To divert his mind from his hopeless passion and kill time, Vincent did some drawing, disappearing into the fields for hours. It was one way of avoiding the questions in people's eyes. If his mother praised something he did, he immediately disparaged it. This was habitual with him from an early age. Johanna Bonger was told of one incident from his childhood which she included in her memoir: 'At the age of eight he once modelled a little clay elephant that drew his parents' attention, but he destroyed it at once when, according to his notion, such a fuss was made about it. The same fate befell a very curious drawing of a cat (climbing a leafless apple tree), which his mother always remembered.'[16] Praise from undiscerning parents is often suspect, seen as hypocritical and placating. Vincent would have been shamed by rewards he did not feel he had earned. The sin and remorse in him that were without apparent cause could not be praised away lightly. Better to destroy these imperfect extensions of himself, attempts by his imagination to make amends, than have them condoned by a sickly false love. Now he was home, reclaiming his lost world on walks, but in the house he sat tensely, lean and abstracted.

We have to ask why it was that this setback in love, bitter and desolating though it had been, should have dealt him such a blow. The truth is that it was not one rejection, but two. Mrs Loyer was a motherly widow. Her late husband was a curate. Wedded to the church like his mother and then set free, she was better able to love him than his own mother had been when he was in her womb, before his ill-omened birth. His fantasy may well have conjured up marriage as a way of getting the mother he longed for, as well as leading to an almost unthinkable heaven of conjugal bliss.

Whatever the actuality of the event was, his over-intense craving for normal joy must have alarmed the girl. His eagerness to merge, to reach his goal, was so fierce and strange, so total, that it would have seemed like a threat to her person. He would be driven to the same extreme again, later, and just as disastrously. But this first double rejection was like no other. It condemned him at the outset, or so he believed, to a life bereft of family happiness, with no outlet for his inordinate intensity of feeling, and no chance of intimacy. How could he endure such a prospect? With the extremism of youth he saw the rebuff as absolute. No reprieve was possible. He had been shut out rather than in, sentenced to live as a man in a world where he would be less than a man; half man.

He described later how Rembrandt's portrait, *The Jewish Bride*, had affected him when he looked at it in the Rijkmuseum in Amsterdam. It shows a man tenderly embracing a young woman

36

in a glow of amber light. Vincent said he would give ten years of his life if he could go on gazing at it. What did he see? A Rembrandt sets forth the achieved reality – in this case the reality of united love – that a work by van Gogh is forever yearning towards, and more compulsively than any other painter. When Vincent was censured later for living with a whore he replied that anything, even death, was better than separation. Attachment and loss are the clues to the frightening acts that punctuate his life. He strove to attach himself, by any means, by all manner of substitutes, because the alternative was intolerable.

'With this first great sorrow his character changed,' wrote his sister-in-law.[17] His sister Anna wanted to look for a post in England as a teacher of French, so he went back with her. He took a furnished room in a house covered in ivy, Ivy Cottage, 395 Kensington New Road. Instead of trying to share in his landlady's family life he kept to himself. Most evenings he stayed in. If he did go out, it was only for an evening stroll with his sister. Nothing was sure any more: he had lost his way. He wished he was older. His letters home dwindled. His father said anxiously that 'his living at the Loyers'' with all those secrets had done him no good.' Relieved now that Vincent had left, he nevertheless worried over his son's isolated existence. Uncle Cent told them to urge his nephew to mix more. 'That's just as necessary,' he said, 'as learning your business.'[18]

Vincent, who had turned a deaf ear to that kind of advice for years, was not likely to heed it now. Hiding away in his room 'he vented the grievance of many bewildered men who have been disappointed in love.'[19] A woman is a completely different being from a man, he reflected, 'and a being we do not yet know, at least only superficially,' adding wistfully his theoretical belief that 'man and wife can be one, that is to say one whole and not two halves.' This had echoes of Michelet, a deity now about to be displaced. Vincent's spirits were too low, and idealism about women couldn't heal his wounds. Soon, only the Bible could.

He was casting about, not knowing what to do with the shame of his disgrace. Mindful of his father, still the apotheosis of good in his eyes, he first of all turned to God. But God was a vast space, a darkness of unknown stars. The white stars with their unearthly beauty were cold, like his isolation. He went instead to Christ. 'Let Christ be the centre of your longing,' he wrote to

Theo. His compulsion to read the Bible incessantly began now. It was a kind of solution. By absorbing him totally, it blotted out everything else. And it brought him close to his father. It was full of human voices. The sorrow and loss it recounted was like his own. Then he found a new father figure in the French philosopher Ernest Renan, whose *Vie de Jésus* spoke to him so sweetly and consolingly, and he quoted Renan's injunction with approval: 'To act well in this world one must sacrifice all personal desire . . . . Man is not on earth only to be happy . . . . He is there to realise great things for humanity, to attain nobility, and to surmount the vulgarity of nearly every individual.'[20]

So his loss could be a gain, even a virtue. Reading further, he learned that a loving mother existed who would, under certain circumstances, feed his hunger. She dwelt in the New Testament for those, like Vincent, with eyes to see. And she was in the earth, in nature. One day he would worship her compulsively in paint.

Because God the Father was lost in space, and his own father and mother were too far off to sustain him, he would find all three in Jesus Christ. In a long, barely coherent letter, giving chapter and verse but quoting selectively to achieve the transformation he wanted, he managed to change God into Goddess. 'Can a woman forget her suckling child, that she should not have compassion on the son of her womb? Yea, they may forget, yet I will not forget thee.' This could only mean that he was not abandoned, not utterly alone, though his own mother may have lapsed away from him. He cited Paul: 'Strengthen thy charity,' and asked, 'What is this Charity Paul speaks of? This Charity is Life in Christ, this Charity is our Mother. All the good things of the earth belong to her, for all is good if enjoyed with thankfulness. But She extends much further than those good things of the earth. To Her belongs the draught of water from a brook or on a good hike or from a fountain in the hot streets of London . . .'.

Finally, out of dire need, the transference is made. Femininity can still be reached, though Eugenia has denied him: in fact, 'All thy lovers have forgotten thee. I shall restore health unto thee, and take the plagues away from thee.' The Great Mother who thus waits to cherish and nurture him is none other than Christ, who can be all things to all men. 'As one whom his Mother comforteth, so will I comfort you, saith the Lord.'[21]

The insistence on sorrow as a thread running through the whole of human life begins now. Only by staying close to sorrow could he guard against the sort of illusion that had ensnared him. Eugenia's silken tresses and her mother's warmly open arms were no longer to be trusted. 'Our nature is sorrowful.' He went further: 'Sorrow is better than joy,' he declared, and one could be at the same time sorrowful and able to rejoice, by drawing near to Christ.[22] In fact, serenity could only be reached through the 'worship of sorrow', he now maintained. Falling ill could be counted as a blessing, since 'we get new ideas and new intentions that would not have come to us if we had not been ill'.[23] Faith and trust were tempered by adversity.

He was living in a house smothered in ivy. The symbolism would not have escaped him. For Christians, ivy is said to represent death, immortality, and affection. Vincent saw it too as an image of that patience he must cultivate if he was to survive this crisis. If he crept along from day to day, tenacious in his belief, he would come through. He would describe a painting of his, *Tree with Ivy and Stone Bench*, as depicting 'eternal nests of greenery for lovers.' The moss and ivy with its clinging love would always appeal to him, though in certain moods he seemed to fear the ivy's power to engulf.

He often talked of suicide, but only by way of rejecting it as a solution to his or anyone else's problems. Even before the crisis with Eugenia had devastated him he was saying in a postscript, 'Theo, I strongly advise you to smoke a pipe; it is a good remedy for the blues, which I happen to have now and then.' Smoking a pipe was one of his few ordinary pleasures. He saw it later as an antidote to suicidal thoughts, taking his cue from Dickens: 'Every day I take the remedy which the incomparable Dickens prescribed against suicide. It consists of a glass of wine, a piece of bread and cheese, and a pipe of tobacco.'[24] Years had to pass before he could throw off a dejection that was only deepened by his inability to accept that Eugenia wanted nothing to do with him. When he did try to face up to the truth, it was only after a fashion. He suddenly began to speak in veiled terms about 'the man whose little boat capsized when he was twenty years old, and sank, did it not?' This man, he explained needlessly, was 'your brother Vincent, one who had been down, yet came up again.' He went on even more obliquely: 'What kind of love did

I feel when I was twenty? It is difficult to define – my physical passions were weak then, perhaps because of a few years of poverty and hard work. But my intellectual passions were strong, meaning that without asking anything in return, without wanting any pity, I wanted only to give, but not to receive . . .'.[25] On he rambled, ever more vague and preachifying. What was being enacted here was the liberation from Eugenia and all she had come to mean to him, together with an attempt to reconstitute himself. He ended in obscurity: 'What helped me recover my balance more than anything else was reading practical books on the physical and moral diseases.' His sympathetic brother must have wondered what lay behind this devious and tormented confession.

As soon as a career of any kind ceases to have meaning, it becomes a bondage. Vincent no longer cared about selling pictures. Disaffected, he now saw everything differently. 'The exhibitions, the picture stores, everything, everything, are in the clutches of fellows who intercept all the money.'[26] Moreover, most of the clients, and in particular those who purchased expensive pictures, were nothing but speculators. 'There are real, serious connoisseurs, yes, but it is perhaps one-tenth of all the business that is transacted . . . that is really done out of belief in art.'[27] How could he, engaged in this sort of activity, justify his life? He was now alienating colleagues and bewildered customers alike. Only his influential relatives were saving him from dismissal. At home, his parents fretted because he seemed so cut off. Was it the London fog that was depressing him? His sister Anna, out of patience with him, told them shortly, 'He's only in a bad temper.' An aunt gave them her opinion: 'It's that girl.'

Partly it was his proximity to Eugenia that unsettled and tortured him, yet he had come back to England to be near her. It was all a waste, everything. A career didn't matter, nor did personal gratification. None of it amounted to anything: it led nowhere. All it produced was nausea. How loathsome the self was, burdened with itself.

Finally it was Uncle Cent who came up with a solution. A change of surroundings would do the trick, was his forecast. An essentially practical man, he arranged for his nephew to be transferred to the head office in Paris. By October, 1874, Vincent was installed there. He was still fond of his uncle, finding him admirable as a person as well as enormously clever. He liked him even more when he realised they both admired a painting by Gleyre called *Lost Illusions*. Uncle Cent was a shrewd businessman who seemed to have an understanding of his nephew's psychological problems. Vincent, summing him up appreciatively to Theo, wrote: 'Saint-Beuve said, "In most men there exists a poet who died young, whom the man survived." And Musset said, "Know that often a dormant poet is hidden within us, always young and alive." '[28] He thought Uncle Cent belonged to the former group. Encouraged by their friendly relationship, he tried to alleviate his loneliness by suggesting that his uncle transferred Theo to Paris too. It didn't work.

He made frequent pilgrimages to the Louvre and to the Luxembourg Museum. Everything he saw confirmed his new conclusion. What mattered, first and foremost, was a man's soul. Trading in art was a degradation, no better than most petty commerce. He wondered how much longer he could submit to it. He went on out of deference to his parents, simple souls ignorant of this market place disguised as a temple to art, which was how he now saw Goupil's. The Paris experiment was a failure. At the end of December he went back to London.

Why he was then transferred permanently to Paris in May of the following year is something of a mystery. One explanation could be that the London management were at a loss to know what to do with this well-connected ex-apprentice who was now so subversive. In Paris, under his tolerant uncle's eye, he could be kept under special observation.

They put him in charge of the picture galleries. He much preferred being in his little cabin of a room in Montmartre, which had a view from its window of a tiny garden full of ivy and Virginia creeper. He shared a room with a young man of eighteen, Harry Gladwell, thin as a stick, with protruding ears, a colleague at Goupil's whose father was a London art dealer. Gladwell, an amenable youth, shared Vincent's preoccupation with religion. They studied the Bible together (in French), and also a new obsession of Vincent's, Thomas à Kempis' *Imitation of Christ*.

At work he offended as before. One of his bad habits was the criticising of engravings he didn't like – and presumably was supposed to be selling – in front of customers. Reprimanded, he wanted to know how he could stand by and admire the choices made by vulgarians after he had spent time drawing their attention to the best there was. How would he stay silent when they picked the worst – were his superiors asking him to be dishonest?

This couldn't go on. He was making it impossible for his employers to go on tolerating him. It is legitimate to ask whether his self-alienating behaviour was deliberate or unconscious. When finally asked to leave, he made no attempt to defend himself. By all accounts he was only too glad to go.

It has been suggested that Vincent's fear of failure was matched by his alarm at the possibility of success. Nothing is worse than success for someone who finds his career more and more hateful to him. He was perpetually discontented; he could find no fulfilment. Renan had warned that if the soul was black, one went on dragging out a weary existence. Renan's 'great things' were waiting out there to be accomplished. He had no idea what they were to be, he only felt them stirring like monsters in the blackness. He yearned to know. Like a monk he prayed and listened, and put curbs on his flesh. Soon he was advising the eighteen-year-old Theo not to read the dangerous Michelet any more, 'or any book (except the Bible)' until they met again and talked.[29] He was half unhinged with mad zeal. On his wall were the icons of his gospel, the 'woman in black' and a portrait of Thomas à Kempis.

The very idea of Vincent as an art dealer now seems preposterous. So does any profession for this man who could only ever think in terms of vocation. 'Painting is a faith,' he was to proclaim. Nevertheless, he had served a seemingly successful apprenticeship and now was all set to jettison the fruits of it. This was a bitter blow to his father, who had hoped his son might eventually succeed Uncle Cent in the business. With no vocation in sight, to sabotage his chances so arbitrarily instead of delaying until he had some idea of his next move seems on the face of it inexplicable. The truth may have been that he was haunted by the fear that he might, against all the odds, eventually succeed in it. In his mind at least he was being threatened with the finality of a life mistake. Again and again he would veer violently away from such 'mistakes'. Towards the end of his life, when the tide seemed about to turn for him, he referred to his 'horror of success', and quoted Carlyle: 'You know the glow-worms in Brazil that shine so that in the evening ladies stick them into their hair with pins;

well, fame is a fine thing but look you, to the artist it is what the hairpin is to the insects.'[30] Another time he resorted to a ferocious image. Fame was like 'ramming the live end of your cigar in your mouth'.[31]

When he listened submissively to Boussod, the new partner at Goupil in Paris, insisting that he would have to leave in April, and then made his laconic report to Theo about it, he was in another world. His struggle to be transfused, and to live again, in the 'zone of pain' he had entered since leaving London, implicated his whole being. He was like a piece of darkness, unable to attend. His inner life so exhausted him, the darkened river of his feelings flinging him to and fro, that the world outside made no sense. Only his reading and his thoughts counted.

One book especially was to prove seminal. As with everything that touched him deeply, he recognised a part of himself in it. His account of one of its stories gives us a strikingly accurate foretaste of the pattern his life was to take. Here in advance were his self-neglect, his bad eating habits, his alignment with the poor, with their squalor, even his attempted reform of a drunken prostitute and his own early death: 'I have just read a very fine book by George Eliot, *Scenes from Clerical Life*: three tales, especially the last one, 'Janet's Repentance', struck me very much. It is the story of a clergyman who lived chiefly among the inhabitants of the squalid streets of a town; his study looked out on gardens with cabbage stalks, etc . . . and on the red roofs and smoking chimneys of poor tenements. For his dinner he usually had nothing but underdone mutton and watery potatoes. He died at the age of thirty-four. During his long illness he was nursed by a woman who had been a drunkard, but by his teaching, and leaning as it were on him, had conquered her weakness and found rest for her soul.'[32]

4

THE SOUL IS A MIRROR

Vincent's release from what he now saw as the parasitical world of art trading, and from the misery of exile in France – he would always be intensely homesick away from Holland – meant that he could now find a pretext to get back to England and be near Eugenia again, nursing his unrequited love. His father, discussing with his younger son the problem of a job for Vincent, wondered if he ought to help Vincent start up in a small art business of his own. What did Theo think?

Reverend van Gogh now had a living at Etten in the Brabant. Vincent arrived there at the beginning of April. He was glad to be home. It was much more to his liking than before, and he was thankful to immerse himself in a religious household. He had washed his hands of commerce, he told them – no more compromises for him. When asked what he proposed to do, he said he would try to teach and be a lay preacher. His qualifications were nil, but for someone young and idealistic as he was, with a knowledge of languages, getting a job proved easy enough. He wrote off and soon found a post, with board and lodgings but no wage, at the small private school run by the Reverend William Stokes, a Methodist minister who lived at Ramsgate.

On the train and steamer he jotted down a sort of travel diary for his parents. He wanted to say what they all meant to him, his mother and father and little sisters, and his other, baby brother, and how his heart broke when he had been taken to Mr Provily's school as a child, and he stood on the steps to watch the carriage leave. He could see the little yellow vehicle as it shrank, far down the road, wet with rain among the bare trees, running away through the meadows as if leaving for ever. And he recalled his joy a fortnight later, standing in the playground, to hear someone say that a man was asking for him. 'I knew who it was.' He remembered throwing his arms round his father's neck and weeping. 'And that first homecoming at Christmas!'

On Saturday, still travelling, he reported that the weather was good, the dunes dazzling in the sun as he set sail for England. His last glimpse of Holland was of a tiny grey church spire. He stayed on deck until it was too cold and rough to remain.

Sunday found him on the boat train at dawn, heading for London through fields, the grass sparkling with dew and night frost.

When he reached Ramsgate, Mr Stokes was away but he met his son, a young man the same age as himself, and at dinner he saw Mrs Stokes with all the pupils, twenty-four boys from ten to fourteen years old. The school faced the grey sea. That evening Mr Stokes returned, and the new assistant went with the Stokes family and the boys to church. He didn't fail to notice an inscription on the wall of the church: 'Lo, I am with you always, even to the end of the world.'

And he added a postscript: the little room where he slept, in another house nearby, needed prints on the wall to make it pleasant.[1]

Mr Stokes was bald, a man of medium height with side whiskers. The atmosphere seemed good; Mr Stokes was liked and respected. Vincent taught elementary French and arithmetic, and after school was expected to keep an eye on the boys, supervising their baths and so on. It would do for now, though what he really wanted was to be a London missionary in the slums, he confided to Theo. He had written to another clergyman applying for such a position and would see what happened. Meanwhile, he seemed unusually content.

A month after he arrived, he was setting out to cover the huge distance to London on foot. Starting on Saturday morning, he reached Canterbury in daylight. The act of walking always lifted his spirits. So life was nice after all! Thank God, he could stand cleanly upright, his shame in abeyance. He relished his own company once more. This was the greatest blessing, and it had been granted him. Like many adults who tend to despise themselves he had spells of ecstasy when he felt himself magically transformed into his own opposite.

It was warm weather. In the dusk he went on until he came to a pond by some large beeches and elms. There he had a rest. At three he was hiking again, and soon the birdsong started: it was nearly dawn. He tramped on into the sunrise and by afternoon arrived at Chatham, and saw partly-flooded, low-lying meadows that reminded him of Holland, and the Thames with its ships. A friendly carter gave him a lift for a few miles, then disappeared inside a tavern, so he pushed on alone. He began to enter the London suburbs when it was evening. He stayed for two nights with the parents of his friend Harry Gladwell. Harry's father kissed him goodnight as he went to bed, and he felt happy. On his second day it was pouring with rain and he wanted to go on to Welwyn to see Anna, his sister. At four the next morning he walked through London to Hertfordshire and reached Welwyn at five in the afternoon – a distance of over thirty miles.[2]

He loved to walk at night. His amazing marathon walks, so punishing and exhausting, were in part a necessity – he had little free time and no money – but also a form of catharsis. He would be restored to wonder and simplicity in the dead of night. On the road, as he sweated over the huge distances, his old sense of helplessness left him and he felt he was on a pilgrimage. It was as if somehow the twilight and then the all-enveloping, alive night dissolved his doubts and troubles and obliterated his failures. He was absorbed in something greater than himself, yielding and other-worldly, infinitely delicate and tender. Truly it was the mother of all things.

His attitude to darkness was complex. The night was essential if there was to be a dawn, and so his belief in rebirth was bound up with it. Because of this the night was palpable, like a throbbing cave or a wood. It aroused his expectancy. The engulfing darkness of the grave, of death, was another aspect of the night, linked in his imagination with his mother's grief for her dead son and with his father's death-centred religion. As well as those morbid aspects, it excited and stimulated him because it contained the seeds of resurrection. Death was a threat and also to be welcomed.

Depression, when it struck and disabled him, was like walking around as if dead. A woman in sorrow was to him always a potent symbol of death. Death was a threat, a doom, signalled by the flapping of crows over a wheatfield, or a glorious promise of the immortality to come. The Crucifixion had brought 'darkness over all the land', but only after it did so was a world of love possible. Never was so much love shown to Jesus as after he suffered and died: so death was a means of obtaining love. The theme of death is coupled with a mother's love in much of Vincent's life and shows itself in a number of his pictures. He was often afraid of life, but said more than once that death held no terrors for him.

While at Ramsgate, and then at Isleworth, he visited London at weekends whenever he could, sometimes calling in at Goupil's to look at paintings. Two of his favourite pictures at this time were G H Boughton's *Deserted*, a desolate flat landscape of stunted storm-torn bushes and water-logged fields, and Millais' *Chill October*. Both pictures exude that melancholy for which he felt such a strong affinity. Boughton often painted in Holland, the bleak terrain appealing to him. When Vincent was working at Goupil's he caught sight of the artist but was too much in awe of him to speak. He did pluck up sufficient courage to approach another admired painter, Thijs Maris, a fellow countryman as lonely and introverted as himself.

In London, apart from the galleries there was his sister to visit, and the Gladwell family; and he kept in touch with one or two friends he had made while working at Southampton Street. He may once have called at the Loyers, turning up out of the blue in order to greet Mrs Loyer on her birthday. If true, it has all the impulsiveness of a van Gogh action. So does the story of him standing for hours outside the Kennington house, only to run off when the door opened. Whether fact or fiction, it is more pertinent to ask why he should have felt compelled to enter the centre of London time after time, after experiencing so much anguish and humiliation there. Perhaps he half hoped for more.

Albert J Lubin, in his study of van Gogh, devotes a whole chapter to Vincent's melancholy disposition and the benefits he managed to derive from it. When Vincent remarked to Theo that sorrow was better than joy, he wasn't referring to bouts of paralysing depression but to something he later called 'active' or 'healthy' melancholy. We are reminded of Keats' notion of negative capability, defined in a letter to his brothers George and Tom as 'when a man is capable of being in uncertainties, mysteries, doubts, without any irritable reaching after fact and reason'.[3] The Scottish poet William Soutar expands this idea in his *Diary of a Dying Man*, calling it 'the readiness of the being to accept life with no dogmatic assumptions; and from this passive receptiveness to learn how to act creatively. It is a willingness to be guided by the event and not to set up any ideal by which we would judge beforehand: it is, in short, submission to experience'.[4]

Vincent was once told by his father that 'Sadness does no harm, but makes us see things with a holier eye.' Though they became estranged later, Vincent never forgot his father's words. A J Lubin maintains that Vincent learned to convert his periods of depression into masochism, and thus into a rejuvenating activity, since the masochist tends to exhibit his misery and turn it to his advantage. By creating difficulties for himself which he then has to overcome, he can as it were 'enjoy' the sensations of martyrdom.[5] Here is where Christ came in, and proved such a valuable asset. To identify with Jesus was to make his own sufferings acceptable. Equally important, he was able to resemble his father, a god to him since childhood.

Vincent was only too willing to admit his tendency to depression, a word he used freely in his letters to Theo. We can see him seeking to ally himself with it, even at times appearing proud of it, and doing his best not to be overwhelmed by it. When he did become a painter he sought to transform it to what he called 'pure gold' by the alchemy of art. In a sense, therefore, it would be wrong to label him a depressive. 'Depression,' says John Leyard, 'is withheld knowledge.' From an early age Vincent was uneasily aware of the demon within him. His struggles for salvation were really attempts to combat the *rigor mortis* of morbid melancholy that a collapse into meaninglessness brings. Impelled at first to commit wildly impulsive acts, he would insist later on that his psychic health depended on his ability to work. If a fascination with looking was one impetus which pushed him into art, another was his pressing need to circumvent a misery that would come flooding up from a formless darkness to threaten him with horrible collapse. After one such crisis, he wrote: 'Well, even in that deep misery I felt my energy revive, and I said to myself: in spite of everything I shall rise again, I will take up my pencil, which I have forsaken in great discouragement, and I will go on with my drawing, and from that moment everything has seemed transformed in me.'[6]

All the time at Goupil's there had been something urging him to put an end to a career that betrayed his hope. Under the apparent unreason of his new stance lay a sense of the growing discrepancy between his inner and outer life. One was passionate, mystical, his heart hushed and pregnant in it as though in a church, the other a sham and a vulgarity that led only to material success. 'I believe and hope that I am not what many people think I am at this moment,' he had written haltingly to Theo, only half sure of what he meant. It was as if he feared the consequences of spelling it out.

Released now from a code and system alien to him, he was close to bringing the two halves of his life together. His letter applying for a religious post listed a few attributes he thought might influence a decision in his favour. He was a clergyman's son; he had three generations of pastors behind him; his upbringing had been austere. Lately he had been teaching Mr Stokes' boys some Old Testament history. What else? Nothing, except 'my innate love for the Church and everything connected with it. It may have slumbered now and then, but it is always roused again.'[7]

All at once Mr Stokes moved his school to a fine house in Twickenham Road, Isleworth. Vincent approached him to enquire meekly about the possibility of a salary. There was nothing doing: teachers willing to accept board and lodgings while they acquired experience were easy to find. Vincent intensified his efforts to obtain another post, and found one near at hand. The Reverend Jones, a Methodist minister at Holme Court, Isleworth, took him on as a sort of curate and assistant teacher. His joy can be imagined when he was asked not long afterwards to preach a sermon at Richmond.

As a public speaker he was ineffectual, like his father: his manner was diffident, his delivery mumbling and jerky, his English pronunciation eccentric. The words of his sermon, recorded in full in the Letters, are a different matter, strong in faith and powerful in expression.

After this debut he led the service again, at Turnham Green and again at Petersham. But this first sermon was a turning point. In the body of it he sounded all his important themes, on a rising note of triumph. The series of past failures and defeats was vindicated by this breakthrough. Through his awkward and sincere language ran an emotional charge. Like George Eliot's Felix Holt, he had looked behind the word 'failure' and found 'tribulation', which, if one submitted, became a blessing in disguise. 'Eat your bread, but live simply,' he advised Theo. It was to be his lifelong creed.

The text he chose for his sermon came from Psalm 119:19: 'I am a stranger on the earth, hide not Thy commandments from me.' To get to the church he walked from Isleworth along the riverside path, noticing how the big chestnuts loaded with yellow autumn leaves and the clear blue October sky were mirrored in the water. Ahead of him in the distance was Richmond, its houses with red roofs piled on their hill, above the long bridge thronged with black moving figures.

Standing in the pulpit was like a redemption in itself. He shed the errors and confusions of his recent past like someone stepping wonderfully out of a dark cave and finding the 'friendly daylight' he had known once and then lost. He had emerged from underground, like someone entombed. A few days later, at Richmond again one evening on his way to the church, he saw a woman 'dressed in black' under the trees, with beautiful grey hair.

The tremulous young preacher – 'preaching to the congregation he was also preaching to himself, and of himself'[8] – began by saying that we are all pilgrims, our life a long walk or journey. We – the lonely 'I' was now subsumed in Christian fellowship – had much sadness to experience, for 'our nature is sorrowful', but despair was unnecessary for those who believed in Jesus Christ. 'There is only a constantly being born again, a constantly going from darkness to light', and life was 'evergreen'.

He would define his painting in these magical terms, and refer to art as the creation of himself. Holding to his text, he proclaimed that the journey of our life began at the loving breast of our mother and ended in the arms of our Father in heaven.[9] With this familial image he endeavoured to console his fellow pilgrims as he wished to be consoled; it was a vision of intimacy arising from a longing he could never satisfy. Solitude, he had found, was better than being a witness to the love of others. Failure was better than success. At least it could not disappoint. At Arles, no longer a Christian believer, he would describe himself as a bewildered traveller, following the same road as everyone else but not knowing where it led, if anywhere. A few years earlier he had said he was a homeless vagrant, ever on the move. Rimbaud, his near contemporary, also wandered restlessly over the countryside like a hungry wolf in all weathers, deprived of security and warmth, and even when he did not, *felt that he did.*

In late October Mr Jones gave Vincent a job to do that he soon found distasteful. Some of the pupils' parents were in debt with their fees, and Vincent went marching off towards Whitechapel in his new role of debt collector. He enjoyed the long walk to town and out to the East End, but the Zolaesque tragedy of the slum streets shocked him. He loathed his task of extracting money from these impoverished people, in the midst of foul smells, surrounded by large families shivering in rags over putrid food, gaunt ill faces staring from the windows of bare ugly rooms. Had he become a preacher for this? What he was doing was a mockery, when he wanted to alleviate suffering and minister to the sick and distressed.

Home again for Christmas, he must have unburdened himself to his family. Theo was there too. Although Mr Jones was paying Vincent a small wage, the situation gave no promise of leading anywhere. There was some discussion as to what he should do next. The influential uncles were consulted, and once again it was Uncle Cent who came up with something practical. This was magnanimous of him in the circumstances, to say the least. A brother of one of his employees ran a bookshop in Dordrecht. Vincent went off there to be a bookseller's clerk.

Theo next heard from him at the beginning of the new year, 1877. He was lodging with the Rijken family. Rijken was a corn and flour merchant. His wife had half a dozen lodgers. Another motherly woman, she scolded her other charges when she heard them teasing Vincent for being 'a queer freak'. Not that he cared. His piety was now unshakeable. At dawn he would be up and about, reading the Bible.

He shared a room with a young teacher, Görlitz, so he had a

congenial companion. To cap it all, his window had a view that delighted him, overlooking the backs of some old houses covered in ivy. What could be better? Dordrecht wasn't too far from home: he was back in Holland, near to his mother and father and brother, sharing with them a countryside to which he had always been deeply attached – as dear as an old friend, he called it. Now and then he would be torn at the thought of England, of Eugenia, but – it was better this way.

Restless all his days, wanting another form of life, straining to go forward and at the same time to put down roots, he was often humbled by whatever seemed still, unchanging, and eternal. He wrote to Theo: 'It is good to love flowers, and ivy, and fir trees, and hawthorn hedges – they have been with us from the very beginning.' When he thought of the world of his childhood it was of a world without stress, a poor village where everything stood still. It lacked enterprise, it made no progress, the inhabit-ants lived on tiny patches of fertile land, the branching horns of the cattle swung placidly in the barns in winter, or out on the pasture if it was summer. Church was a place to kneel in simple worship, and to hear the latest gossip. He had been free then, sharing the open secret that was nature, that everyone understood though no one had words for. In the lonely settlements, a lantern going out in a window would hold a meaning. To re-enter such a world it was necessary to unlearn everything, to be humble as grass. The only books he needed now, he said, were Thomas à Kempis, *Pilgrim's Progress*, and the Bible.

Yet in spite of this he was a child of the times, where old forms were in dissolution, and others, some of them not yet above ground, were clamouring to be acknowledged. Strindberg characterised the hero of his novel *By the Open Sea* in the follow-ing terms: 'Having been brought up in the era of steam and electricity, when the pace of life had quickened, he, like the rest of his generation, was inevitably afflicted by bad nerves . . . . These symptoms of illness were an expression of increased vitality, the result of extreme sensitivity, like that of the crayfish when she changes her shell, or the bird when it moults. It was the creation of a new race, or at least of a new type of human being.' His book, he declared, was 'a modern novel written in the footsteps of Nietzsche and Poe, and showed 'the ruin of the individual when he isolates himself.'

In Mr Braat's bookshop he was allowed to serve customers, even though his ignorance of the book trade seems to have been matched by his lack of interest in it. Apart from selling the odd quire of letter paper or the halfpenny print every so often, he sat at the back of the shop at a desk, supposedly occupied with deliveries. He started work at eight, had a lunch break from one to three, and at midnight was often to be found there. Doing what? One of Braat's sons, talking thirty-seven years later to a Rotterdam journalist, recalled that Vincent, instead of working at his job, would be translating the Bible into French, German, and English – in four columns, one of which was the Dutch text. 'At other times when you happened to look, you caught him making little sketches, such silly pen-and-ink drawings, a little tree with a lot of branches and side-branches and twigs.'[10] In other words, he was doodling. After Vincent was famous, Mr Braat ransacked the desk drawers from top to bottom in the hope of finding something of value. Alas, not a doodle remained.

He came to work in a top hat, one so much the worse for wear that it was as if he were caricaturing his previous incarnation at Goupil's in London and Paris. But if he had begun to regard himself as a drop-out and a rebel, no one would have guessed it from his behaviour. He went out of his way to be obliging, to cause no trouble, to remain as invisible as possible. All his conflict was internal. Religion, nature, and art pulled him first one way, then another. Guilt-ridden at the thought of past failures, hurt by his family's 'torrent of reproaches', he dreamed continually of becoming a Christian worker in emulation of his father – and of course, of Christ.

If his lodgers at the Rijkens and his colleagues in the shop saw him as strange, this actually gave him pleasure. It made him feel he was on the right track at last. Hadn't Christ been accused of strangeness? His identification with Christ seemed to intensify almost daily, as he worked away at what he saw as his own rebirth. What could be more important, more urgent? He pointed to II Corinthians 5:17: 'Therefore if any man be in Christ, he is a new creature.'[11] During his stay at Dordrecht he laboured away at his real occupation, which was to work through the whole story of Christ 'in all places and circumstances.'

He was soon given a chance to exhibit his new Christlike persona and translate his thoughts into deeds. Flooding in these parts was a frequent hazard, and one night Mr Braat's storehouse was awash, as well as the street outside. A small boat went up and down. Vincent waded over to his employer's house to warn him, then spent hours carrying heavy wet sacks of paper to the floor above. His endurance and willingness earned the man's gratitude. Others admired the young man's physical strength. Years later, striving to project another wished-for persona, this time one which united him with the underdog, Vincent would say hopefully that he was being mistaken for a bargee or an ironworker.

If he wasn't always popular at his lodgings, this was mainly because of his practice of nailing up prints and sketches on the walls of his room. He wasn't averse either to scrawling annotations underneath them. 'Mind the wallpaper!' his landlord would yell. Under one print, Vincent had written: 'Take my yoke upon you, and learn of me; for I am meek and lowly of heart. . . . In the Kingdom of Heaven they neither marry, nor are given in marriage.'[12]

More and more he kept to himself. At the table he preferred not to eat meat or gravy. Whether this vegetarianism continued for any length of time is unclear. But not once did he visit Mr Braat's house socially. Only his room-mate Görlitz really knew him at all intimately. In a letter written in 1890, the year of Vincent's death, he set down a few impressions. The reclusive Dutchman was well-made, and his reddish hair stood up on end. His face, usually abstracted and gloomy, would light up marvellously in moments of enthusiasm – as it did when he suddenly shouted with laughter. Görlitz went on to express astonishment at the other's church-going. Vincent went off to the Dutch Reformed Church but also to Lutheran and Catholic services. Tackled about this, Vincent retorted: 'Do you really think that God cannot be found in the other churches?'[13]

He was living now as ascetically as a monk, his one luxury his pipe, which he smoked all the time. Once, when Braat asked him bluntly why his mind wasn't on his work, Vincent replied, 'I want to be a pastor like my father.'

Braat could be tactless. What a shame it was about Vincent's father, he said: he had been a clergyman for ages and yet was stuck in a place like Etten. Roused to anger – it was the first time Braat had seen him like it – Vincent's eyes flashed and he looked suddenly like an excited evangelist. 'My father's a true shepherd, he is in his right place,' he told Braat.

When his friend Görlitz went off to be interviewed for a teaching post at De Leur, he was given a bed for the night by the van Goghs at Etten. Asked how their son was faring, he told them what Vincent had deliberately left out of his letters home, namely that he was no happier in the bookshop than he had been at Goupil's. What he wanted was to be a preacher and nothing else.

Touched by this, his family set about trying to make it possible. After all, the bookshop had only been a stopgap. First, though, he would need to complete his education privately at Amsterdam and then take the state examinations, enter university, and study theology. This meant a crash course in Latin and Greek, mathematics, geography, and history. Once again the uncles came to the rescue. This time it was the turn of Uncle Jan, commandant of the Naval Yard, who provided accommodation, and Pastor Stricker, who seemed just the man to organise and keep an eye on Vincent's studies. Stricker had married into the family as the husband of one of Vincent's mother's sisters.

Uncle Jan was a real discovery, an old sailor who had travelled the world. Settled now, he was an open, straightforward man, with an aura of travel about him. Vincent had difficulty in remembering him from his childhood. Uncle Jan didn't seem to notice – or was not put off by – his nephew's habit of introspection, and anyway he liked young company. He took Vincent on walks around the town and on his tours of inspection in the Yard. He approved of the serious young man's decision to study for the ministry. Vincent for his part liked the old man's homely turns of speech, his quaint proverbs. 'The devil,' he'd say, 'is never so black that you can't look into the whites of his eyes.'[14]

Later, left to himself in his comfortable quarters in the vice-admiral's residence, Vincent was at a loss. It was hard to settle in, and even harder to accustom himself to having everything, a spacious bureau, a wide soft bed, a study table, when he had been used to hardship for so long. He walked out and across the Dam in search of prints. Making for the waterfront he came on a street of booksellers with prints hanging up in open kiosks. He bought a heap of prints from a Jewish trader, and was soon back in his room tacking them up and feeling better, taking care this time not to damage the wallpaper. The costly fabrics intimidated him.

On Sunday he was invited to dinner by Uncle Stricker and his family. The Strickers lived in a fine street of aristocratic houses, a boulevard in the shape of a horseshoe that ran alongside one of the more important canals near the harbour. He was struck by the tranquil beauty of the tall narrow house's interior, with its subtly filtered light.

More memorable still was his first meeting there with his cousin Kee, a tall slender girl, her hair blonde but with reddish tints. Later her husband Vos came in, and their little boy of two, his eyes as blue as his mother's. Vincent sat absorbing the happiness of the family group, the exchanged kisses, Kee's flushed cheek. They asked him to visit them. One Monday he did, and wrote wistfully to Theo that 'they love each other truly, and one can easily perceive that where love dwells, God commands his blessing. . . . When one sees them sitting side by side in the evening, in the kindly lamplight of the living room, quite close to the bedroom of their boy, who wakes up every now and then and asks his mother for something, it is an idyll.'[15] So deeply did it affect him that he tried, a few years later, to reproduce it exactly – and not far from here – though on his own terms, and in circumstances anything but idyllic.

He was moving again among the genteel and well-to-do, in a world of servants, and no doubt his parents were ashamed to think of him letting them down with his unkempt appearance among these well-heeled relatives. On one of his visits home they tried to smarten him up a bit by 'putting him in the hands of the best tailor in Breda', and arranging for him to have a decent haircut. Meanwhile, Uncle Stricker had found him a tutor, Dr Mendes da Costa, a young scholarly Jew, with whom he was to study Latin and Greek.

To start with, all went well. Teacher and pupil liked each other, and they were of a similar age. Mendes da Costa was alarmed at first by Vincent's rough exterior. Then he noticed the nervous hands, contradicting the homely-seeming face 'which expressed so much and hid so much more.'

Vincent, he soon saw, was eager to prove his good intentions. 'I succeeded in winning his confidence and friendship very soon,' he said, and 'we made comparatively good progress in the beginning – I was soon able to let him translate an easy Latin author. Needless to say, he, who was fanatically devout in those days, at once started using this little bit of Latin to read Thomas à Kempis in the original.'[16]

Before long, peculiarities and difficulties began to surface. Growing restive as he fought to master Greek verbs, Vincent confronted his tutor with an unanswerable question: 'Mendes, do you seriously believe that such horrors are indispensable to a man who wants to do what I want to do: give peace to poor creatures and reconcile them to their existence here on earth?'[17] Off the troubled man hurried to consult the Reverend Stricker, and was told to keep trying.

Mendes da Costa has painted a forlorn picture of Vincent clamped into the strait-jacket of a curriculum. He would catch sight of his unhappy student hurrying across the square from the direction of the Herengracht Bridge. In winter he would be without an overcoat. Books were under his right arm, pressed against his body, his left hand clutching the bunch of snowdrops that were meant to placate his professor. His face would be set grimly in a despairing mask. His half-grown beard didn't help the impression of misery, nor the fact that he had probably got himself locked out deliberately the night before, sleeping on a pile of sacks in an outhouse as a penance for neglecting his studies. He confessed one day to Mendes – they didn't 'mister' each other now – that he would beat himself on the back with a heavy stick if he felt especially remorseful.[18]

Vincent was in a double-bind. He could see no sense in what he was doing and yet he badly wanted to succeed in it, so as to avoid further condemnation. 'Don't be mad at me, Mendes,' he would plead in a mournful voice. The sensitive Jewish scholar found it impossible not to feel sorry for this man who clearly had a need to torment himself, and who kept repeating that he only wanted to help the unfortunate. He wasn't merely sounding pious. Mendes had a deaf and dumb brother, to whom Vincent was drawn. He also went out of his way to spend time with Mendes' aunt, 'an impecunious, slightly deformed woman who was slow-witted and spoke with difficulty, thus provoking the mockery of many people.' She mangled Vincent's surname, calling him 'mister van Gort', but he told Mendes not to worry, she was a good soul and he had grown fond of her.[19]

We could ask ourselves the question: how did he occupy himself for a whole year in Amsterdam when it must have been obvious to him that he was marking time? He did what any bored student does – loafed around, went on jaunts as far as the Zuider Zee, drew large-scale maps of the area to amuse himself, and explored all the bookshops. To believe, as his mother and father did, that serious study was beyond him because of his fragmented early education is to underestimate his ability. A person of his intelligence and breadth of learning would, one imagines, have coped perfectly well if only he had been able to concentrate properly and put other interests out of his mind. In the first of his letters to Theo from Amsterdam he said, revealingly, 'A great deal of study is needed for the work of men like Father, Uncle Stricker, and so many others, just as for painting.'

There we have it. Instead of studying, he did a great deal of *looking*. He fed his sensations, becoming obsessed with twilight. He experienced terrors which transformed themselves into ecstasies. 'I got up early and saw the workmen arrive in the Yard while the sun was shining brightly . . . that long line of black figures, big and small, first in the narrow street where the sun just peeps in, and later in the Yard . . .'.[20] Something impelled him to peer into dark interiors thrown open to the light that were perhaps analogous to Christ's open tomb. Walking along a street past the huge dark cellar of a wine warehouse with its doors yawning open, he had a vision of hell, but one redeemed by light – 'men with lights were running back and forth in the dark vault.'[21] He was given an awful feeling, followed by an ecstatic one.

In his London sermon he had said that life was 'a constantly going from darkness to light', and he equated this with dying and then being born again. Albert Lubin has noticed that there are literally hundreds of references to the theme of light in his letters. Many of them link light with its opposite. Twilight, which affected him profoundly at this time, could have been seen as a God-given means of reconciling these warring opposites in his mind. Commenting to Theo on Dickens' 'blessed twilight', he went on to describe lovingly a drawing in sepia, charcoal, and ink by Rembrandt of the house in Bethany. Jesus, Mary, and Martha are shown wrapped in that mystical twilight evocative of family happiness and communion which so stimulated him in art and in life whenever he came upon it.[22]

A great deal of his energy was being consumed in allaying his fears about another regular occurring obsession, the idea of a wasted life – 'une vie, une existence, manquée.'[23] The Hammachers remind us of the frequency with which it haunted so many nineteenth-century artists and writers. Vincent's great contemporary, Tolstoy, is a case in point. Unlike Tolstoy, however, whose life in this respect was a reverse image of Vincent's, the painter eventually married himself to art, making a sacrifice of the dream of family harmony which had so entranced him. But he would never cease to regret the absence of human love in his life.

Mendes soon gave up trying to discourage his student from vehement displays of emotion and acts of self-punishment. The fellow had something biting him and there was nothing he could do about it; he was zealous in a way inimical to sound scholarship. Yet he appreciated the man's sincerity and directness, the very qualities Vincent admired in his beloved Thomas à Kempis. Grateful for Mendes' forbearance, Vincent would talk to him as if addressing someone he had known for years. He wanted to know what Mendes thought of 'hating one's life for the sake of some great ideal,' and went on, 'Doesn't Thomas à Kempis say the same thing when he speaks about knowing and hating oneself?'[24]

One day his father paid him a visit. He had to find out for himself what was going wrong, and he went with his son to see Mendes and then Stricker. Vincent's lack of progress must have dismayed him. After he left, Vincent struggled again to persevere. It was as hopeless as before. Worse, because his father's visit had unsettled him and he longed for home. 'After I had seen Father off at the station and had watched the train go out of sight, even the smoke of it, I came home to my room and saw Father's chair standing near the little table; and though I know we shall see each other again pretty soon, I cried like a child.'[25]

Saying farewell to someone dear often seemed a devastation. The image of an empty chair would soon be a potent symbol. He had already drawn attention to a painting by Fildes, *The Empty Chair*, a view of Dickens' study the morning after his death. Chairs were reminders of absences; farewells were a kind of death, as were sickness and old age. 'Empty chairs – there are many of them, there will be even more, and sooner or later there will be nothing but empty chairs,' he wrote.[26]

Shortly before he gave up and went home, he urged Theo to read George Eliot's *Adam Bede, Silas Marner, Felix Holt*, and

Romola (Savanarola's life), and to be sure to look at Millet's etching, *The Diggers*. He was himself digging his way towards the light with tremendous stubbornness and consistency, and at a time when most people condemned him for floundering helplessly without purpose or direction. Mendes seems to have been an exception. He did, at any rate, leave Vincent to his own devices. Something about Mendes, his features, perhaps a certain rapt expression, reminded Vincent of the *Imitation of Jesus Christ* by Ruyperez, he told Theo.[27]

His power of transference was formidable. Already full blown, it is concentrated here on the personality of Jesus. Sometimes he would pour himself into the characters of novels he was reading, or into aspects of paintings he admired, or real persons would become the crucible into which he would release feelings with which he then passionately identified. When he came to embrace art, the process of creating self-portraits and symbols under various guises was as natural to him as breathing, even though the road to that naturalness was a long and painful one.

In life, things were inevitably more devious. He would praise a painting or a book extravagantly, and be utterly sincere in doing so, but at the same time he would be finding things to say which he wanted to hear said about his own work. How this expressed itself negatively is harder to see, but one can detect it all the same in his dealings with his 'loved' brother, whose goodness he sometimes resented and on whose loyalty he utterly depended. His letters – the bulk of them are addressed to Theo – are a quarry of biographical information, and overwhelm the reader with their acute self-knowledge. Nevertheless, the ingenuity required to conceal deep wounds and jealousies from his consciousness was equally a test of his skill. He had to go on telling all in this process of continual therapy and yet protect himself from a revelation of his own capacity for hatred. In this sense, of repressed and revealed knowledge going hand in hand, the letters can be regarded as symbolic works in their own right, to be set beside the paintings and evaluated accordingly.

Even their serpentine, heavily surging style seems to be telling us something. A muscular energy informs them, as it does the paintings. The man behind them was mysterious, as capable of deceptions as he was of standing before us naked. Sometimes the two were inextricably combined. The Vincent we think we know is contradictory, out in the open and out of sight, both aware of his own nature and yet hidden from himself.

In Amsterdam he worked again at the art of 'failing', so as to avoid being further enmeshed in activity that his instincts told him would run counter to his future development. He had enlisted Christ in this strategy because His failure was exemplary and His dying led to rebirth. None of this could have been conscious, for he was soon bitterly accusing himself once more of being a disgrace, a disappointment to all and sundry, as well as clumsy, ill-dressed, thoughtless, uncouth, selfish, evil – the list of his self-accusations grows and grows. One suspects an element of pride, almost arrogance, certainly satisfaction at the way he always 'chooses whatever leads to trouble', as his father complained, or 'the dog's path',[28] to use his own words. Ernst Pawel notes in his biography of Kafka – another ferocious self-punisher – that 'Self-flagellation is a not uncommon form of self-abuse, and the sinner lustfully wallowing in his guilt was known to perceptive inquisitors, grand and petty, long before Freud and Dostoevsky.'[29]

Vincent would evolve more complex strategies later, using his 'health' to extort sympathy from those close to him, notably Theo. This manipulation would intensify as he came to accept an image of himself as unwanted and unlovable, seeing it as a condition likely to remain permanent. He submitted to this fate while always protesting bitterly against it as intolerable, and tried to mitigate its worst effects by the use of illness, acting like a child and parading a host of mysterious ailments.

Sitting up late one night to write to Theo, looking out on a view of the deserted Yard down below him, the lamps burning and above it all a starlit sky, Vincent quoted from a book he was immersed in, Lamartine's *Cromwell:* 'The soul is a mirror before it becomes a home.'[30] At roughly the same time his mother was writing about him to the son who gave them no cause for anxiety whatsoever. 'He really takes no pleasure in life, always walking around with head bent, although we have done all we could to bring him to some honourable goal in life.'[31]

Vincent's agonising was about precisely this, but it had to be his goal, not theirs, and he had to find a way out of the cage of self to it. Choices bewildered and blocked him. There were so many branchings, as he tried to decide on the right road, the road meant for him, laid out for him by his fate and leading to the work he must do. Once found, the anguish of postponement would be over. Never able to separate life from work, he would walk down the road of his life towards a death that he seemed to see ahead of him, as if it already existed and was lying in wait for him. After the road was known, his crises would be to do with failures of nerve and the loss of faith, when the source of his power reversed its flow, and what had been fecundating dissolved his will to water.

5

LOWEST OF THE LOW

Disillusioned with the ministry before he had even entered it, Vincent now said damningly that to trade in religion was on a par with trading in art or tulip bulbs.[1] That, one would have thought, was an indictment sweeping enough to settle the matter once and for all.

But it was not. He still burned to preach the Gospel to the poor and to help them. Back again at the parsonage at Etten, he must have pleaded with sufficient eloquence to convince his father that he should be allowed to try. His stay at home coincided with a visit from the Reverend Jones of Isleworth, who had kept in touch and was now a friend of the family.

The two clergymen went with him on a trip to Laeken near Brussels. Vincent's father knew of a school there for training mission workers. It was an establishment that placed more emphasis on public speaking than on a knowledge of the classics, and the course was shorter and more intensive than anything comparable in Holland. So on 25 August 1878, the failed scholar, bookseller, and art dealer arrived in Laeken to start a three-month trial period. In his first letter from there he makes a significant little admission to Theo, and encloses a sketch: 'I should like to begin making hasty sketches of some of the many things I meet . . . but as it would probably keep me from my real work it is better not to start.'[2]

Poised to begin his 'real work' as a missionary among the wretched of the earth, a holy man at last, he is paralleled in time with Tolstoy. In this same year, 1878, by an extraordinary

65

confluence, their spiritual paths crossed, though they were travelling from opposite directions. Vincent would move on from evangelist to artist, and the great Russian, determined to live a life modelled on Christ, was beginning to regard all art as frivolous. In July, the month in which Vincent was enrolled at the mission school, a desperate Tolstoy and his friend Stakhov set off on a pilgrimage to the Optina Pustyn Monastery not far from Moscow. Tolstoy, uneasy about his wealth, wanted to reject violence in all its forms and live like a peasant. Vincent would soon see the struggle to turn himself into what he called a Peasant Painter as his prime aim. In a diary started in the spring of 1878, Tolstoy wrote: 'Read the Gospels. Christ says everywhere that everything temporal is false, and that only the abstract is real.' The terms would not have been Vincent's, but the note of absolute certainty could be his. The religion Tolstoy was to advocate was remarkably like the only one Vincent could wholeheartedly contemplate, 'a practical religion, not promising future bliss but bliss on earth.' Close to the end of his life, Vincent referred approvingly to Tolstoy's *My Religion*, and spoke of his hopes for a 'private and secret revolution in men from which a new religion will be born . . . something altogether new which will have no name, but will have the same effect of comforting, of making life possible, which the Christian religion used to have . . .'.[3]

His probationary period nearly over, he was suddenly hauled before the committee on evangelisation and told that he was unsuitable. Vincent was shattered. His state was serious enough for his father to be called. He had failed because of a lack of talent for impromptu speaking, considered essential for the task he was contemplating. He was also, it seems, notably short on humility. Two of Vincent's instructors later described their impressions of this eager novice who 'did not know what submission was'. According to one report, Vincent was as dismissive of academic study as he had been in Amsterdam. A master asked him on one occasion whether a word was nominative or dative, and back came his answer: 'I don't really care, sir!'[4]

Another time, in a French lesson, when the word *falaise* (cliff) was being discussed, he jumped up and asked if he could illustrate the word by drawing a cliff on the blackboard. The master said no. At the end of the lesson the excitable Dutchman got hold of a piece of chalk and began to draw a cliff on the board. One pupil, laughing behind his back, tugged at his jacket to distract him. All at once Vincent swung round. His face contorted with rage, he lashed out, shocking everyone with his show of violence. Clearly he had little aptitude for meekness either.[5]

Where next? While at Laeken he had seen miners, strange grisly beings to him. He made a sketch of the inn they frequented, adjoining a big coal shed. They would call in for a glass of beer on their way back from a shift. Enclosing this sketch in his letter he mentioned a district he had heard about, called the Borinage. It was possible that even a reject like him could be of use in such a godforsaken spot. He made enquiries. Yes, he could go there if he wished as a lay evangelist. Fired with enthusiasm he wrote to Theo: 'Experience has shown that people who walk in the darkness . . . like the miners in the black coal mines, for instance, are very impressed by the works of the Gospel, and believe them, too.'[6]

The Borinage, desolate and impoverished, was a coalfield in the south-west of Belgium near Mons, a region of flat blasted lands surmounted by slag heaps of waste. One assumes that his father financed this latest venture. He probably thought it would be short-lived. In fact Vincent spent twenty-two months in this terrible black country, a period nearly as long as his stay in France. For thirty Belgian francs a month he lodged with a pedlar by the name of van der Haegen who lived at Paturages, not far from Mons (the house was demolished in the early 1960s to allow for road widening). As soon as he got there he set to work. He visited the sick, taught his landlord's children, and gave Bible readings in the locality.

He was as shocked here as he had been by the scenes he had witnessed in London's East End. These were the realities of grinding poverty, the price paid in human terms for that age of worldwide industrial expansion into which he had been born. It festered here under his nose. And somehow, in a setting that had once been rural, it seemed yet more dire. The place was indescribably filthy and hopeless. The miners were emaciated, old before their time, and so were their bedraggled, staring women. At the centre of all that lived and moved in this ghastly universe was the mine. Around it clustered the settlement of miners' huts. Dead trees stuck up, together with blackened thorn hedges, dunghills, heaps of worthless coal. In the middle of his harrowing report he let slip a sentence, and we hear from that monster of objectivity inside every artist who sees everything as grist to the mill. 'Maris,' he wrote, 'could make a wonderful picture of it.'[7]

It was a hell of human vileness he had fallen into, a great raw wound crying out to be bandaged. But what was one person able to do here? So many sickly and feverish people were wandering about, some of them half-maimed, some burned from explosions. All were trapped in something inhuman, into which they had dumbly delivered themselves.

The only real life, curiously enough, was underground, in the pit of hell itself. Out on the surface the villages struck him as being stunned, dead, and forsaken. The men themselves could hardly bear to be above ground; at least down below they had each other. Vincent asked to be wound down to the pit bottom. He saw the weird underworld life for himself, and heard the horrible drip of water leaking through. Children, boys and girls, were loading small carts to be dragged along by old horses. Vincent spoke almost enviously of the miners' darkness, and the chance it gave them to reclaim the light. He soon came to appreciate their special character, their solidarity and mutual trust, their innate hatred for anyone who was domineering, their intelligence and quickness in spite of being unable to read or write. Above all he was impressed by their bravery, and the haunting mournfulness of their deep-set eyes.[8]

Winter was soon upon him. It gladdened him to see how even these degraded surroundings were touched by a curious beauty, as he watched the little gangs of miners making their way home, black as sweeps, in the white snow at twilight. Their houses, no more than huts, were scattered along the sunken tracks or half hidden in woods, or else perched on the slopes of the low hills. You could see the candlelight flickering through the small-paned windows, under roofs covered in moss. It was somehow medieval and hushed, in the shadow of the pit and its fiendish machinery.

These squat, frank men, working skilfully and terribly hard, who said little but had quick nervous responses, were not his equals – he saw them rather as his superiors. How could his role, safe on the surface with the women, be compared with theirs?

Everything here fed his masochism – as he had known instinctively that it would when he applied for a similar position in the

English coalfields some years before, only to be told that he was not mature enough. Now there were other motives being satisfied, and scores being subtly settled. Vincent's father spent more time ministering to the Catholic majority than to his own Protestant flock in the Brabant. Vincent, in Catholic Belgium, although emulating his father once again was also mocking him, by going to the limit in a way that passed judgement on his parents' safe Christianity, while putting himself beyond criticism. Christ would surely have acted as he, Vincent, was doing. Therefore he was the true follower of Jesus Christ. Instead of lagging woefully behind, he had surpassed them.

He had come to the Borinage as his parents' representative, dressed correctly in the approved manner, his accents refined, and 'showed in his appearance all the characteristics of Dutch cleanliness.'[9] But not for long. Spiritual instruction was the last thing these downtrodden people needed, he argued. Instead of Bible teaching, he ought to be translating fine words into deeds. He changed direction almost overnight.

Then in January 1879 the Mission School committee relented and informed his father that he could have a temporary post after all. Vincent was sent to near-by Wasmes and given a salary of fifty Belgian francs a month. Overjoyed at having a recognised part to play, he taught the Scriptures, but spent most of his time assisting the poor and the ailing. Even in this hell-hole he found a kind of salvation. Being a combination of social worker, medical auxiliary, and teacher to these miners and their families meant that he was able to break out of the prison of his hateful loneliness. Besides, it was fitting that he should serve a people who were so obviously more admirable as human beings than himself.

His compulsion to be of service and to act from his feelings had found its outlet. He had been pressing for the opportunity to abandon himself, free of dogma, and here it was. He was his own master, dedicated only to Christ, who had asserted the brotherhood of man. If he neglected his physical body, there was no one here to reprimand him, for the whole community was woefully neglected. His heart was appalled by what he saw, but in his heart also there lurked a triumph. This hell he had entered could be his heaven.

Soon, whatever he did, no matter how hard and long he worked, it was not enough. Apocryphal stories abound. Like

Walt Whitman, who became a wound dresser in the American Civil War in order to draw closer to the simple young soldiers he adored and whom he wished to tend, Vincent sought to draw nearer to Christ. First he threw off his respectability, exchanging it for 'an old soldier's tunic and a shabby cap'.[10] Nothing was enough. Nothing satisfied his urge to descend lower, until he was low enough to identify with these men who lay entombed in cramped cells, and crawled on all fours in the dark. Through them he would know Christ.

In Wasmes he lived at first with a baker called Jean-Baptiste Denis and his wife Esther. Then he thought he was being pampered, so he moved into a dirty hovel, 'where he lay on straw like a beast'. His habit of Dutch cleanliness was no more. He stopped using soap. What he wanted was to be as dirty as the miners, covered in coal-dust like them. In the end he was even dirtier than they were. Following his own desires and urges he lay on straw in his freezing barn, after giving away his bed, his decent clothes, and his sound shoes. When Madame Denis asked him why he went to such lengths, he answered, 'Esther, one should do like the good God; from time to time one should go and live among His own.'[11]

Monsieur Bonte, a pastor recently installed in the neighbouring village of Warquignies, saw nothing odd in his amazing behaviour, which, he said, 'revealed the originality of his aspirations'. However, less flattering reports were beginning to reach the Mission School and also Vincent's family in Etten. And there was worse to come. A series of firedamp explosions shook the mines, causing fearful injuries – though the high accident rate was a commonplace in these parts. Vincent was involved in one disaster at the Marcasse mine. He worked frantically to help the casualties, tearing up what was left of his linen for bandages and soaking them in olive oil and wax to apply to burns.

Having got rid of his shirts in this way, he was reduced to replacing them with crude garments made out of sacking. Tralbaut mentions an old woman who knew Vincent well, and who told him, many years ago when he began his researches, 'There aren't men like that nowadays.' Vincent would enter houses and tell exhausted women to go and rest, and then take over the family wash. There are even rumours of near miracles he accomplished, such as the conversion of a foul-mouthed old alcoholic, hurt in the Marcasse pit disaster, who told him in no uncertain terms to clear off, he didn't want 'rosary-mumblers' around him, and then was converted by Vincent's sanctity.[12]

The more tender-hearted biographers have pictured Vincent as a St Francis, lifting straying caterpillars from the ground and placing them gently on branches, leaving cheese and milk for the mice while he starved on bread and water. In the words of others he springs into action as a political firebrand, marching into the coal-owners' offices and demanding justice for their exploited work-force, only to be told that the coal seams were too meagre and the profit margin too small to provide improvements in safety standards. Contradictory stories tell of Vincent coming into his own as a pacifier, quelling an uprising of vengeance-bent miners by persuading them that violence only begets violence.

The truth seems to have been less dramatic. At no time during his life did Vincent show any sign of wanting to involve himself in the socialist movements of his day. A J Lubin does suggest that his experiences in the Borinage fostered a revolutionary spirit in him. This was no doubt true. In the coalfields he read as avidly as ever, including in his reading books about the French revolution by Michelet and others. Lubin comments that 'Shyness probably made concrete political action impossible, for this would have required direct action with other people. But in art the revolutionary in van Gogh could find a place.'[13]

As he went on abasing himself in this extraordinary fashion, the Synodal Evangelisation Committee were taking steps to dissociate the Church from his unseemly conduct. It was decided that he was bringing them into disrepute and should be dismissed summarily. The Committee's 23rd report refers to the failure of the experiment of accepting the services of a young Dutchman, Mr Vincent van Gogh, and goes on to cite his spirit of self-sacrifice, his admirable qualities in aiding the sick and wounded, and his devotion, 'of which he gave many proofs'. Unfortunately he was, in their opinion, such an indifferent speaker as to render 'an evangelist's principal function wholly impossible'.[14]

But nothing could stop him now. He was living on dry crusts and frost-bitten potatoes. Somehow his constitution, always incredibly strong, held up. He was indistinguishable now from the ragged half-starved men, women, and children he struggled day and night to help. The sufferings he saw everywhere piled up more and more tasks and threatened to overwhelm him. At night he was heard weeping in his miserable hut.

It may seem strange to suspect such a man of inflation – the psychoanalyst's term for a tendency to grandeur, the obverse of a patient's self-denigration and depression. A famous example nearer to our own time is that of the Christian martyr Simone Weil, who joined the Renault workers on the assembly line so as to share their debasement, and worked on the land for the same reason, absurdly so in view of her frail physique. In England during the war, she literally committed suicide by refusing her food rations, thus expressing her solidarity with the starving of Europe. In both cases, a strong sense of shame is combined with the arrogance of a person who insists on suffering more than anyone else, and justifies such action by invoking the name of Christ. From being despised, feeling inferior, wanting to be invisible, one is lifted up in full view on a cross of one's own devising.

None of this would have mattered, of course, to the crushed but undefeated people he was trying so hard to help. So as to be like his fellows who had been turned into slaves, he slaved tirelessly himself. The Decrucqs were one family who could never get over the loving care he lavished on their small son when he fell desperately ill with typhoid fever. A portrait he drew of Madame Decrucq coming home from the pit has since vanished. Theo's salary was a small one, but out of it he managed to send Vincent a pittance from time to time. As soon as he received it, the holy man who now looked like a scarecrow gave most of it away.

Struggling to survive the discouragement of another rebuff, Vincent walked on foot from the Borinage to Brussels to plead his case with the Reverend Pietersen, one of the more sympathetic members of the committee which had just sacked him. The door was opened by the clergyman's daughter, who ran off terrified when she saw the fearsome-looking tramp standing docilely on the pavement. Nevertheless, it seems that the journey was worth making. Pietersen, a kindly man, invited the apparition in and made him welcome. An amateur artist himself, he was intrigued by the drawings Vincent had brought along with him. No one until then had considered these subjects suitable for art. The man wrote to the young man's parents that their son 'strikes me as someone who stands in his own light'.[15] This was shrewd comment, to say the least. He urged Vincent to go back to the Borinage and continue with his work there, though without promising to intercede. And he could hold out no hope of any financial assistance.

Back once more, Vincent moved to another village, Cuesmes, where he lodged in a house divided in two. In one half lived the miner Charles Decrucq and his family, and in the other a fellow evangelist of whom nothing is known, except that his surname was Frank. Theo was about to travel from The Hague to Etten, en route for a new post in Paris, and Vincent pressed him to 'leave the train' on the second leg of his journey and stay with him for a day or two. Then he could show him the dismal landscape, and drawings he had done recently, some of which he had shown the Reverend Pietersen. One of these early pictures may have been *Miner with Shovel on his Shoulder*, a clumsy Expressionist drawing in black chalk and wash. It hits us with that familiar thump of veracity we experience before one of the 'dark' paintings of Josef Herman, an exiled artist of this century who made his home in Britain and painted the miners of the Welsh valleys.

Vincent's figure, head shrouded with a sack, leans forward to attack a steep hill. Encased in work before the workplace is even reached, the striding man is so grainy that he seems made of coal particles. Describing this drawing or another like it, Vincent said he had tried to reveal 'something touching and almost sad in these poor obscure labourers – of the lowest order, so to speak, and the most despised.'[16] His choice of words shows how thoroughly he has identified with his subject, and for what reason. In drawing a miner he has made a self-portrait. In his letter asking Theo to come he mentioned a novel of Dickens, *Hard Times*, as one which had particularly impressed him. 'Excellent: in it the character of Stephen Blackpool, a working man, is most striking and sympathetic.'[17]

He often draws far into the night, he tells Theo. Mr Tersteeg, his ex-employer at The Hague, has sent him a box of paints and a sketchbook. Already he has half-filled the pages. Are we to assume then that he had now switched over from being an evangelist and was a deliberate artist in the making, out in the open for all to see? Things are rarely that simple – and for a van

Gogh, never. Theo did break his journey and came to spend a day or so with him. Vincent – partly because of exhaustion – had not written to a soul in months. Sunk in religious doubts, he was being supported by a father whose profession he had ceased to respect. And was Theo for or against him? Brooding over it all in his weakened condition brought him low, in a dangerous state of depression.

Theo's visit was intended by both brothers to heal a rift which had developed between them. To judge by Vincent's subsequent letter of 15 October, it did at least bring them back into contact. But a closer reading tells a different story.

From start to finish it is a bitter refutation of whatever advice Theo had seen fit to give him. They hadn't clashed openly. It seems that on reflection it wasn't so much what Theo had said but how he had said it that had generated such despair and fury in him. His letter, veiled and angry, makes clear how violently disturbed he was, hating his whole family and Theo most of all. He had felt betrayed by the visit, after hoping to be lifted out of his crushing depression by it. Rather than swallow any more of what to him was the worst kind of mealy-mouthed claptrap, he gave up the vital therapy of letter writing and lapsed into total silence.

The falling-out lasted eight months. Forced to reply the following July to acknowledge a sum of fifty francs from Theo, he said grimly that he was writing 'with some reluctance' because 'you have become a total stranger to me, and I have become the same to you.'[18]

What was this half-smothered vituperation all about? After all, grievances had been aired before, plenty of times, usually with Theo acting as peace-maker.

Well, it was the last straw, apparently, to be told by this cultivated, clean, excessively reasonable, and controlled favourite son, in these hideous surroundings, that Vincent really shouldn't have come here; that it was more foolishness, another dead-end, when he could have gone to university and made everyone happy, including himself. How could he, Theo, have forgotten what it was like for him in Amsterdam? The whole enterprise was a terrible joke, misguided, utterly stupid. 'I still shudder when I think of it.' It was the worst time he had ever lived through. Compared to that unspeakable calamity his days here in the

Borinage, for all the filth and hardship, had been almost pleasant. If he followed more of their so-called 'wise advice', where would he end?[19]

Theo insisted that he should concentrate on improving his life – whatever that meant – and that he seemed intent on doing the opposite. Vincent retorted that he *did* wish to be better than he was, and feared stagnation, but was 'even more afraid of remedies that are worse than the evil itself.' He was searching for the right doctor – he meant a doctor for his soul – and kept falling into the hands of quacks.[20]

At some point it seems that Theo made a most fatuous comment. Wasn't it unwise – that word again – for Vincent to spend his days idly? Wouldn't he become fond of idleness if he wasn't careful? Surely it was better to follow any occupation, even a baker's, a barber's, a librarian's, than commit the cardinal sin – for a Dutchman – of doing *nothing*.

Vincent's reply was heavily ironic. 'May I observe that this is a rather strange sort of idleness . . .'[21] and he went on to admit that, although it was difficult for him to defend his present way of life, there *was* purpose in it, even if that purpose was an obscure one. It was certainly obscure to Theo, who had gone off sadly shaking his head. For Vincent, it rankled most that his sensitive brother had defected to the other side, seeing him as the cause of discord and anxiety at home, just as 'they' did. The realisation left him with a feeling of anguish so great that it threatened to engulf him. Perhaps, he concluded, in his letter terminating their correspondence for months to come, it was all just a terrible nightmare which would only be understood later?[22]

Another cruel winter was about to start. He had done all he could here, but instinct warned him that it would be a mistake to go home. Instead of being condemned to death he felt condemned to life, like these worker-convicts in the rain and cold and mud of a no-man's land. He belonged with them. They were like him, as undernourished in one way as he was in another. He would go on living on scraps like they did. He would freeze in hell with them. Somehow he managed to end his onslaught – like so many of his attacks it was also an apologia – on a note of hope. The bitter frost would last interminably, and then suddenly, 'with or without permission', it ended. There was a change, a thaw. He would hang on for that.[23]

The following July, 1880, he got the fifty francs from Theo and made reluctant contact again. The one and only period of estrangement in their short lives was over: the frost had ended. Theo's fears that his brother was on a self-destructive course must have been at least partly eased by this letter. But A J Lubin is mistaken in thinking that he now announced his intention to become an artist. There was no announcement. What artist – or writer or composer – ever makes it? The whole question is hedged about by doubts. Does he have the ability, is he fooling himself? Usually someone sneaking towards an artistic niche does so in a sideways, disguised fashion, and under cover of darkness, like a smuggler. And artists are not the only ones to take a roundabout route. One of Isaac Bashevis Singer's characters in a short story tells the narrator-author: 'You once wrote that human nature is such that one cannot do anything in a straight line. You always have to manoeuvre between the powers of wickedness and madness.'[24]

Nevertheless, his letter was crucial and marked a real turning point. Vincent declared that as a man of passion he was prepared to try anything. Here in the Borinage, he admitted, he was 'often homesick for the land of pictures',[25] uniting in the same phrase his love of home and his longing to see paintings. Here too occurred the first mention of the beneficial effects of what he called 'active melancholy'.

His passion for books still raged, and so did his desire to study, to instruct himself. But he had to be untutored, a free agent. He swung back again to the imputation of idleness that had so hurt him. He had been more or less unemployed for five years, wandering about. Did this mean he had deteriorated, fallen apart? No, he had been moulting, like a bird. Out of the moulting stage a bird emerged renewed. This is the nearest we get to an announcement that his long hibernation has transformed him. He has gained a new identity, but its nature is unclear to him. Interrogating himself, he asks: Do I have a definite aim? The answer is not forthcoming. Instead, he rambles on some more, to ask why he is still unemployed when he feels such a sense of renewal. 'It is simply that I have different ideas than the gentlemen who give places to men. . . . '.[26]

In the same letter he mentions his fondness for Dickens' Sydney Carton, and for Kent in *King Lear*. 'My God, how beautiful

Shakespeare is! Who is mysterious like him? His language and style can indeed be compared to an artist's brush, quivering with fever and emotion. But one must learn to read, just as one must learn to see and learn to live.'[27]

So this is what has kept him employed through these 'misspent' years: he has been learning to see, and to live. 'Maybe for a short time somebody takes a free course at the great university of misery, and pays attention to the things he sees with his eyes and hears with his ears.' Doing this, 'he will perhaps have learned more than he can tell.'[28] What he had learnt in the Borinage was that human suffering of the most basic sort somehow activated his creative energies, as well as enabling him to gain access to the depths of his own nature. He loved the superb art of the Dutch Golden Age, but he wanted to master a different, rougher, Adamistic art, purposely naive, one that satisfied his demands for simplicity and truth and vindicated his distaste for luxury. It had to be an art that did not separate him from the uncultured poor but was founded in them, gathering them to him in a home of art they could all share, a home that sheltered and consoled; a warm place.

How this would come about was as yet unclear. For all that, it was a key letter and sounded a new note, and it was his first written in French, as if to underline his sense of liberation from the worst aspects of things Dutch – their narrow-mindedness, their lack of joy. Back again to the fundamental question of whether or not he was idle, he worried at it like a terrier, then laid down a challenge. Perhaps Theo could tell him the difference between the two types of idleness, he asked slyly. There is the fellow who is idle from weakness, born idle as we say, a lazy character, and there is the idle man whose idleness imprisons and tortures him, because like a caged bird he longs to fly. His idleness is involuntary; he dreams of actions he can't perform. Because in the cage 'he does not possess what he needs to become productive. . .'.

This was spelling things out with a vengeance. He ended with one of his most beautiful and profound utterances: 'Do you know what frees one from this captivity? It is every deep, serious affection. Being friends, being brothers, love, that is what opens the cage by some supreme power, by some magic force. Without this, one remains in prison. Where sympathy is renewed, life is restored.'[29]

He didn't as yet quite dare to imagine himself as a real artist. To move over from religion into art with his newly liberated soul, he badly needed a bridge – a Dutch bridge. The bridge was Rembrandt. Didn't great art lead to God? he asked himself. 'One man wrote or told it in a book (the Bible), another in a picture.' Furthermore, 'there is something of Rembrandt in the Gospel, and something of the Gospel in Rembrandt.'[30] He had closed the circle. Now he could begin.

The picture we have of Theo as a man is extremely hazy. Like an angel, he is not easily seen. Always attendant, from now on he will occupy a position that is centre stage, yet invisibly as it were.

What is his story? Vincent blocks our view of him. Information about him is scant, partly because he was by nature self-effacing. His widow tells us the things we expect to hear; that he was good, kind, gentle. Friends and relatives speak of him in glowing terms. He was a loving husband and, briefly, an adoring father.

Did he have off-days? Did he ever lose his temper, raise his voice? Were his money worries the main source of his anxiety? We know they were a contributory factor, but our curiosity is aroused by the hints of maladies of which we know virtually nothing. Vincent once tried to persuade him to give up his safe career and join him as a fellow painter – like other famous brothers in art history. Was he tempted? If he had been, it would have meant the end of Vincent's support-system. Are we to deduce from this that Vincent saw Theo as an artist-manqué, or was he simply trying, not too hard in this instance, to shift the guilt a child feels before a self-sacrificing parent? These are speculative questions. One thing is certain: the burden this younger brother assumed, of caring for Vincent like a parent – sometimes a mother, sometimes a father – extended him both financially and emotionally to a dangerous extent. Vincent's demands mounted over the years until they seemed to flood in – as they often did – by every other post.

Theo's occasional complaints, hardly ever voiced directly, were usually muted and so we fail to take note of them. His constitution was delicate, and the strain on his health would have been considerable. He suffered, like Vincent, from depressive attacks, of a kind now seen as indicating acute anxiety neurosis. Otto Rank describes the neurotic as someone who, faced with the proposition 'All or nothing', chooses the nothing.[31]

Rumour has it that he contracted a venereal disease at some point and sought medical treatment. This only comes as a shock if we insist on seeing Theo in terms of sainthood. He was, after all, living in Paris, which had dozens of brothels and hordes of prostitutes on the streets. Access to whores. was sanctioned by male tradition and by his class, if not by his upbringing. He kept company with a crowd of painters and with businessmen. As a man whose sensibilities would be troubled by these liaisons with 'beastliness', a basically tender-hearted man, it was perhaps in compensation for his acts of relief that he tried to befriend and help women in trouble, as we shall see.

For all his determination to break the mould, Vincent was in a sense always typically Dutch, and never more so than in his obstinacy. Here was a trait that Theo could wholeheartedly approve and support. And he did, up to the hilt, as soon as it was clear to him that Vincent had chosen his life's work and intended to concentrate on it enthusiastically, against all the odds.

Vincent made a start by setting himself exercises from a popular drawing manual, the *Cours de Dessin Bargue*, and by painstakingly copying prints. Theo was soon keeping him well supplied with prints and etchings as well as art materials. Vincent's aim, naive though it now seems, was to turn out drawings presentable enough to bring in a few francs. His father cheered him by ordering copies of large maps of the Holy Land at ten guilders each. He still drew from life, of men and women filing towards the mine shaft through the snow and of miners holding lamps, bent double under loaded sacks. He drew stiffly, crudely, full of feeling but with faulty technique. He had so much to learn. He asked for and was sent *Sketches of Anatomy for Artists' Use*, and struggled to teach himself the complexities of bones and muscles by endless copying. And what about animals? Where was the nearest veterinary school? If only he could make contact with a genuine practising artist he'd be able to discuss all these things and get proper advice.

A painter he especially admired, Jules Breton, lived thirty-five miles away at Courrières. He went tramping off one day with ten francs in his pocket, hoping to call on him. He was on the road for a week, making sketches in villages along the way, intrigued particularly by the lives of weavers. Miners he saw as men of the abyss, and the weaver as a different type of character altogether, dreamy, something of a somnambulist. He made detours and slept in the open, 'once in an abandoned wagon, which was white with frost the next morning.' Then, as he got near to Courrières, a steady drizzle of rain descended.

When he located Breton's studio he was immediately put off by its exterior. The new raw brick had a cold, Methodist-like aspect and that discouraged him, he said. In fact he had lost his nerve and was too shy to go up and knock on the door. Embarrassed by his lack of courage, he wandered forlornly about the town, finding in an old church a copy of Titian's 'Burial of Christ' that *might* have been done by Breton.

He went from there to a café called Café des Beaux Arts, decorated inside with rather dismal and bad frescoes. He came out again. He had to compensate for the waste of a visit with his encounters, and with the countryside around the town, the haystacks, the brown earth speckled with whitish spots where the mark showed, so unlike the black earth of Holland. He was heartened too by the French sky, clean and limpid after the smoke and fog of the Borinage. Leaving Courrières he saw a small colliery. The day shift was coming up into the twilight, miners with tired and miserable faces trooping out, their clothes as tattered as those of the miners in the Borinage. One man was wearing an old soldier's cape.[32]

Now that he was working and studying with real purpose, he had a problem. His cramped room in the Decrucq house, that he shared at night with two small children, was no good for his art work. As well as the lack of space, it was ill-lit. A larger room was taken up with the endless daily washing that miners' wives were obliged to do. They might have swapped with him, but he couldn't ask it: their need was greater than his.

He kept drawing. 'It is not surprising,' writes A J Lubin, 'that the pictures he drew in Holland (and in Belgium) had Dutch qualities, for he was thoroughly saturated in his youth with knowledge of Dutch artists of the past and the present. . . . Much of it resembled the old Dutch genre paintings that had "a touch of the curious and a moral to be learned".'[33]

Drawing was always to be a liberation for him. He told Theo that the act of drawing enabled him to see things differently. In everything he attempted, the religious ingredient, essential from the first, remained paramount. His drawings and paintings were part of a gospel. In time he would say, 'I want to give the wretched a brotherly message. When I sign myself "Vincent" it is as one of them.'[34] Socialism is here coupled with a vision of the artist as a kind of Christ.

Unable to cope any longer with his conditions of work, he moved abruptly to Brussels and took a room in a cheap hotel at 72 Boulevard du Midi. His unexpected changes of direction would take people by surprise. He had moved out to escape distraction and improve on the bad lighting, but more than anything he wanted space, so that he could draw from a model occasionally. In addition to this, he thought it might be possible to work with a sympathetic artist in a good studio, and perhaps take lessons at an academy. The Brussels Academy, he reminded Theo in his next letter, had one great advantage over the academy in Amsterdam – it was free of charge.

M E Tralbaut recounts the story of Vincent's actual departure from Belgium's black country, as told to him by his old friend Louis Piérard, who knew the widow of the pastor of Warquignies well. Vincent had called to say goodbye to them, Madame Bonte remembered. He looked terribly pale, and said sadly, 'Nobody has understood me.' Then he walked away on bare feet, his bundle (or cross) on his shoulder. His identification with Christ, whom he called 'the greatest of all artists', is here, in defeat, at its most sublime or its most ridiculous, according to one's point of view. As he walked off, village brats ran after him, screaming, 'He's mad, he's mad!' The pastor stopped them. Turning to his wife, he said, 'Perhaps he's a saint?'[35]

He stayed in Brussels for six months. During that time he made important progress in a number of directions. He did apply at the Academy for a place, but although his name is there in the archives for 1880, whether he actually attended is a matter for conjecture.

Living in a city again meant that he would have to stop looking like a derelict. In a very Vincent-like move he wrote home to say that he had had to buy two secondhand pairs of trousers and two coats, as well as underwear and shoes. He enclosed a sample of cloth with his letter to prove his words and demonstrate that he wasn't being unduly extravagant. Really he was inaugurating a procedure that would become permanent, providing itemised details of his budget, first of all to his parents and later only to his brother.

Once a week without fail a breakdown of his expenses would arrive. We are intimately acquainted with the state of this painter's worn-out trousers, decaying coats, leaking boots, the money spent on his teeth, his food, his rooms, more so in fact than with any other artist. Here he is, at the outset, reporting from Brussels: 'You must not imagine that I live richly here, for my chief food is dry bread and some potatoes or chestnuts which people here sell on the street corner, but by having a somewhat better room and by occasionally taking a somewhat better meal in a restaurant whenever I can afford it, I shall get on very well . . . . The expenses here . . . .'.[36] And so it goes. Realising that his whole future depended on it, he perfected the art of talking 'poor-mouth'. At the same time, as with so many of his ploys, he was telling the absolute truth about his situation. Art is a matter of timing, selection, emphasis.

Whether he attended the Academy or not, what is certain is that he wanted to live with a practising painter as a working apprentice. Just to dream of their stimulating discussions was enough to make his head spin. Theo, ever-helpful, arranged for him to meet a Dutch artist in Brussels, Anthon van Rappard, a young man in his early twenties.

After meeting him for the first time, Vincent thought that he must be wealthy. The touch of luxury put him off, and so did his work, which he found charming enough but 'a little more passion, please'. All the same, in spite of these initial reservations the two got on well. Van Rappard was willing to let his intense young friend share his studio for a while. And now Vincent could realise another of his dreams, which was to draw from the nude in heated premises. What a luxury – and what sensuality!

Back at his hotel room, he was bringing in an odd collection of characters, presumably off the street, to use as models: a porter, a snow shoveller, old women, a soldier, various working men.[37] Before long, objections were being made to these practices, and to his old habit of hammering up etchings and drawings on the wall. He had also for some reason tried to mask part of his window.

Acting on his own initiative he found a mediocre painter whose technique was sound, and took some lessons in perspective from him. His comments, taken out of context, read comically. 'I should have written sooner, but was too busy with my skeleton.' Working through the *Bargues* manual he laboured to produce a drawing of a large-sized skeleton on five sheets of Ingres paper.[38]

All in all, he was a good deal happier now. But how he missed the country! And every so often, of course, things fell apart. He couldn't draw properly, he lost confidence and floundered horribly. One letter in January finds him apologising to Theo for composing his previous letter in 'a moment of spleen'. He should have waited for a better moment instead of acting impulsively. Then he went back to the attack. Exasperated by what he saw as Theo's heartless neglect of him, he unleashed a volley of angry questions to a brother he relegated to the third person: 'Why doesn't he write? If he is afraid of compromising himself in the eyes of Messrs Goupil and Co by keeping in touch with me, is his position with those gentlemen so shaky and unstable that he is obliged to be so careful?' He followed this with the unkindest cut of all: 'Or is it that he is afraid I will ask him for money?' If so, Vincent rushed on, Theo might at least have waited until Vincent tried to squeeze him, 'as the saying goes'.[39]

By his next letter he had recovered his good humour and was asking to be forgiven. He went on to say that he liked van Rappard in spite of his lifestyle, because he took things *seriously*, underlining the word. This of course impressed him. It always did.

His father came on a visit to see him, and inevitably he was left feeling homesick. But he had discovered something surprising. Theo had been sending him sums of money from time to time through their father, keeping his name out of the transaction. He thanked Theo, and hoped he wouldn't live to regret the investment. His plan, he explained, was to become a good enough draughtsman to earn a hundred francs a month and so support himself modestly without assistance. It remained a dream. Money and how to get hold of it were the perennial problems that refused to go away. If he forgot it, some well-meaning or malicious busybody would be sure to remind him of it. People would talk about 'the strange and unaccountable fact' that he was perpetually hard up, and yet belonged to a well-connected family. These days his reply, a lame one, was the same one repeated, only with variations. It was temporary, things were about to change, his prospects were improving. Tersteeg, his ex-employer and for long a friend of the family, wrote him a disapproving letter. He had got wind of a rumour that Vincent planned to sponge off his rich relatives and he hoped it wasn't true. This kind of gossip and these misunderstandings only served to bring home to him how grateful he should be to Theo, who was now a believer and supported him willingly.

Writing to his mother and father, he said he wanted to explain that it wasn't extravagance that had led him to buy not one coat but two, and two pairs of trousers. No, he had a definite reason in mind. He intended to build up a small collection of workmen's clothes, a Brabant smock, a fisherman's outfit of yellow oilskin and a sou'wester, a grey linen suit of the sort worn by miners, straw hat, wooden clogs, so that he could dress his models in them. If this strikes us today as quaint, peculiar in its literalness, we have to remember that he was addressing, through his parents, a nation that prized practicality. Dutch to the bone, his ambition was to paint the world realistically. There were problems, however. His realism was not the realism of his forebears. It included the supernatural, and it contained the soul. Nature was dead unless it had his soul in it. The Dutch tradition of realism, together with his never-sleeping Protestant conscience, forced him to find an outlet for his visions and fantasies subversively, under cover of symbols, by depicting men at work, portraits of common people, street scenes and fields as everyday subjects in an ordinary light, and simultaneously as expressions of a state of mind. Like his fellow countryman, Spinoza, he believed that God was nature and nature was God.

Hearing that his friend van Rappard was going back to Holland, he saw little point in prolonging his own stay in Brussels. Anyway, living in a city was more expensive than a rural existence would be, he reasoned, thus rationalising his longing to return home.

Once his mind was made up he packed hurriedly and started out, in April, 1881. He was looking forward to a reunion with Theo in Etten on Easter Sunday. A year later, Tolstoy, another peasant-lover, would clear out of Moscow complaining of city life with its 'stench, stones, luxury, poverty, debauchery'.[41] He too was only able to relax in the heart of the country, seeking its isolation instinctively, just as Vincent did, and like him unable to breathe freely inside any mainstream.

6

'THE FACTORY IS IN FULL SWING'

It was good to be home. Nothing had really changed. He was glad to be included in old routines and in a family which he always thought, while he was away from it, he had outgrown. Surprisingly, he had not.

His father was touching, grown older, less sure of himself. His mother ran the household, and seemed as always the stronger of the two. In fact she had been the powerful sustaining force for as long as he could remember. Now he knew it consciously, took note of it. His sisters were still at home, unwilling as ever to comprehend him, only making him feel oafish, prematurely old, unclean. To them he was the same rough dog, running into the room with wet paws to be disparaged. In short, 'a foul beast'.[1]

Nothing had changed. The only surprising thing was that it was all less irksome than he had imagined. His mother's dark nature and her rather cold surety still shut him out, but he expected it. And there were compensations. He liked to come in and find the family gathered under one roof. He loved to wake and hear the large house stirring, with himself enfolded in it.

It was spring, the beginning of May. His ink drawing of the parsonage (and the church with its tower across the road) and a photograph of it show a large, long, impressive building on two floors, the front door surrounded by thirteen windows.

He had plenty of space to work at his drawing and to study. He doesn't seem to have expressed a wish for a studio – that would have been to declare himself too soon, to stretch his confidence too far. Most of his art activity went on out of doors. If it rained, he continued with the exercises in the manual: he had reached the Holbeins.

He looked forward to the promised visit of young van Rappard. When his friend did come, Vincent's parents approved of him, charmed by his personality. He stayed for twelve days. For Vincent this was a dream come true, working alongside a fellow artist in collaboration – two comrades, shoulder to shoulder. The two men went off deep into the surrounding countryside on a series of expeditions, to the heath near Seppe, and to a big swamp, the so-called Passievaart. They separated briefly, Rappard to paint a large study and then some sepias, and Vincent to another spot nearby where the water lilies grew.

Another day they went to Princenhage. Vincent wanted to introduce Rappard to his uncle, but when they got there, the old man – never in good health – was ill in bed.

Left alone, Vincent did some drawings of his sister, Wil. She was the one sister who was sympathetic to him; that is, when he was able to detach her from the others. She posed well, sitting at a sewing machine. He would have preferred a spinning wheel for her to sit at, but one had to move forward with the times.

Moving into summer, he took advantage of the dry weather and lived more outdoors than in, drawing the same subjects repeatedly if they appealed to him, toiling incessantly in an effort to improve himself. His parents, perplexed by this endless repetition, thought it meant that he was unable to get anything right. A stickler for realism, he was frustrated by an obstinacy in his models as strong as his own. He wanted their gardener, Piet Kaufman, to pose holding a spade, and if possible in his own garden or in a field where he would feel more natural, but the fellow objected. He insisted on wearing his Sunday best for such an important occasion, and as a mark of deference to the young master. Have pity on these small miseries of the draughtsman's life, Vincent wrote humorously to Theo, adding proudly that 'The factory is in full swing'.[2] He was now churning out drawings at a tremendous rate.

Like Hokasai, the old man mad about drawing, he drew everything in sight, insatiably. 'And finally, he doesn't even notice that he's stopped talking and is only drawing. And from then on,

that's all he does . . . .'.[3] Well, not quite: not yet. Only too painfully aware of his inadequate technique, he went off one day to
see his cousin-in-law, Anton Mauve, a successful painter of the
Hague school – armed perhaps with a letter of recommendation
from dear Uncle Cent. Vincent, eager to consult Mauve, was
hungry for any advice he could get, willing to kneel at the man's
feet if necessary. He took along a portfolio of his drawings, and
received 'many hints which I was glad to get'.

He reported back faithfully to Theo, who had provided his
train fare. Mauve expressed interest in his work, he said. He had
seemed puzzled but intrigued by the clogged, uncouth sketches
of peasants. He urged Vincent to clean them up, get them clear
of the earth they stood on. His stubborn cousin, who saw his
models as a kind of earth, part of the body and blood of the soil
they dug, one impregnating the other, failed to see how the
interchange he saw stamped on the dazed faces of these men could
be smoothed away without losing the secret of how they lived,
rooted and dumb and rough-barked as live willow trees. Something was being gained by the roughness of his work; what it
was he couldn't explain. He did say that by concentrating on
types of labourers, and learning from the studies of life he admired
so much in work by Gavarni, Daumier, Dore, De Groux, and
Rops, he hoped one day to produce acceptable illustrations for
the magazines and newspapers, and bring in a small income.
Mauve approved. He showed Vincent a whole lot of his own
studies, and told his eager listener that he ought to start painting
soon.[4]

Vincent didn't act on this heady, alarming advice for some time
to come. 'Painting is drawing at the same time,' Mauve had told
him. Exactly how he saw it. Hence his reluctance to start painting
before he had mastered the incredibly difficult art of drawing –
and drawing the figure especially. If you mastered the figure, that
was bound to influence the drawing of landscape, he believed.
The muscularity of his fields and trees – even the skies knotted
with clouds – would soon bear this out. There was also the totally
unexplored domain of colour, rearing in his mind as a great
seduction, a temptation to be fought off until he could enter it
willingly, and then occupy it, live in it, like a paradise regained.
This could only happen when the time was ripe, which would
be when he was worthy.

On this same trip he also called in on Tersteeg – who complimented him on his progress – and on another painter, de Bock. He took in several exhibitions, seeing a large figure drawing of a girl and two children by Neuhys which he thought splendid, and the paintings of an artist new to him, Clara Montalba. Her talent was a peculiar one, he commented ambiguously. And he saw the work of an old favourite of his from the London days, J Maris, who had some beautiful things on show.[5]

Home again, he shot off an urgent request to Theo for some Ingres paper that was not blindingly white – the whiteness hampered him – and stout enough to withstand his attacks on it with a reed pen. Could Theo lay his hands on some that was the colour of unbleached muslin or linen? Otherwise he was forced to waste time giving the whole paper a wash of flat tone each time.

People would say – usually his father – that if he was determined to be an artist, well and good, but why did he spend so much time with books, and silly French novels at that? Where was the connection? He replied politely that just as he studied the whereabouts of bones and tendons and muscles so as to know more about the figures he tried to draw, in the same way – if he was attempting a portrait – it helped to know something about the working of people's minds and how their characters had been formed.

He would draw the same figure over and over again, trying to get what he wanted. All his subjects were workers of one kind or another: 'a man with a spade, a sower (twice), a girl with a broom twice. Then a woman in a white cap peeling potatoes; a shepherd leaning on his staff . . . an old sick farmer sitting on a chair near the hearth, his head on his hands and his elbows on his knees.' 'Diggers, sowers, ploughers, male and female, they are what I must draw continually. I have to observe and draw everything that belongs to the country life . . . I no longer stand helpless before nature, as I used to.'[6]

He began as he continued. The nameless, the humble, the ignorant and the overlooked were his chosen material, to be recorded and given their true place, and if possible to be transformed by love. Why, then, were these early drawings such examples of ugliness? No one can pretend that his stooping, kneeling, and digging figures are beautiful, either by contemporary standards or our own. Ugly and irregular in their bodies as in their features, delineated in harsh thick outlines, these creatures are either static, frozenly waiting – as if for blows – or blackly and stiffly at work, or walking down roads with the clumsy, painful gait of arthritis sufferers.

His first drawings mount, whether unconsciously or by design, a direct assault on our concept of beauty, obliging us to re-examine it. Concentrate on the truth, advised Eric Gill, and let beauty look after itself. In Vincent's case there were precedents to be found among his Dutch artistic forebears. The searching self-portraits of Rembrandt in approaching old age, as he became uglier and poorer and more grimy, were acclaimed as master-pieces in preference to the earlier elegant portraiture of his society period. Frans Hals had painted portraits of girls who could only be described as plain, but something lively and piquant redeemed them.

Vincent had come to regard himself as unredeemably ugly and unkempt. One suspects him of seeking equivalents in others and in nature. It was one way of justifying his own self-image as an 'unfortunate' and at the same time masochistically drawing attention to it. Certainly the paradoxical view of ugliness as a special kind of beauty appealed to him from the start. 'I do not want the beauty to come from the material but from within myself,'[7] he wrote later, taking direct responsibility for this pro-cess of redemption. Suffering, commonly seen as ugly and distort-ing, stirred emotions in him that brought the word beauty to his lips. Some of his preferences were so extreme as to appear per-verse. He found beauty, or so he claimed, in a broken old woman bearing the marks of poverty rather than in a beautiful young woman who was the essence of grace.

On rainy days he devoured books, recommending *Shirley* and *Jane Eyre* by an author known to him as Currer Bell. Theo should try Balzac again, he thought – *Père Goriot*, for instance. And whatever he did he shouldn't neglect Victor Hugo. Later he would see Hugo's Quasimodo as having a direct bearing on his as yet unformed philosophy of ugliness, and he remembered a saying: 'In my soul I am beautiful.'[8]

Another time, noticing the pain of a cow in labour and a small girl who shed compassionate tears as she watched, he thought the scene 'pure, wonderful, beautiful'. Beauty to him came from the soul, as we say, and he saw it as his task to exteriorise it in some way that harmonized with the subject matter. But how? He spoke once of 'a rough man who bears blossom like a flowering plant' as being beautiful. Soon he was seeking analogies in nature for the human beauty he wanted to unearth. Gnarled old trees were drawn and modelled later on as if they were figures. Of the host of trees he painted, how many should we see as self-portraits?

Dozens of his drawings from Etten and elsewhere are concerned with diggers. It is such a prominent theme that we are compelled to ask why. On the face of it, of course, nothing could have been more natural. Diggers were everywhere around him, the most commonly seen labourers, cutting the peat and reclaiming the land of this 'sinking boat' called Holland. In Vincent's case, however, there seemed something obsessive going on. The endless repetition strikes one as inexorable, like a recurring dream. Vincent made several copies of an influential painting by Millet, *The Diggers*. As well as its obvious appeal as a peasant painting, Lubin suggests another reason for his fascination with this one. In the picture are two men, almost interchangeable, working side by side as they dig a ditch. To see this double image as joined to a symbol of the grave 'that linked one Vincent to the other'[9] is not as far-fetched as it appears when one sees the multiplicity of twinned and fused pairs appearing later: pairs of cottages, trees, and chairs, as well as of people on roads or seated at tables, overlapping or merged or shadowed. What are we to make of these coded messages that go on bombarding us in their attempt to break through?

Vincent, steeped in the realism of his culture, could never have settled for external appearance only. He had to drag out of nature whatever lay hidden and 'inferior' – to use Jung's word – and exhibit it on the opened-out surface of a work of art. Grappling with nature's secret meant being prepared to wrestle with 'her'. This involved constant vigilance and stubborness. To illustrate the problem, and explain why he saw the whole business in gladiatorial terms as a contest resulting in victory over a subdued female Nature, one that became the opposite of what it seemed, docile and yielding instead of cold and repelling, he invoked the example of Shakespeare. 'The struggle with nature sometimes reminds one of what Shakespeare calls "the taming of the shrew" – that means conquering the opposition by perseverance.'[10] Perseverance in the face of bitter discouragement, such as feminine

92

resistance to his approaches, were factors he was now trying to incorporate in work habits that would be essentially him, original to him. Opposing forces were in precarious balance, and resolving their tug-of-war was his prime concern. Good work could only arise out of peace of mind. Victor and vanquished, he was beginning to think, came together in art and were one and the same.

The busy 'factory' went on producing, running on nothing but aspiration, perseverance, and the passion for art. One day, a woman turned up who must have seemed the very embodiment of that nature he was tussling with daily. Presumably his parents had told Vincent that they had invited her. It was a Christian act. Kee, the daughter of his mother's eldest sister, was recently widowed. This was the young woman Vincent had called on at her home in Amsterdam when he was studying there. He had met her husband, Vos, a young clergyman, and seen their baby son. The family scene had enchanted him. Now Vos was dead. Here was the grieving widow, his cousin. She had come with her little boy of four to stay for a fortnight because the van Goghs felt so sorry for her. They felt a change might do her good.

It was full summer. Kee was dark, striking rather than pretty, with wavy hair. But what was beauty? Her sorrow and evident loneliness struck him as beautiful. Her chin was distinctly pointed, her mouth clenched as if withholding a cry. Vincent saw the pallor of her face, its sad lines, her eyes inward-looking, and felt that his soul was in correspondence with her. At once he wanted to heal and restore her. First, though, she had to be saved from her sad trance.

The immediate effect she had on him was to make him strong, sure, steadied on himself as never before. He knew all about unhappiness: she had come to the right place. Bereavement was something he understood. Hadn't the losing of Eugenia been like one? Since then he had survived a whole series of setbacks. He had learned to live in himself and be self-sufficient. Instead of feeling Kee's presence as an intrusion, upsetting his concentration at a critical stage, he was inspired by her. Instead of fearing her as a sensual temptation, a bringer of chaos into the monastic order and productivity of his life, he was able to work harder and better.

His one-man factory became a powerhouse. Drawings flooded

from him – not as the result of battling, but from the rare relaxing of his will. He stopped fretting about his life and about the future, about what was good or bad in it. He had faith, he believed. We hardly need to ask where this faith and belief came from, pouring in from a source previously untapped. He was in love as never before.

He poured this love back into his work, happy to keep the source of it secret. He was twenty-eight. She was a few years older, mature, a mother. Everything he desired in a woman was in her. The pattern is ominously familiar. Like Eugenia, she was someone who had committed her love to another. Like her, she had a clergyman father. Like Vincent's mother, she had married a clergyman, and like his mother she had known bereavement.

Blissfully, quietly happy, he went through the village with Kee and the little boy, taking them on walks. He led the way through the fields along paths only he used, pointing everything out to them. He loved the child, and was endlessly kind and thoughtful towards it, as fond of it as if it were his own. His tender consideration touched her. She said how grateful she was.

Her words ran into him as love, like a shy declaration. When his heart brimmed and overflowed, he told her he was in love with her. She replied with three deadly words: 'No, never never.' The past and the future were one, she explained hastily, and that was how it had to be. The next day she left for Amsterdam, earlier than expected, after asking him not to try to get in touch with her there. Distraught, he went to his parents, thinking they might be able to intercede in some way. Then he set to work laying siege to her with letters. According to Tralbaut, his letters went unread.

Like a drowning man he snatched at anything, just as he had done in London. Kee wanted to love him but her guilt prevented her. Also her parents objected, he imagined. To them, an approach to their daughter when she was still in mourning was 'indelicate', a word he now heard from his mother. It made no difference what anyone said. In Kee's fine dark eyes he had read a call for help. She was a sleeping beauty: he would wake her. He had strength enough for them both. The old ones, fearful and suspicious, jealous even, were attempting to stifle young love. Somehow they must find the courage to accept the challenge. A new world was calling them. How happy they had been together, he and she and the little lad in the drowsy heat of the meadows. How gorgeous it was to be alive! Once safely through the fire of this opposition they would move into a future that was free of the dead past, lovely as cowslips and silent like a miracle. A love such as his could never be 'untimely' and 'indelicate'.[11]

He comforted himself with the saying of Uncle Jan – 'the devil is never so black as he is painted' – and dreamed of what he might accomplish in the company of such a woman, in collaboration with her soft femaleness. It was destined that it should be 'she and no other'. He talked of her as a goddess beyond reproach who was being restrained against her will. More realistically, she was an iceberg that he would thaw with the fire of his blood, the warmth of his heart. If he went on courting her *in absentia* it was because he had no choice. His parents and hers were afraid of change, as the old always are. The only thing that would change them, he commented savagely, was when he became someone who earned a thousand guilder a year.[12]

Only Uncle Cent acted unexpectedly. He admired Vincent's refusal to take Kee's 'no, never never' at its face value. Vincent, baffled and angered by his parents' pessimism, lost his temper when they told him not to write to his uncle and aunt in Amsterdam. He refused to promise anything, just as he turned a deaf ear to their prayers for his 'resignation'.[13]

Surprisingly, he told Theo nothing of this drama until the late autumn, when he wrote that 'perhaps you know about it already and it is no news to you'.[14] Theo must have known in any case: he was always his parents' confidant and advisor, as well as his brother's.

Out it all rushed in a torrent, the whole story so far. In the midst of this pain and uncertainty, the wonder is that he could still produce work. There was no creative stasis. Tralbaut comments that he seemed to be almost glorying in his failure to break down the barriers and 'storm the fortress' of his love's frozen heart.[15] More probably he had tapped a fresh source of energy in himself – call it the power of love – which made him feel invincible. Any obstacle could be overcome. 'For love is something so positive, so strong, so real,' he wrote exultantly to Theo, 'that it is as impossible for one who loves to take back that feeling as it is to take his own life.'[16] Everything was now irradiated by this feeling, which was bound to affect his work for the good. 'Did you receive my drawings? Yesterday I made another, of a peasant boy lighting a fire early in the morning on the hearth over which a kettle is hanging; and another, of an old man putting kindling wood on the hearth. I am sorry to say there is still something harsh and severe in my drawings, and I think that *she*, her influence, must come to soften this.'[17] In his joy at being in love, all he saw was now sparkling like the illuminations in a missal. He was full of an incandescence that 'no pails of cold water' could put out. He felt prodigal. Love was the new axis of his world.

For all his fortitude, and his determination to throw off what he called the 'yoke of despair', screams of pain would be suddenly torn from him. 'Do you think Kee knows how terribly she unintentionally thwarts me?' Even with his new source of strength there seemed little he could do. At times he was irrationally optimistic. 'Well, she will have to make up for it afterwards! That means I count on her joining in many artistic campaigns, you see.'[18]

He reread Michelet's *L'amour et la femme*, hoping for guidance, desperate to solve the burning problem that forever eluded him, the reality of being a woman. If only he knew what he was up against. Michelet was now reinstated, and indeed elevated during this crisis to 'Father Michelet', faced as he was with a father painfully unwilling to advise him. 'I told Pa frankly that under the circumstances I attached more value to Michelet's advice than to his own. . . . But then they bring up the story of a great uncle who was infected with French ideas and took to drink, and so they insinuate I shall do the same.' As usual, a French book meant only 'thieves and murderers and immorality' to his father.[19]

He went on to quote Michelet: 'A woman must breathe on you for you to be a man. She has breathed on me, old fellow! On the other hand, must a man breathe on a woman for her to be a woman? I most certainly think so.'[20]

He must have asked himself, perplexed as to how to act, whether he would ever again get near enough to 'breathe' on Kee with his ardent breath, so as to melt their horrid separateness into one glorious entity. 'But she has loved someone else and her thoughts are always in the past; and her consciousness seems to bother her even at the thought of a possible new love.'[21]

He warned Theo not to be confused, to get his priorities right at all costs, and to take care not to bow down before the 'money devil'. Keep reading the Bible, but even better, read Michelet. The Bible was true, eternal, and everlasting, but for clear advice, directly applicable to the hurry and fever of modern life, he was indebted to Michelet, who said aloud what the Gospel only whispered.

Moreover, if Theo wanted to love – and he knew he was as desolate and starved of love as he, Vincent, had once been – then a belief in God was an absolute necessity. Not that he should listen, he hastened to add, to all the sermons of clergymen or the arguments of 'bigoted, genteel prudes'. He should just remember that there was a God, and *feel* that there was, 'not dead and stifled but alive', urging us towards more love, more life. In other words: Good News, God is Love.

Resolute again, as though energised by his own words and thoughts, he told Theo to stand firm and take the broad view. They were moderns, they must keep faith with their generation and not look back towards the old one. That was fatal. If they were misunderstood, so be it. In the future it would be seen that they were right. Let the old things die. Be soldierly.

Inside, his heart would be strong one day, and quivering like a hurt bird on the ground the next. Heartbreak, then hope, then heartbreak again. He rose and fell on the sickening see-saw of his terror and delight. How long could such anguish last? How much punishment could the heart take before shattering into fragments? He repeated once more, for Theo's benefit, his fateful words on that summer day: 'Kee, I love you as myself . . .' and her reply, 'No, never never', which fell on him like a death sentence, 'and for the moment it absolutely crushed me to the ground'.[22]

Only he had the inside story. What did they, on the outside, know? He and them, inside and outside: only in art was this dichotomy ever really clarified and brought to rest. Now the focus for his interminable dilemma was Kee, held away from his sight in a kind of darkness. He struggled on alone, as against a blank wall of darkness and silence that blocked his light, stifled his breath, and threatened to make him mad. Why were they being held apart? It was terrible, wonderful, the 'peculiar discovery of love': it was like 'the discovery of a new hemisphere.'[23] He wanted to shout with glee and with despair, both together, locked in the birth-pain of this love. He kept summoning up more strength to attack the 'fatal evil of burying herself in the past.' It was like a disease she suffered from. One thrust of the surgeon's knife – that was all it would take.

In spite of this agony, there was one sure reward. Fall in love; he said to Theo, and you'll discover another force, stronger than any other, 'and that is the heart.'

Sometimes the pain of unreturned, unacknowledged love turned to frenzy in him, exalting him to worship. Sometimes he felt he had been made whole, delivered, in a kind of fantasy, by his very longing. 'There is a feeling of deliverance within me and it is as if she and I had stopped being two, and were united for ever and ever.'[24] At other times his need to go to her was awful. He wanted them to complete each other, to be made fully whole and created by her, instead of enduring the throes of his uncreated self. He preached to Theo like a priest of marriage, outdoing his father in unshakeable belief. 'A man and wife can be one, that is to say, one whole and not two halves.' His father could only say falteringly that 'My conscience has never allowed me to influence two people to marry.'[25] Vincent's conscience was telling him precisely the opposite, and at the top of its voice. When he came to move among artists he would sing the praises of marriage, he vowed. An artist would be more productive with a wife, he went on to declare, theorising wildly, than if he stayed unmarried and took a mistress. Then he uttered the simple statement of his faith, one which read more tragically, in retrospect, than any other single thing he wrote: 'In order to work and to become an artist, one needs *love*.'[26] Meanwhile, his father and mother drove him frantic with their endless harping on irrelevancies, such as the 'means of subsistence' and his inability to provide it. As if it were a question of an immediate marriage! Couldn't they see that he was simply dying for want of a word from Kee, that not seeing her or being able to write or talk to her was killing him, and that nothing else mattered? They could only see an obdurate, ungrateful son, old enough to know better, selfishly concerned with his own desires and no one else's. And of course the dreadful thought gnawing at him like a rat, that he refused to allow into his conscious mind, was the fear that she might already be complete in herself, and because of her love for her dead husband have no time for his helpless need, just as his mother had once been complete, in her sorrowful love for the stillborn Vincent who had preceded him.

In Arles, Vincent painted a picture based on memory of the parsonage garden at Etten. Two women, Vincent's mother and a younger woman, walk together in a garden, so close as to be almost overlapping. The younger figure is taller, but the mother is in the foreground and dominates. Although the younger woman has been taken to be a likeness of his sister Wil by many biographers, misled by an ambiguous comment of Vincent's, Tralbaut sees in it a close resemblance to Kee. This leads A J Lubin to speculate on the 'close psychological kinship' between the two women in Vincent's mind.[27]

There was still the countryside, and he would never relinquish that. The black gloom of his anger was effaced when he stepped into the open air. 'I began to draw a man busy digging potatoes in a field again. And I put in a little more of the surroundings. Some bushes in the foreground, and a streak of sky. I cannot tell you, boy, how beautiful that field is!'

Apart from D H Lawrence, no one has written so fervently about modern marriage as Vincent in 1881. 'I do love, and I am loved,' wrote Lawrence in a letter. 'I have given and I have taken – and that is eternal. Oh, if only people could marry properly. I believe in marriage.'[28] And there are other resemblances. Aldous Huxley said that it was impossible to write about Lawrence except as an artist. He could have been writing about van Gogh. Both men were prolific letter-writers, both allowed their correspondents generous access to all their moods, and gave intimate details of their daily lives. Both saw a beauty in vitality; both preached a gospel. This list could be extended. They believed that emotions should be let out and then mastered; there was their Protestantism, fighting the good fight, the insistence on going their own way; their fear and dislike of cities; their psychological as well as actual isolation from the body of mankind; their awareness of the stigma of art; a distrust of the intellect when fed on abstractions; a desire to get 'beyond' art to a kind of heaven and a paradoxical belief in art activity as a means of shedding psychic sickness. Both were intuitive first and rational second, men who lost their composure, were impetuous, and dreamed of peace as a great goal, a heaven on earth. Both were dogged by homesickness. Most striking is the tenacity they had in common. Frieda Lawrence said of her husband: 'I must say he is like the English in the bulldog quality of hanging on. They say the English never are really roused till they are beaten – I do love that – though I am never *quite* sure whether I love or hate it.'[29] They both hoped to found colonies, brotherhoods of kindred spirits in warm climates. Vincent would have applauded the religious tenor of Lawrence's Foreword to *Sons and Lovers*, and especially this: 'So there is the Father – which should be called the Mother . . .'[30]

Vincent lived by gusts; he was always on the move inside himself. His gusts were disrupting the drawing room. It is easy to sympathise with his parents as these whirlpools of feeling kept arising out of nowhere. Driven by the thought that he was nearly thirty, his impatience consuming him, he was the cause of almost daily tension and argument at the parsonage. They were at a loss to know what to do with this sullen rebel who kept bursting out against them so unjustly.

Vincent wrote more impassioned letters to Uncle Stricker. No reply. In his correspondence with Theo he suddenly dropped his role of wise counsellor and turned into a beggar. How could he make his drawings saleable, he asked angrily – and then came abruptly to the point. If he could earn some money for a railway ticket he would go straight off to Amsterdam and 'fathom' the deafening silence which was tormenting him. Swallowing his pride, he came out with a proposal. The relevant passage, in his letter of 12 November 1881, makes heart-rending reading. He had hit bottom. He could take no more nail-biting suspense; he must act:

'Theo, I want money for the trip to Amsterdam; if I have but just enough, I will go. Father and Mother have promised not to oppose this if only I leave them out of the matter . . .

'Brother, if you will send it to me I will make lots of drawings for you of the Heike, and whatever you want. . . . Could you help me with the money, boy? If it is only 20 francs, Father will perhaps give me another 10 . . . and then I'll rush off at tremendous speed.'[31]

First though he had to make sure that the person he burned to confront was in fact there. His sister Wil was going to Haarlem, and then to Amsterdam. She would spy out the lie of the land and write to him. He sent off three drawings for Theo's delectation – 'Dinner Time', 'Lighting the Fire', and 'Almshouse Man'. By 19 November he had the whole amount, 30 francs, from Theo, and was writing to say how kind and humane it was of him to let him have the ticket money.

His letters to his brother were now naked as never before. It takes little effort of the imagination to put oneself in Theo's shoes, and feel the grey, correct, judicious side of his character flinching from the terrifying sincerity of Vincent's outpourings. At home, his protests died down. He relapsed into a dangerous silence when they accused him of 'breaking family ties' by his refusal to stop writing letters to the Strickers' home. This retaliatory silence was apparently even harder to take than his outcries had been. When they did get him to speak, after several days, he said, in effect: This is what it would be like if family ties *were* broken, and how does it feel?

His father shocked him. He swore. Then he ordered his son out of the room. In his rage, the clergyman 'who is used to having everyone give in to him when he's in a passion' told Vincent to clear out of the house if he couldn't mend his ways. He didn't mean it – it was said in passion, Vincent assured his brother, knowing how profoundly the news would disturb him.[32] But here, out in the open, was the first real break with his father. It would widen over the years. He had worshipped his father, identified with his work, his faith, his church. All these things were bound up together and by defying his father he was in effect abandoning them. Before long he would react even more extremely, exclaiming bitterly, 'There really are no more unbelieving and hard-hearted people than clergymen, and' – taking a vicious sideswipe at his mother – 'especially clergyman's wives.'[33]

At last he took the train to Amsterdam. He went straight from the station to the Keizersgracht where his uncle and aunt lived. He rang the bell, and was asked in by the maid – only to be told that the family were at dinner. Entering the dining room shortly afterwards, he looked around in vain for Kee. Her plate was missing, too. Had they taken it away so as to fool him?

Asked where Kee was, they looked at each other and said she

was out. His uncle hesitated a moment and then said she had left the house as soon as she realised Vincent had come.

Vincent didn't believe them. She was in the house somewhere, kept from him, probably against her will. The famous incident of the ordeal by fire then occurred. He put his hand over the flame of the lamp and said to Stricker: 'Let me see her for as long as I can keep my hand in the flame.'[34] The tone is biblical. Horrified, his uncle blew out the lamp, said Vincent would never see her, and ordered him from the house. Several months later he told Theo the full dramatic story, ending sadly: 'Then, not at once, but very soon, I felt that love die within me. A void, an infinite void, came in its stead.'[35]

The protracted struggle Vincent waged against impossible odds raises a number of questions. Did he surrender, walking in the summer with Kee and the child, to his craving for a wife and family, to such an extent that an invented relationship became true – only to collapse, tipping him into shock when she abandoned him with her 'No, never never'? Just as a distraught person will deny an unbearable piece of news and act as though the opposite were true, so he kept repeating in his letters, 'she and no other'. Or was he courting pain? Converting a forbidden sensual yearning for a 'pure widow and mother' into the voluptuousness of half possession. To possess someone in the mind is to be saved from a brutal repudiation in reality, and instead to love the ethereal, which can neither disappoint nor satisfy, but only act as a goad. So we find him circling for months around the insoluble problem of Kee, exulting and then despairing, then exulting again. He could not lose, but nor could he win.

He was twenty-eight, a young man strange and violent in his being, as well as in the eyes of others: sensual in spite of himself. Sublimation was not working any more. His alliance with his work, with nature, excited him with the nearness of a goal he had not yet reached. And the same with books. It all swung him towards the burning reality of Kee. Her proximity had overbalanced him; physically and in the spirit it had to be 'she and no other'. Now it was finished.

It is reasonable to ask whether there had been an element of choice in it all. Kee loved a dead husband who was now angelic, beyond criticism, perfect. Had Vincent sought pain for himself, putting himself forward as the rival of a man who was bound to triumph over him? Did he will failure on himself for the sake of his solitude? Did his spirit want one thing and his body another?

This time the defeat of his hopes didn't crush him for more than a few days. On the contrary, it made him blaze up into action. Harking back to 'the first case – that of the man whose little boat capsized when he was twenty years old,' he said that then he had been prepared to give but afraid to take. He was 'foolish, wrong, proud, rash'.[36] Since then he had gained insight into himself, and into a woman's heart. It was different this time.

All the same, he hung about dismally in Amsterdam for three days, beginning to sink. Something forced him to move, to act. He went to Haarlem and spent time with his sister Wil, walking about with her but not confiding anything. From there he went to The Hague. At seven in the evening he was at his cousin Mauve's.

Before his last throw of the dice he had been hanging on at Etten in hopes of a visit from Mauve, who had half promised to come and initiate him into 'the mysteries of the palette'. Mauve was an artist who could be generous and expansive, but as a personality he was unpredictable, not to be depended on because he was so self-absorbed. Vincent was frank with Mauve. He would dearly like to spend a month taking lessons from him, starting now: would that be possible?

Mauve answered without hesitation: yes. Vincent was never to forget the straightforwardness of this man and his direct, open way with him, though they soon quarrelled and parted company. Both had irascible temperaments, but for the moment all was well. Vincent found a room in an inn nearby, going to Mauve's studio mornings and evenings. The artist looked over Vincent's recent work and his comments were honest and constructive, not in the least 'Jesuitical'. He had thought his young cousin's stuff dull when he had seen it previously. Now he saw something else there, a rough groping for some unformed, folded life. He muttered gruff compliments and showed his student how to prepare a palette. Vincent, overcome with gratitude for this ready help, apologised several times over for his presumption in landing on Mauve's doorstep without warning. But you see, he said, 'the sword is in my loins'.

One impulsive act had paid off. Now for another. 'Why don't we live more?' he had exhorted Theo. Dissatisfied with work and nothing else he went on the streets to experience life in the raw. What had happened in Amsterdam at the Strickers' had stunned him – as if he had been standing too long 'against a church wall'.[37] The antidote was at hand; it was any real, warm, live female. If she was outcast as he was, so much the better.

Perhaps it was no more than frustration, a demand for physical relief. In Vincent's day, prostitutes were – in liberal circles at least – a recommended healthy alternative to masturbation and its frightful supposed dangers – paralysis, blindness, insanity. Brothel-going was thought preferable to the guilt and fear induced by self-abuse.

Suddenly, shockingly, the clergyman's son was a desperado. He prowled the streets looking, hoping to be picked off. He was no longer at odds with himself; he had declared war on all those who were out to suppress or castrate him, for whatever reason. Let them try: he was his own man now at last, at twenty-eight.

Though he often knew fear, and rage, and self-disgust, he was not a vengeful man. It wasn't to take revenge on Kee that he wanted a woman – a want he now confessed to Theo. If it was contradictory to say that he was ready to go to another woman so soon after declaring Kee to be the one 'and no other', very well then, he contradicted himself. He sounded a grandiloquent note: 'Who is the master, the logic or I?' Blame the church wall, the indifference, the freezing-out treatment he had received. 'I need a woman,' he wrote defiantly, shamelessly. It is as though he is amazing himself with his own lust. 'I am a man, and a man of passions; I must go to a woman, otherwise I shall freeze or turn to stone . . .'.[38]

So he set out to look for one. 'And, dear me, I hadn't far to look.' The woman he found, or who found him, a nameless prostitute, was neither young nor beautiful. He spares us the details, saying only that she was tall, well-built. He take a rather gloating pleasure in setting her beside Kee, and one imagines his expression as he writes – the isolate, turning over his secrets to make capital of them. The woman's hands, he says, are those of someone who works for a living – not those of a lady like Kee. But she isn't coarse or common, he insists. She is in fact perfectly ordinary, with nothing to distinguish her from a thousand others. Wonderful. At this point his desire to embroider intervenes, and he somewhat patronisingly brings art into it. She reminds him of

something out of Chardin or Frère, or is it Jan Steen? And he
waxes portentously for a moment. 'Every woman, at every age,
if she loves and is a good woman, gives a man, not the infinity
of a moment but a moment of infinity.'[39] Insufferably put, and
probably not his own thought but something he has read, out of
one of his damned French books that his father loathed seeing
about the place – he had a phenomenal memory for things he had
read. But what is this about love? What has happened to the
stalwart Dutch realist?

We have to allow for some license: he is writing to his brother
in Paris about this street pick-up and doing his best to make it
palatable. He drops another little bombshell. It's not the first time
this has happened: he's gone with prostitutes before. And what
the devil, Kee isn't without sexual experience after all: she has a
past. Then, being human, he indulges in a spurt of malice. One
warms to him because of it. If Kee, who is far from ignorant in
these matters, wanted to go on starving herself for the sake of an
old love which is dead and rotting in the ground, well, so be it,
that is her business. Don't expect him to do the same. He refused
to freeze. When he said he wanted the 'spark of fire' and intended
to have it, it wasn't spiritual love he was talking about.

He sang in praise of prostitutes. There was no reason to withhold any of this from his brother, he said wickedly, because surely
Theo was no stranger to these experiences himself. And 'so much
the better for him'. More revelations followed. He didn't spend
very much on the woman, since they had no need to make
themselves drunk in order to feel human. What he had to spare
he put in her pocket. 'And I wish I could have spared more, for
she was worth it.'[40]

She had humanised him. They talked freely together about
everything, about her sad life, her worries, her bad health, about
how foul the world was, and it was more illuminating than plenty
of conversations he had had with educated folk. 'Sin, bah! Is it a
sin to love, to need love, not to be able to live without love? I
think a life without love a sinful and immoral condition.' As we
take in the tale of this encounter, which clearly did him a power
of good, we have to translate the euphemisms. He had nowhere
to go, so she took him to her room, such as it was. His lyricism
takes flight as he remembers waking in the morning to find 'a
fellow creature beside you; it makes the world look so much

105

more friendly.'[41] A friendly whore! The scene, which should by now be exuding sentimentality like syrup, somehow does no such thing. Everything pleased him; it was good, it was right. More to him perhaps than the relief afforded by the crude sex was the fact that he woke up in the meagre home of a real working woman, warm like a picture by Chardin; 'a wooden floor with a mat and a piece of old crimson carpet, an ordinary kitchen stove, a chest of drawers, a large simple bed.' Note the one touch of extravagance, the tool of her trade – a large bed. Though she was only a part-time whore who 'had to stand at the washtub next day.'[42] A brutal life, which had not extinguished her humanity. That was what he found memorable. It *was* love he felt – and not only for her: for the pathetic room, the faded carpet, the floor boards, the stove, everything. And what he felt was a fraternal love.

Living in The Hague was expensive. He soon got through 90 guilders, which his father thought an excessive amount. He hated having to account for every cent, he complained to Theo, not least because sooner or later everyone came to hear about it. A room with breakfast at the inn cost 30 guilders, and for double that he could rent a decent-sized room for a year in Schevengin, a poor district behind the station. Mauve had said, on seeing his studies, 'You are sitting too close to your model.' Passing this on, he was making a plea for more funds.

When his money had gone he went back home, in time for Christmas. The humiliating financial dependence on his parents, a fact of life ever since he had been dismissed from Goupil's, was being gradually shifted on to Theo, who would soon find himself shouldering the whole burden. Probably one immediate result of this change was Vincent's growing rebellion against the restrictions that went with the use of his home as a base. In addition, the Kee affair had put him on a collision course with his parents. On Christmas Day, he met the opposition head-on. Vincent waded into his father with such anger that his expulsion from the house inevitably followed: such grossness was an offence to the fragile truce they were only just sustaining. Was that what he intended? If he hadn't provoked the argument then he had certainly seized on it with relish. The apparent cause was his father's

attempt to force him to go to church. He had been going regularly, but out of courtesy. To stop going was, of course, a hostile
act, as he well knew. 'But in truth there was much more at the
back of it all, including the whole story of what happened this
summer between Kee and me.' He worked himself up into the
kind of rage that leads to unforgiveable things being said. He told
his mother and father that he found their whole system of religion
abhorrent. The violent scene ended with his father telling him to
leave the house, 'so decidedly that I actually left the same day.'[43]

He packed there and then and returned to The Hague. Presumably he gave Mauve an edited version of what had happened, said
he couldn't stay any longer at Etten, and he would like to stay
in The Hague. Mauve, a man of few words, said, 'Stay then.'
And that was that.

On hearing this dramatic piece of news, Theo wrote at once,
promising as much support as he could afford until Vincent was
in a position to earn his own money. He then proceeded to read
the riot act to his headstrong brother. It is one of the few letters
from Theo that we have, and a remarkably frank one. Pulling no
punches, he asked Vincent what on earth had possessed him to
behave so grotesquely. It was callous of him to embitter and spoil
their parents' lives. What was he doing, acting the liberal again,
and in front of country people who couldn't be expected to
comprehend modern attitudes? 'I don't understand you.'[44]

Vincent replied by return of post, writing his answer on the
back of Theo's letter – but not, he hastened to add, 'with the
intention of insulting you.' Why then? He defended himself vigorously, and took Theo to task for parrotting their father's words.
Admitting the affront, he made capital out of certain phrases.
That expression 'embitter and spoil' was in reality 'a Jesuitism of
Pa's,' he pointed out, and so typical of their father, who said
things like that when in fact he had no answer to the charge. It
was just rhetoric. For example, he would be sitting there calmly,
reading his paper and smoking his pipe, and say to Vincent, 'You
are murdering me.' It was nonsense, it meant nothing. 'Because
Father is a tired old man I have spared him a hundred times, and
tolerated things which are little short of intolerable. This time,
however, there was no question of fighting at all, but simply of
saying "Enough!" '[45]

Anyway, he has since wished his father a Happy New Year.

The van Goghs must have been relieved as well as saddened when their rumbling volcano of a son departed. A semblance of peace descended on the parsonage once more. The Reverend van Gogh's servant girl remembered later that Vincent, who had turned a ground floor room into a makeshift studio, would sometimes work all night. His mother would find him still at it when she came down to breakfast in the morning. Called for lunch, he kept answering, 'Yes, I'm coming,' and often didn't put in an appearance until an hour or more later. He walked around with a portfolio under one arm and a folding campstool under the other, his head held to one side in a manner considered odd. He passed people in the street without recognising them. He once gave a beggar his nearly new velvet suit – doubtless glad of the chance to get rid of it. Without doing anything that could be described as eccentric, he left an impression of strangeness. He was intensely serious. He made no jokes. He visited the homes of the poor. If one of his drawings went wrong, he tore it in half with an angry gesture. He stared straight ahead. He wasn't in the least bit proud. Once he did a picture of an old farmer ploughing his field. When it was done the old man remarked that his dog was missing from it. Vincent obligingly added the dog.

The evidence of peculiarity accumulates. After his death, country people acquainted with him around Etten were astonished that 'that Vincent' could have ever amounted to anything.

7

CONJUGAL/MATERNAL

He was in The Hague: he had done it. Now it was sink or swim. The rupture with his father would never be absolute, and even now, after a dreadful parting scene, the old man had apparently offered to lend his son money. Perhaps Vincent's mother had put pressure on him, or perhaps he had his own reasons for softening the blow. The gesture may have been made for the sake of appearances: after all, how could a minister be without Christian charity? His actions from now on were to show an increasing ambivalence. Even with his authority flouted, in spite of all manner of provocation, it is possible that he still loved his eldest son, at least when Vincent was absent. Face to face, the son who had wanted to model himself on his father now outraged him, showing him little respect, openly arguing with him. Under Vincent's voice, in his fixed, obstinate stare, he detected a lurking mockery and contempt for everything he stood for. Betrayed into fury, he accused his son of being the cause of his own hatred. It seemed to him that Vincent came home spoiling for a fight. The father felt murdered. He hated the brutal-sounding clumsy speech his son used, the invincibility of his young purpose.

Vincent rented a studio – 'that is, a room and an alcove which can be arranged for the purpose, cheap enough' – on the outskirts of town, at Schenkweg 138, close to Ryn station. He was so near, he could see the trains pulling in and out. He was only a ten minute walk from Mauve, who had promised to help him settle in. The rent was low, 7 guilders a month; the expense of buying furniture was the problem. He only needed the rudiments, a wooden table and a few chairs; he was prepared to lay a blanket on the floor and sleep on that. Mauve said no, he should get a bed: he would lend him the money. He also mentioned an old bugbear – he thought Vincent should dress better.

Vincent reported to Theo that though he had worries, he had a feeling of satisfaction at having accomplished the move. Now the die was cast he felt a certain calm. No use regarding recent events in terms of misfortune; one had to show courage for anything worthwhile to be attempted.

So he began, with his bits of furniture which were in the real 'village-policeman' style, whatever that was. The light was good, the window twice as large as an ordinary window, though it faced south. He could work from the model here, a great improvement on the parsonage. He had overcome the main drawback of living in the country at Etten, since now he could associate with other artists, exchange views, be stimulated by the work and lives of others with whom he had something in common. To do so meant of course to abandon the simplicities of pastoral living. In time he would seek a solution to this problem by envisaging a brotherhood of painters living self-sufficiently, away from the worldliness of towns and thus uncontaminated by modern fevers and distractions. Entertaining such a dream was naive; yet, compared to Cézanne, who shared the instinct to hide away from civilisation, he was paradoxically the epitome of subtle thought, as his letters increasingly testified. Cézanne was phlegmatic, timid, at times virtually dumb. But as well as the instinct to get right away, the two painters were alike in being unable to draw acceptably. Critics have expressed doubts about the draughtsmanship of both artists. Both seemed to lack the facility to make things *look* right. In Cézanne's case this was because at first he struggled to compose in the Renaissance manner, and did it badly. Vincent strained every nerve to turn himself into a draughtsman acceptable to the illustrated papers, and the strain showed.

The truth is that the liberties he wanted to take simply disrupted his attempts to produce marketable drawings for Theo, and for his connections in The Hague (such as his Uncle Cor). His aim at first was to produce a body of work which would sell. During his eighteen months at The Hague he collected about a thousand sheets of contemporary wood engravings and etchings – English,

French, and American. These of course were paid for by Theo. Vincent regularly bought copies of the *Graphic* and *London News*, tearing out sheets to add to his stock. The English artists in particular attracted him, he said, 'because of their Monday-morning-like sombreness and studied simplicity.' He went on admiring them in the face of the snobbish dismissal of them by many artists of the Hague school, who sneered at woodcuts as 'those things you find in the South Holland Café.' In other words, they attached about as much value to them as to the drinks.

None of this hollow criticism deterred him. Like Cézanne he was at war with the cliché, whether religious or artistic. If only he could have preached conventionally he might have been accepted, and if he could have imitated the smoothness of those illustrators he admired, he could have made a living. Each time a drawing came out that looked 'all right', he seethed with dissatisfaction, tore it up and started again. And again. It wasn't what he wanted. Remember, the age of photography had dawned. Illustrators were hard at work representing things with photographic accuracy as a way of ensuring that their scenes and figures were true to life. They weren't to him. His aim was for a deeper realism than that of the illustrators and photographers who called themselves Realists. Why then did he admire them, and collect them so avidly? Partly he was desperate to earn his own living and vindicate his decision to be an artist, and, in spite of everything, to place in front of his father and mother the hard-won gift of his success. But what attracted him above all else to the magazine illustrators was their subject matter. It had the kind of social content which stirred him. It wasn't that he wanted to be more imaginative than them. His future liberties with techniques were all to do with representation. His urge was to deepen. Representation could be more truthful, more profound than that, and ought to incorporate that feeling which had been naively symbolised by the halo in early primitive Christian painting. Blake's 'everything that lives is holy' was now a gospel confined to churches in the care of men like his father. In Vincent's era, as he knew in his nerves and on his skin as well as through his eyes, the new creators were the inventors of speed and progress.

Vincent's early history is the story of a great refuser. He refused outright the advice of his 'betters', either by alienating them in a flash of rage or by stubbornly preferring not to go along with them; rather like Melville's eponymous character Bartleby. But Bartleby by his refusal was preferring not to live. Vincent wanted to cast his skin and emerge shining, like Christ after the crucifixion. After refusing to be a Jesuit, he then refused to be an atheist. He sought the means to do something quite different, creating it out of himself as he went along – but he hoped for everyone: a way of looking that was a kind of worship.

At first, as always, things went well. Mauve put himself out in all sorts of ways – a highly irritable man who could be expansively generous. Vincent went to him for drawing in the mornings, and in the evenings to try his hand at watercolours, as he had done before Christmas. Mauve proposed his name for membership of the Pulchri Art Club, where Vincent could draw the models available without extra expense. The more he was involved with Mauve, the more he saw how the man's work drained him. They were too alike, they annoyed and inflamed each other now and then, which made for a tricky situation. 'I think we are equally nervous.'[1]

Watercolour was a revelation. Vincent was soon absorbed in trying to master its alchemy, daubing and washing out again. Something though was eluding him. Either things came out too harshly, heavy, muddy and dull – Mauve called it his 'yellow-soap style' – or else the tenderness wasn't tender enough. He turned back in despair to drawing. When he went out, he tried to infiltrate the soup kitchens, the third-class waiting room at the station, anywhere in fact where the poor gathered. Working in the open was too bitterly cold at present. He even ate at the soup kitchen to save money and time.

Drawing was now an abiding passion, and 'it is a passion just like that of a sailor for the sea'.[2] He lost himself in its possibilities, its immensity, he went far out, and came back dazed, stunned by horizons, often with sketches he had done in a hurry and afterwards flew at with the axe of a black crayon, or a pen loaded with black ink, hacking at them fiercely, savagely, to kill off the sentimental and picturesque that was so much in vogue. In his rage and despair he became a vivisector.

At the beginning of February he confessed to a whole list of ailments and obscure setbacks. Some were psychological; or perhaps they all were. He had headaches, toothache, his anxiety about the coming week and how he would cope with it had given him a fever. He was depressed, so severely that he took to his bed. He got up, then went back to bed again.[3]

Next came a litany of his material difficulties. His clothes, some of them old things of Theo's which had been altered for him, were shabby, and were getting spattered with paint. His boots were dilapidated. His underwear was falling apart.

He gives as his reason for this sudden discouragement the feeling that his strength was failing him. Also he was worried about a model he had arranged to hire through Mauve, and then doubted whether he could pay the price. Mauve would think he lacked guts. So was the whole epistle an elaborate begging letter, or was it voicing a loss of nerve, a fear of life, an attack of what we now call angst? In his next letter, on his feet again, he thanks Theo for the enclosed 100 francs.

We shall become accustomed to these inexplicable relapses. They punctuate the log of his days and weeks throughout his months at The Hague. This time he seems to be picking up the signals of some approaching hostility towards him. He was a man excessively sensitive to the opinions of others. Disapproval would at first enrage and then devastate him, and these warning messages apparently arrived visually. He observed people closely, as was only natural for a painter, and he was already watching Mauve, the friendly mentor who might at any moment turn into an enemy. Feeling unloved, he half expected to be hated. People at Etten had recently commented on his habit of walking along while staring straight ahead, and this was perhaps his protection against unfriendly glances. His sister Elizabeth remembered that as a child he half closed his eyes at meal times as he sat with his family.

He was burdened too during this difficult winter with a sense of the loss of his youth. Nearly thirty, at the mercy of involuntary depressions which seemed causeless, and which struck at him 'just when one is feeling cheerful', he analysed his feelings with considerable insight and honesty. 'At such a moment one feels as if one were lying bound hand and foot at the bottom of a deep dark well, utterly helpless.' He admitted that it saddened him to realise that 'my youth is gone – not my love of life or my energy, but I mean the time when one feels so lighthearted and carefree.'[4]

He offered Theo some startling advice. 'And I tell you frankly that in my opinion one must not hesitate to go to a prostitute occasionally if there is one you can trust and feel something for. . . . For one who has a strenuous life it is necessary, absolutely necessary in order to keep sane and well. One must not exaggerate such things and fall into excesses, but nature has fixed laws which it is fatal to struggle against.' Another desolate little thought followed swiftly on the heels of this one. 'It would be well for you, it would be well for me, if we were married – but what can we do?'5

What indeed. Nothing prepares us for his next move. He was about to experiment with a drastic remedy – not only taking his own advice but overriding that 'occasionally' by cohabiting with a prostitute as a common law wife. This done, though not yet admitted to his brother or, presumably, to anyone else, he found all the justification he wanted in the words of 'Father' Millet – another of his father-replacements. 'Art is a battle,' Millet had said in his autobiography. 'In art you have to risk your own skin.'

Biographers, notably A J Lubin, have suggested motives which may have prompted him to choose such a woman for a partner. One immediate result, once the news leaked out – and he made no attempt to hide his new circumstances from Mauve and others in his immediate vicinity – was swift condemnation by all his middle-class associates. This one act of his expelled him into the wilderness more forcibly than any other, just as it did the novelist George Gissing in England. In Vincent's case, this may have been the very reaction he wanted. The neglect of his appearance had already caused him to be shunned, in the Borinage and elsewhere. Justifying this self-neglect to Theo in 1880, he also commended it as 'a good way to assure the solitude necessary for concentrating on whatever study preoccupies one.'6

Barriers and handicaps were always contributing to the alienation he bemoaned and yet instinctively courted. When his teacher, Mauve, and then Tersteeg, the manager at Goupil's whom he had counted a friend, both turned against him, he was at first bitterly hurt. Then he managed to stand their opposition on its head. 'And though some people may damn me irrevocably and for ever, in the nature of things my profession and my work will open new relations to me, that much fresher for not having been frozen, hardened, and made sterile by old prejudices.'7

In the light of these observations, the act of living with a prostitute takes on another meaning. Relationships were perhaps being tested and found wanting. Hopefully he would be led to others which were more fruitful in the long run. By ensuring rejection in this way he was also ensuring that he would not be enslaved by anyone else's methods of work. His attitude to others and towards mixing with them was rooted in an ambiguity that was fertile for his art but disastrous in his dealings with people. He was hungry all his life for friends and friendly environments, vilifying and imploring as he shifted about restlessly and unpredictably like a Lawrence, never finding the right place, the right person.

Often he acted in ways that made him seem like a child demanding to be looked after. Falling into depression, he appealed to Mauve to call and see him. In spite of his bitter criticism of his father, he still asked for help from him. Theo was soon changed into the loving father he believed was his due. Later on he would utter cries for help and expect to be nursed back to health by sympathetic doctors, demanding attention as a substitute for love and taking masochistic pleasure in its denial. When he declared, 'I resign myself to everything and put up with everything,'[8] he was rejoicing in his discovery that to behave like a child sometimes worked. It also aligned him with the underdogs, helpless like children under the blows of fate.

He chose 'the dog's path', and chose it consciously, because it was the crooked rather than the straight, it created difficulties, and those difficulties fed his art. By accepting the role of victim he glorified his own suffering and was brought close to Christ. 'It is better,' he concluded, 'to be a sheep than a wolf, better to be ruined than to do the ruining.'[9] Failure was more honourable than success. It became a matter of pride to be 'chained to misfortune and failure', like the picture 'The Prisoner' by Gérôme, showing a man lying fettered.[10] The hardships he accepted with a kind of satisfaction would benefit others and do their work a power of good, he said, and cited as an example a painter friend at The Hague, Theophile de Bock. 'I should be sorry for him if he did not land more in the thorns than in the flowers – that's all.'[11]

Vincent remarked several times that he had no fear of death. On the contrary, he welcomed it, befriended it. At the end, he chose it. He was afflicted by the modern malaise of instability and a fear of life. To fear life is to fear the world. A lifelong fear of the world means that one is afraid of the outside, of society, and erects what bulwarks one can against it. Nothing, he found, was more effective – as he tried to devise an inner world that at the same time avoided the black hole of dejection – than work, solitary work, work in which one was gladly buried. Dostoevsky had come to a very similar conclusion when he came to write about his four years of penal servitude in Siberia: 'I felt that work might be the saving of me, might build my health, my body.' His letters at this time were – like van Gogh's throughout his life – full of references to fainting fits, spasms, weakness, nervous attacks of various kinds. Vincent said categorically: 'Work is an absolute necessity for me. I can't put it off, I don't care for anything but the work; that is to say, the pleasure in something else ceases at once, and I become melancholic when I can't go on with my work.'[12] On another occasion he reflected that only hard work saved him from 'that melancholic staring into the abyss'. His aim, in fact, as he freely admitted, was to *forget himself* in his work. Forget his disappointments, forget that he was unmarried, childless, forget his hunger for a loving mother, forget that he was ugly, freezing cold, in disgrace. As A J Lubin movingly observes, 'His pictures became his companions, his mistresses, and his children.'[13]

Now, however, he had a real-life mistress, a mother with a child of her own. A van Gogh scholar, Jan Hulsker, has unearthed the following facts about her. Her name was Clasina Maria Hoornik and she was born at The Hague in February, 1850. This makes her three years older than Vincent, and roughly the same age as Kee. Vincent called her Sien, the familiar version of her Christian name. Her parents had eleven children legitimately and probably others besides. Before their encounter Sien had two illegimate children, in 1874 and 1879. These children were dead. Vincent knew nothing of them. Sien had a five-year-old daughter, and she was pregnant.

The poor woman was a wreck, addicted to drink, ill and half starved. She scrubbed out the houses of Dutch burghers when she had the strength, or she took in washing. Too weak to do either, she had gone on the streets. It was an old resource. Her own mother had done the same.

Where did they meet? Possibly in one of the cheap wine-shops he frequented at the back of Ryn station. He may have taken pity on her and bought her a drink, at the same time buying a little companionship for himself, easing the ache of his loneliness. It was winter, bitterly cold outside. Wherever it was, she attracted his attention by her deplorable state. He found himself confronted by a sorrier specimen than himself.

They met towards the end of January, and he kept the news from Theo until April. When he did let it out, he did so in a rather peculiar fashion, linking it to a quarrel with Mauve and casting it in a dramatic mode, with himself in the first and then third person. 'They suspect me of something – it is in the air – I am keeping something back. *Vincent is hiding something that cannot stand the light.*' This narrative flexibility indicates the extent to which he now saw himself as a character in his own drama. To put it another way, he was aware of the idea of divided consciousness, much discussed in his day, and here and elsewhere he can be seen applying it to his own actions.

No doubt attempting to forestall criticism and evoke compassion, he began with the pregnancy, highlighting it twice. 'Last winter I met a pregnant woman, deserted by the man whose child she carried. A pregnant woman who had to walk the streets in winter, had to earn her bread, you understand how.'

Kenneth Wilkie, asked in the early 1970s to write a feature article on van Gogh for the *Holland Herald*, has done his best to show that Vincent was the father of Sien's unborn child. One warms to Wilkie's enthusiasm for detection and admires his industry, but the evidence he puts forward is somewhat shaky. Dr Jan Hulsker had told him that after Vincent's departure from The Hague, Sien had given custody of the baby Willem to her brother, Pieter Hoornik, before going back to a life of casual prostitution and drink. She drowned herself in 1904. The brother, Pieter, had a son of his own. This boy became the Dutch poet, Ed Hoornik. Wilkie, who describes himself modestly as a working journalist, then tracked down the poet's widow. Mies Hoornik-Bouhuys, a writer and broadcaster, said that her late husband succeeded in tracing Willem, after being told by Jan Hulsker that the prostitute Vincent lived with was his aunt. Then follows more hearsay evidence, and the trail peters out on a question mark.[14]

For all the fascination of this quest, we have to ask whether its

117

outcome really matters. It is not nearly so intriguing for this writer as is the closed book of Vincent's intimate life in this unlikely household, with a woman who allowed him to clean her up, who tended and fed her like a mother, rocked the cradle of her newborn baby, and shared his food and his room with her.

We do have a few glimpses, through the keyhole as it were. It makes more sense to enquire into his attempts to reform this woman, and then to glorify her and her child in a whole series of marvellous drawings, than to establish a dubious fatherhood he in any case assumed at the outset, emotionally and spiritually and with the utmost delight. The horrible emptiness of his heart, mocked in a cruel doubling by his empty room, was now filled with a domesticity he had thought would never be his.

Every extreme action produces its reaction. From an idealised, spiritual love for Kee which always had something sickly and perverse about it, he plunged into the lightless sub-world of labour, submerging himself in its mean and desperate poverty, as if to kill off once and for all the romanticism which had brought him nothing but pain. The joyless cynicism, vicious cruelty, and ugly surroundings of his new life were his punishment for living so long in foolish illusion. Here there were no facades, no masks, no appearances to be kept up. Faces were stripped of pretence by the pitiless bombardment of harsh reality. A crust was a crust. You snatched at it and gobbled it down, before someone else did. Fine feelings were soon mauled and discarded. It was the Borinage all over again, but with one essential difference. He had no shreds of status clinging to him. The Church was unaware of his existence. An unsuccessful artist was no better than a lunatic in the eyes of these people. Only one person really cared whether he sank or swam, and he was far off in Paris. Cohabiting with Sien made him a denizen of the slum district she knew intimately. He had moved in, not only with her, but with Jack London's 'people of the abyss'.

He was in fact a man of two worlds, as he would always be. Balancing between them took a great deal of agility. There were risks, deformations, and there were compensations, artistic seams to be mined. He set about exploiting this one with tremendous zeal.

Pleas for understanding began to pour from him in a stream. 'Poverty has advantages and disadvantages.' 'I am not living in a bed of roses but in reality.' By living with 'the woman' he was undeniably saddling himself with more expense, but consider the gains, he implored. He now had a permanent and very willing model, and not only one; he had several. The mother was a good subject, and the little girl, and soon there would be a baby. He spoke already in terms of collaboration – 'I sent you a few studies because you can see from them that she helps me a great deal by posing. My drawings are done by "my model and me". The woman in the white bonnet is her mother.'[15]

A row blew up between him and Mauve. The truth was that Mauve only wanted to spend time on a large painting of sailing barges which he was getting ready for an exhibition. Vincent's constant demands for attention were becoming a pest. Mauve's critical comments, at first sympathetic, were now unpleasantly caustic, and, as far as Vincent was concerned, unjust. What had he done wrong? Why had the man turned against him? As always, when he was criticised unkindly he smelled persecution. Who had been whispering against him – was it Tersteeg?

As it happened, he was right about Tersteeg. The man was a snake. Beneath his refined manners and superficial elegance lay something treacherous. God knows, there was little about Vincent to inspire jealousy, but jealous the fellow undoubtedly was. His favourite line of attack was to start talking about finding useful employment for Vincent, and to issue veiled threats. Vincent translated these to mean: Take my advice or I'll use my influence with Theo to cut off your subsistence allowance. Then Vincent heard, in this nest of artistic vipers, that Tersteeg was laughing at Vincent's absurd ambition to be a painter. He was going behind Vincent's back with his 'hatred, grudges, chicanery, sarcasm'.

And now Mauve too was suspect. Agitated, Vincent went running to a painter called Weissenbruch to see if he was another one who had been poisoned by the gossip circulating against him. He was reassured by the man's friendship. He liked Weissenbruch's gaiety, and the man had a reputation for telling the truth. The painter said frankly that he had told Mauve: 'I could work from his (Vincent's) studies myself.' This was praise indeed.

Mollified, if not entirely convinced, Vincent went back to Mauve and tried hard to knuckle down. Tersteeg had finally told him venomously: 'You failed before and you'll fail again – it'll be the same story all over again.'[16] His security undermined, he was now more vulnerable than ever to Mauve's voice and its cutting edge, to his cold eyes, the touch of condescension. Things were disintegrating between them. It was hideous, unfair. He did what the established artist ordered, and felt the ignominy of it, of what his instruction had turned into – a succession of orders.

Finally his anger boiled over. Mauve kept insisting that he should concentrate more on studies from plaster casts. It was perhaps a strategy for dissuading him from coming round so often. Vincent loathed the grey, dead plaster. Mauve had given him a few casts of hands and feet to take home and study. A day came when Mauve lectured at him, 'as the worst teacher at the academy would not have spoken.' He swallowed his pride and kept quiet, but was so furious when he got home that he hurled his hated casts into the coalbin. They lay there, smashed and filthy. He was done with them: from now on he would draw from living hands and feet, and no others. At Mauve's studio the next time it came spilling out. In a pitch of frenzy he stammered, 'Man, don't mention plaster to me again, because I can't stand it.' A curt note arrived shortly afterwards from Mauve, telling him to stay away for the next two months.[17]

It was soon after this incident that Sien moved in with him. Overjoyed to be of use to someone, and by his role of rescuer, he expressed his happiness to Theo obliquely, in a rushing torrent of plans. He wanted to be out in the open street working, so as to catch things 'in motion'. Industrial subjects interested him. He had just come in from sketching workmen out on the Geest, where they were laying water and gas pipes. It was difficult to draw well in such conditions, among the noise and confusion, standing in mud in the squalls of rain, but worth it for all that. They were the kind of difficulties he thrived on.

He made out a case for dressing down rather than up. 'When I wear a fine coat, the working people that I want for models are afraid of me and distrust me, or they want more money from me.' The real reason was that he felt at ease; he was no longer a figure of fun or an eyesore, he had a place – just as he did at first with Sien. The metamorphosis he felt was an inner as well as an outer one. 'I am a different person when I am at work on the Geest or on the heath or in the dunes. Then my ugly face and shabby coat harmonise perfectly with the surroundings and I am myself.'[18]

Figures, the human body in motion or at rest, would be his prime material for the immediate future. Landscapes were empty and without meaning unless they could be related to an inner view, to a feeling of emptiness or apprehension, a sadness, a surge of hope, an ecstasy. When he turned to attack landscape he would either include a figure smudged on the periphery, dwindling in the distance, or portray anonymous couples or figures imprisoned by fences and obstructed by walls and trees. Landscape only became meaningful when he found the confidence to treat it subjectively. He equated a lone tree with a lonely person, and paired trees in the same way that he paired humans.[19] His work, nearly always typographically accurate, had himself projected into it. The earth he painted was impregnated earth. His skies boiled and burned, or they reflected the eternal in the eyes of a baby. His perspectives led the eye obsessively to some place out of reach, that he could long for but not have.

Sien had made him strong and potent again. It was not the sex. Without knowing it, she bestowed value and purpose on him. He could help her regain her health, even give her a sense of her own worth if he persevered. He saw her as a person injured by life, as he was injured. He encouraged her to take public baths, he saw that she ate properly – though indifferent to food himself – and behaved with her like a caring mother, the kind of affectionate mother who had always inspired him. The mother-daughter relationship he had witnessed in London had moved him so profoundly that he had fallen in love with them both.

Sien's own mother was inadequate, often drunk. He would stand in for her. His description of Sien bears a remarkable resemblance to the image he had now formed of himself. She inspired disgust in other people. She threw angry tantrums. Her health, like his, had been impaired by malnutrition, and 'her mind and nervous system were also upset and unbalanced.' In moments of extreme stress Vincent could barely speak, and when he did his words would sometimes be mangled. Sien's speech was ugly. 'Nobody cared for her or wanted her, she was alone and forsaken like a worthless rag.'[20]

Seeing her as innately beautiful, especially after she gave birth to the child she was bearing, was to applaud her regeneration and at the same time redeem his own unattractiveness. Out of sorrow and ugliness emerged freshness and grace. Depravity and a wasted body and spirit could give birth to health. In taking refuge with a submerged class, which by its toil serviced the spotlessly clean houses of Dutch society, he was laying down a challenge to his privileged friends and relatives. It was this implied indictment that was soon to bring so much wrath down on his head. Yet he was no revolutionary. He had a hatred of cant, but his eyes were wide open. After his liaison ended and he was alone again, he wrote simply and forlornly, 'I hated being alone so much that I preferred being with a bad whore to being alone.'[21]

For all his apparent certainty, the decision to throw in his lot with her must have weighed heavily. He held back at first, but only until she was confined in the hospital at Leyden. Sien as a nursing mother was irresistible. What he found in her was what he wanted to find: a sickly, faded woman as beautiful in his eyes as a Madonna. He made a simple crib for the baby, and heaped praise on Sien whenever she acted maternally. The inferior and degraded had become the norm. A later friend, the painter Emile Bernard, remarked that 'Vincent showed extreme humanity for prostitutes', and said he was a witness to 'sublime scenes of devotion on his part.'[22] By subjugating himself, Vincent replaced their bad image with a good one, and not only theirs but his own.

He wrote enigmatically to Theo, urging him to come and meet Sien. He thought he would be reminded, as Vincent was, of their childhood nurse at Zundert, Leen Veerman. Sien, he stressed, was that kind of person: in other words she was a substitute for something else – as prostitutes are – and from an inferior class. He went on to say that meeting her would be like meeting an apparition from their past . . . 'you will rediscover yourself in her'. And he went on more explicitly to speak of that period 'some ten or even twenty years ago.'[23] It was all a roundabout way of saying that Sien was synonymous with sorrow, and perhaps as well he was referring to the sorrowing mother of their childhood. Sien had 'that Dolorosa expression' which had affected him so deeply when he had seen it depicted in the picture *Woman in Mourning*. Somehow this sad and pitiful woman, 'already pock-

marked, already withered and prematurely old,' has been fused
with Michelet's 'woman in black' in his imagination. Women cast
down, on whom life had left its mark, were to him sisters under
the skin regardless of station.

In the hard light of day, of course, he had no illusions about
her. Nevertheless, he thought Theo unduly alarmist in warning
him that women like her were out to fleece him. Before he had
become involved with Sien he had used her for some time as
a model. One incident in particular had convinced him of her
genuineness. They had been working together, and she had asked
about the following day. No, he couldn't afford her. The next
morning she came knocking on his door. He opened it shaking
his head. 'I just came to see if you had something for dinner,' she
said. She gave him what she had brought, a dish of beans and
potatoes.

At about the same time, something extraordinary happened.
Crowing over it to Theo he made it sound like a breakthrough.
'It is almost miraculous!' His uncle Cornelius, head of the van
Gogh art business in Amsterdam, had commissioned him to make
twelve small pen drawings of The Hague. If he liked them he
would take another twelve, at a better price. This was Vincent's
first sale. The day before he had just bumped into Mauve, 'happily
delivered of his large picture,'[24] who had promised to call in.
Another miracle. So his fears about his cousin's strange hostility
were, it seems, unfounded.

Alas, his elation was short-lived. When Vincent wrote impulsively to congratulate Mauve on completing the big work he had
laboured at for so long, he got no reply. Fretting, he thought of
hurrying round to have it out with him, whatever it was. He was
never able to bear uncertainty. He lost sleep, his mind churning,
piling up imaginary complaints and magnifying them. He wrote
again, a careful, stilted letter, expressing gratitude for the help he
had received and suggesting they shook hands and called it a day.
His reserve broke before he had got far and he revealed his own
grievance. If it was hard for Mauve to guide him, it was equally
hard for him to be guided 'strictly'. The stumbling block was the
obedience he demanded. 'I cannot give that. So that's the end of
the guiding and being guided.'[25] He had acted hotly, but with his
usual honesty. It was a manly, proud note. He had no reply to
this letter either.

One day the two men met by chance out on the dunes. It was clear from Mauve's manner that they were finished. Vincent asked his cousin to call and see his latest work, and Mauve shook his head, his face bitter. He turned away, muttering something about Vincent's vicious character. Deeply hurt, Vincent jumped to the conclusion that news of his friendship with Sien had reached him and upset the man. He was in a small world, incestuous, spiteful, and more disliked for his unorthodoxy and his apparent arrogance that he realised. He gave up trying to understand it and vowed to harden himself more. He worked harder still.

He still resisted colour. He had heard enough stories of artists who had started painting too soon, and failed, floundering in a morass without sound drawing and perspective techniques. In a book by Dürer he read a description of a perspective device and made one for himself.

Drawing refreshed him as a long walk refreshed him, and it was part of the art of forgetting slights, frustrations, old wounds, so necessary if he was to survive and stay serene. Nature too was a great balm. He was always grateful for 'the healthy and restorative force that I see in the country.' Yet the Expressionist in him kept seeing psychological equivalents everywhere. Trees, corn, grass, cabbages would all be anthropomorphised, so that 'for instance in trees I see expression and soul, so to speak. A row of pollard willows sometimes resembles a procession of almshouse men. Young corn has something inexpressively pure and tender about it, which awakens the same emotion as the expression of a sleeping baby. The trodden grass at the roadside looks tired and dusty like the people of the slums. A few days ago, when it had been snowing, I saw a group of Savoy cabbages standing frozen and benumbed, and it reminded me of a group of women in their thin petticoats and old shawls which I had seen standing in a little hot-water-and-coal shop early in the morning.'[26]

Whatever he drew exhibited the old traits and gestures for which he had been criticised and condemned, but preferred not to correct: their so-called clumsiness, for instance. John Berger has noticed that his drawings – and later his paintings – contain in their ink, their crayon, their pigment, what he calls 'the labour of being' of what they depict. If he drew a chair or a pair of boots he managed to convey the effort of production that went into them, as if he had shaped them and fitted them together himself.

The spectator is made to feel that without this element their reality would be incomplete.[27]

His pictures were stubbornly *not nice*: he called for carpenters' pencils of rough graphite rather than the refined Fabers, crayons of a denser black, and later squeezed his colour messily and thickly from the tube direct when he was in the mood. It was as if neatness and cleanliness were linked in his mind with the hypocritical.

At The Hague, still aiming at the illustrated magazine market, he concentrated on figures in action, and in the process would be distracted by other subjects: by shabby house fronts, factories, drying sheds, parks, churches, refuse dumps, freight yards. And somehow they all came out as expressive of human beings. The bricks and iron and peeling paint were somehow analogous to the people he saw passing in and out of them, with their dirty faces, stooping postures, and threadbare clothes.

He walked out as far as Scheveningen to draw the fisherwomen there. He drew peasants digging and sowing, and labourers of all kinds, timber men, blacksmiths, hauliers, as well as the sick and the old, the maimed and the deformed. Wanting to capture figures engaged in activities he made quick sketches of people reading, writing, cooking, drying themselves, or huddling close to fires. Women burdened with loads attracted him, as they had done in the Borinage, pushing wheelbarrows, sweeping, and fetching coal.

Once, out at Scheveningen, he was excited by the wind lashing the sea into a fine rage. The trouble was, in all the fury and exuberance the view was half obliterated: masses of water raised fountains of spray and wrapped the fore-shore in a sort of mist. The most impressive thing about the storm was its eerie quiet. The sea was the colour of dirty washing water.

Another time he was out with his watercolour box and a horse suddenly bolted, dragging a coal cart from the entrance to Ryn station at a mad gallop. In his haste to leap out of the way Vincent dropped and broke his paintbox. He reported the event to Theo laconically as 'another expense'.

If it rained or snowed and he was trapped indoors, he composed beautiful word pictures in ever-lengthening letters to his brother, and for good measure added lightning sketches from memory. He complained now and then of feeling curiously weak and faint.

This feeling of exhaustion would pass, he said, if he kept busy. Ryn station was one of his favourite haunts, or rather its approaches, 'the cinder path with the poplars . . . then the ditch full of duckweed, then the brown-grey soil of spaded potato fields, or plots planted with greenish purple-red cabbage . . . behind this stretch of ground the red-rusted or black rails in yellow sand; here and there stacks of old timber – heaps of coal – discarded railway carriages.'[28] His colour sense was demanding to be heard and utilised. He used correspondence as a safety valve, and for imaginary company.

But it was on days like these that one longed for a friend, hoped for a caller. It was on days like these that the emptiness came back and one grew desperate. How essential it was to be able to work, and to be blessed with the will to work.

One solution, of course, providing he was in funds, was to employ a model. Then he had both the work and the company. He described one, a boy who was glad to come in and sit for him, and bring his spade. He was a hod-carrier. The lad intrigued him, with his curiously flattened nose, like a cat's, and his extremely coarse straight hair. For all his simplicity and rough appearance he had a certain grace of figure. Of course, Vincent explained to Theo, he could avoid the expense of models and use his imagination. His tongue was firmly in his cheek. Wrestling with nature – and human nature – was the prime thing. It mattered. The body's terrible corruption, like the earth's, somehow had to be grappled with and known at close quarters, like a mistress. Then all the rest would follow: salvation, resurrection, heaven.

Vincent had grasped early on that his deep-seated, recurring fearfulness in the face of life was a condition he shared with many nineteenth-century artists. His were not merely personal problems. He rejected outright the idea that he was a special case. The loss he felt at times with such anguish, personified by Eugenia, by his mother, by Kee, were the knife-thrusts of a severance from the world itself, from nature. The Renaissance certainty had been exploded by Copernicus, Kant, the French Revolution. How could a man join himself to God's creation again? How did you get back? It was a cruel madness, being so blindingly aware of his plight and yet mired in it, chained down on a rock, powerless to live fully, in the full glory of the senses. The painters and writers with whom he felt an affinity akin to brotherhood were all suffering, in their different ways, as he was. He was convinced of it. He read the signs everywhere, in their books and pictures, their sundered lives. Something had broken down in them. They had got lost in themselves. Their modern subjectivity tormented them with a consciousness of what they had lost. He saw the age into which he had been born as a civilisation in decline, and said so. One did one's best in the face of it.

Why, then, does a contemplation of his life and work leave us feeling zestful rather than discouraged, as if we have been brushed by someone with an incorrigible belief in happiness? The great Italian poet Leopardi had this to say: 'Works of genius have this intrinsic property that even when they give a perfect likeness of the nullity of things, even when they clearly demonstrate and make us feel the inevitable unhappiness of life, even when they express the most terrible despair, nevertheless . . . they always serve as a consolation, rekindling enthusiasm, and though speaking of and portraying nothing but death, restore to it, at least for a while, the life that it had lost.'[29]

But one kind of suffering seemed about to end for him. He was no longer hopeless and defeated: he had a goal. If he could find someone who had been through the mill as he had and then collaborate with them, great things were possible.

He had not yet abandoned the idea of finding a woman who would commit herself totally to him as a life partner. The dream was still alive, and more desirable than ever. He dreamed of a total sharing, body and soul. To combine forces made supreme sense to him, and the more absurd the reality seemed, the more deeply he desired it.

A woman was a world apart, infinitely baffling and mysterious, even when degraded, even screeching in a foul rage. Even falling apart she was amazingly all of a piece. Fluctuating wildly, yet paradoxically consistent and real, as a man never was. Attaching himself to Sien was like fastening himself to something that was eternal, that never changed, for all its mad fits and perversity. He clung to her, at first out of pity, then self-pity, and finally from need. As the voices of respectability rose in unison against him, he clung even tighter.

He set out his position with great deliberation and tenacity. 'I know full well that, frankly speaking, prostitutes are bad, but I feel something human in them which prevents me from feeling the slightest scruple about associating with them. . . . If our society were pure and well regulated, yes, they would be seducers; but now, in my opinion, one may often consider them sisters of charity.' He drove this argument home with a bitter flourish. Wasn't it Jesus who said to the respectable citizens of His time, 'The harlots go into the Kingdom of Heaven before you?'[30]

Oh, he knew perfectly well that women like her could be bad news. They didn't give a damn for what we call reason, they were liable to act wickedly at a moment's notice. He knew all that. In his eyes their saving grace was something he could only define as 'that truly human feeling'. Whatever that was, it made up for everything else. He was brought in touch with reality, he was thawed out. Vain they might be at times, dangerous, vicious even, when the devil was in them. But for all that they had a certain passion.[31]

There were peaceable, calm times. The woman's debility softened her. Sien responded like a weak child to Vincent's ministrations. Sitting quietly with her in a kind of wordless communion, he felt blessed, fortunate to be in her company. She made no objection to his strange ways, his obsessive working habits were his own business, and she found nothing repugnant in his looks, his soiled clothes. What were they to her? Nor was she at all put off or frightened by his intensity, when he flew into a temper if a drawing went badly. He soon calmed down, then went across and fussed over her to make up for the rumpus, though it hadn't bothered her in the slightest. She was only half alive, poor woman. She sat in a chair with a shawl over her shoulders to keep off the draughts. He taught her how to sit, arranged her arms. When he asked anxiously if she minded, she said it was a fair exchange for all his kindness to her.

He was in a quiet heaven of his own making. However, since he had an imagination, he had to use it. Detaching himself from this passionate domesticity, he composed in his mind the kind of picture Rembrandt would have made of it. Only recently he had seen a photograph of a Rembrandt, one he didn't know. It was the head of a harlot. The light fell on the woman's breast, neck, chin, and the tip of her nose, creating that gravity unique to him, which Vincent adored. Rembrandt was for him 'the magician of magicians'. Sitting at peace with his ailing woman, tenderly responsive, he imagined his mouth curved in a mysterious smile 'like that of Rembrandt himself in his self-portrait in which Saskia is sitting on his knee and he has a glass of wine in his hand.'[32]

He also had a mind. While Sien sat to him, a pathetic drooping invalid who wanted to please him, who actually asked him to tell her what would please him, he probed her, observed her, dissected her painlessly, as the masters of literature had done with women, subtly and beautifully revealing their characters. He thought of a Zola, Daudet, de Goncourt, Balzac. He had felt the truth of their analyses in the very marrow of his bones, yet he remained outside, forever outside.

It was during this interval that he drew several versions of a famous picture of the Hague period, entitled *Sorrow*. It was a seminal work. He worked at it obsessively, did versions in pencil and ink, had lithographs made of it, and sat the figure both indoors and out. Each one is labelled clearly with the title in large letters in the bottom right-hand corner. On one he inscribed Michelet's words: 'How can it be that there is in the world one woman alone – deserted?' He combined in it his two great themes of death and rebirth. The figure is Sien, painfully stripped naked, her bony shanks drawn up as she squats on a sawn-off dead tree stump. Her head is sunk on her arms, one wrinkled hand is visible, her black hair straggles down her knobbly back. The swollen belly tells of her condition. Her breasts hang like empty dugs, the opposite of fruitful.

In a letter, Vincent only said that he wanted to express 'the struggle of life in that pale, slender woman's figure.' She was drained of strength and 'would die if she had to walk the streets again.'[33] The words are gentle, the lines of the drawing cruelly incisive. When he drew he put aside all other considerations and reached for the truth. The outdoor version shows the woman in the midst of spurting spring growth. Behind her a young sapling is about to bloom. Flowering plants grow near her feet. She sees none of it. The stump she sits on is as dead as she is blind. Her spirit, wasted, lapses towards death. Yet her belly, in spite of her defeat, goes on filling with new life.

Another picture, a pen and pencil drawing, is a more devastating exposure still. Like the other, it is of Sien, this time sitting in bed with arms folded, propping up her naked breasts. It is of a remarkable ugliness. One flinches, physically hurt by it. The mouth is drawn down in bitter disgust, the eyes nearly closed, unseeing. The scraggy neck and brutally squared and misshapen breasts put one in mind of an old woman, worked over by a lifetime of misfortune. Again, like the other, it is inscribed with a title, the savagely ironic *The Great Lady*. Is this facetiousness?

The woman is on show, held up to be coldly viewed. She is accustomed to being despised. She despises back. Any moment now and she will spit on us, on life. A J Lubin's belief that Vincent was out to mock or deride his mother (why not Kee?) by taking up with Sien, and by thus labelling his drawing, is of course pure supposition. He did tell Theo that the sketch was suggested to him by a poem of Thomas Hood's relating the story of a conscience-stricken rich lady who has been to buy a dress and sees an emaciated, consumptive seamstress in a back room of the shop. The great lady sits up in bed stark naked, with Sien's face and torso, and we have no way of knowing why.[34]

The Roots, a drawing done at about the same time as *Sorrow*, was conceived quite deliberately as a companion piece. He paired them because he was trying to say the same thing in both. 'I tried to put the same sentiment into that landscape as I put into the figure: the convulsive, passionate clinging to the earth, and yet being half torn up by the storm.'[35] The 'black, gnarled, and knotty roots' were in harmony with the woman's limbs.

The Hague school of artists was rife with theories about 'pure' art. Vincent's work was found wanting – when it was noticed at all – by a sniffing, word-of-mouth criticism that condemned him as too literary. He was a van Gogh, and his cousin an established painter, otherwise he would no doubt have been ignored altogether. Vincent was irritated but not dismayed. These were cant phrases so far as he was concerned and they missed the point. He was not in the business of inventing metaphors or illustrating stories with moral cameos. The parallels he noticed occurred naturally, like Henry Moore's found objects. The roots torn up and bleeding on the ground and the woman smashed by life's storms were to him interchangeable images. The same black thread ran through them both. He picked up the thread and followed it. Sometimes the thread was misery, sometimes the black joy of an earth, blasted and left for dead, that went on labouring in darkness to renew itself.

Walking down a road outside The Hague his attention was caught by a dead willow trunk, 'alone and melancholic'.[36] He went back home and returned later to make a watercolour of it. Another time he passed a copse of exposed trees that had been battered by the prevailing wind for so long that the trees were permanently bent over. 'Those trees were superb; there was drama in each *figure* I was going to say, but I mean in each tree . . . . Yes, for me, the drama of storm in nature, the drama of storm in life, is indeed the best.'[37] By its tests and challenges, a storm called up hidden powers of recuperation. Soon the drawings of people with hunched shoulders, their heads bowed, would be filled with this drama.

He had his eye on a bigger apartment next door. Though he didn't say so, he was looking for something more satisfactory for himself and Sien, and perhaps for an extended family if her mother and brother joined them later. The place next door had a large attic that could be divided into two or three rooms – he knew where he could get the partitions for next to nothing. His present place was shaky – a violent gale had just blown in the window panes and the frame was flapping loose. His easel collapsed, his drawings were ripped from the wall. Over the eight square feet of hole he had nailed a blanket. He was denied proper light. The landlord couldn't afford repairs. 'He gave the glass, I paid for the labour.'

Again and again he was at pains to demonstrate to Theo that he didn't live idly on his brother's money. He detailed his expenses, listed work accomplished and projects lined up. Then suddenly Theo was assailed by a series of shocks, without warning and in swift succession. Vincent had up to then only given vague hints about his relationship with Sien. Now he confessed that he had in fact installed her. Immediately after this he announced that he intended to marry her. With this body-blow came a plea for understanding. Nevertheless, he rushed on, if his plans caused Theo to withdraw his support, God forbid, would he please tell Vincent at once. He begged for a letter by return. Meanwhile, he gave Sien a reference so glowing that she sounded positively angelic. It would be wicked, mean of him to turn such a woman out.

The only way he could really help her, that is if he was genuine about it, was by doing it seriously. Carried away by his own eloquence, he said blithely that his father would surely prefer him to be married. A son who accepted his responsibilities and was only concerned to do good was an honourable son. If he really thought this would be his father's reaction, he was cruelly deluding himself.

When his father did hear, he found his son's actions totally incomprehensible. He would disgrace the family name and be destroyed into the bargain. Theo the go-between was soon urgently warning Vincent that his parents believed he should have treatment and were in touch with the lunatic asylum at Geel near Antwerp. Clearly Vincent was out of his mind. There had been plenty of signs: eccentric dress, abnormal behaviour, violent outbursts, irrational hostility. Horrified by his latest intentions, they were perhaps genuinely considering a last-ditch attempt to save him from himself. Or it may have been no more than a ruse to exert pressure and force him to reconsider. Nothing further was heard of this move.

Vincent stood firm. If they moved against him as if he were a common criminal, he would retaliate by standing up in court and defending himself. He was a grown man, in full possession of his civil rights. His attitude to Theo hardening daily, he said he knew very well that 'whether Father and Mother take it quietly or not will three-fourths depend on what you tell them.'[38] Theo wavered, his loyalties hopelessly divided. Vincent turned the screw, painting a heart-rending word-picture of himself and Sien as persecuted victims. 'I ask nothing, not even an old cup and saucer. I ask but one single thing: to let me love and care for my poor, weak, ill-used wife as poverty permits, without their trying to separate, worry, or hurt us.'[39]

This emotional blackmail worked. He even felt strong enough to issue a threat. 'If you oppose me, then the trouble starts.'[40] In the face of such resolve the opposition finally collapsed, at any rate for the time being. But Vincent never forgave his father, holding him personally responsible for this betrayal.

He could exhibit a saint-like submissiveness, become a mere servant of art, willing to learn from anyone; he would sit patiently at the bedsides of the sick and dying, painting unhappy men and women and feeling awe before peasant earth-mothers, but he could never be coerced into doing anything against his will.

He was now more estranged from his family than ever. Theo, too, was under suspicion. In a mounting attack he castigated his conventional father as a Pharisee, one of the most ungodly men he had known. Let him come and visit them, he exhorted, and see for himself what the reality was. 'She and I are two unhappy people who keep together and carry our burdens together; in this way unhappiness is changed to joy, and the unbearable becomes bearable.'[41] Scornful now of church sermons, he thought of them as black in comparison with the light emitted by pictures, and evoked the name of his preferred 'father', Millet. 'Millet has a gospel, and I ask you, isn't there a difference between a drawing of his and a nice sermon?'[42] His transfer from religion to art was now complete. Drawings and paintings took the place of his father's church. Christ, however, remained exempt. As the greatest of all artists, one who worked 'in living flesh', he still reigned supreme.

Niceness had become the number one enemy. In a fury of revaluation he turned Sien into a 'pure' person. 'It is wonderful how pure she is, notwithstanding her depravity.' Something had been reclaimed, saved, changed from bad to good. He no longer saw her as she was but as a Mary Magdalene, fit to mix with his sisters, with his mother, even, dare he say it, with Kee. Whether or not she was saved, it was a fact that she had saved him from a bleak scepticism. 'I think I shall become a better artist with her,' he rationalised, 'than if I had married Kee.'[43]

Sorrowing women in Vincent's past were put into the category of *mater dolorosas*. Eugenia had a dead father, Kee a dead husband, his mother a dead son to grieve over. Eros and death, mingled romantically in his imagination, aided and abetted by Michelet, made these women potent without being overtly sexual. But they had all, in his view, spurned him. Sien enabled him to combine sorrow with sex and yet stay true to the 'eternal poetry' of Christ's story. She was a fallen Magdalene and a lamenting *dolorosa* rolled into one. Above all, she had been mistreated, a sad mother who opened her arms to him.

Another shocking piece of news greeted Theo in June, 1882. A letter came from Vincent bearing the address of the City Hospital (Ward 6, Number 9). He had been admitted with a fever which had lasted for three weeks. He was passing water painfully and he couldn't sleep. Examined, he was told he had a 'mild dose' of clap, hardly surprising in the circumstances. Theo was asked not to worry, and not to tell anyone unless forced. The treatment so far had been innocuous: quinine pills and injections of alum water.

The fact was that he was enjoying the experience. Being cared for in a hospital was like being a child again. The nurses were paid substitutes, like Sien, for the provision of care that a mother was supposed to give naturally. The sensible diet and strict routine also did him good, but the surrogate maternal love was best of all. He was able to lie quietly and calmly without feeling guilt-ridden about his idleness. Nor did he have to present himself as piteous in order to feed his everlasting hunger for sympathy. Here, as an ill person, a patient, he had status. Sien came in to see him on visiting days, and she was keeping an eye on the studio.

He hoped he would be able to reap the benefit of this enforced rest later, and see his drawings more freshly. To help combat the boredom he had brought his books on perspective with him, and a novel, Dickens' *Edwin Drood*. 'Good God, what an artist! There's no one like him.'

Already his fingers were itching for a pencil, though he wasn't allowed to draw yet, and in any case he wasn't well enough. As he was not destitute he was charged 10.50 guilders a fortnight, all in. Food and treatment were the same for paying and free patients. He found the ward as full of interesting types as in the third class waiting room at the station. Weak and feeble though he was, he didn't omit a lucid description of the view from the window of the ward. It was splendid. He could see part of the canal, part of a garden, barges loaded with potatoes, a rear view of houses being pulled down by workmen, and in the distance rows of trees and street lamps, a complicated little almshouse with its gardens, and finally a grand expanse of roofs. In the evening and at dawn the whole bird's eye view was bathed in a mysterious light, 'like a Ruysdael or Van der Meer.'[44] Although he was forbidden to get out of bed he sneaked over every evening and peeped out, unable to resist looking.

Still receiving treatment, he heard that Sien had gone into the hospital for poor patients at Leyden to have her baby. Overcome with pity for her, he exclaimed, 'What are the sufferings of us men compared to that terrible pain which women have to bear during childbirth?'[45] It is startling to read that his father paid him a visit in hospital, though presumably without knowing his son was being treated for gonorrhea. Longing to see something green and to inhale fresh air, Vincent asked the doctor how much longer he would have to wait to be discharged. A prolonged stay of several weeks was advised. The news depressed him. The whole business of lying there inactive was, like his father's visit, now as unreal as a dream.

The doctor, however, acted in ways he found wholly admirable, and he thought that when he did get out he would apply his methods of handling patients – getting hold of them firmly and putting them into the right positions – to the positioning of his models. And what patience the man had, massaging his patients himself and rubbing them with liniment. He admired him as he admired all carers. He had a head 'like some heads by Rembrandt, a splendid forehead and a very sympathetic expression.'[46]

When it came to his own treatment by this doctor, he was surprised to find him more abrupt than gentle. He often inserted the catheter into his bladder with force, causing pain. The details he gives of contemporary medical practice are explicit. Bougies were inserted into the urethra, and these got bigger and bigger, inflicting great pain and considerable nausea. Yet his comments were curiously approving. Either he wanted to suffer, or he liked the idea of being treated less fussily than in the more expensive wards.

On July 1st he was writing to say that he was back at the studio, and how delightful it was to be free of catheters, bougies, and syringes. On the way from the hospital, everything he saw in the streets was inexpressively beautiful, the light clearer than he remembered, 'the spaces more infinite'. He was describing the kind of everyday ecstasy with which his paintings would one day be imbued.

What he had gone through couldn't be compared, he repeated, with Sien's 'grande misère'. He mentions his father's visit again, when they were to some extent reconciled, with Sien sitting unrevealed in the waiting room. She saw Vincent's father as he went upstairs to confront his son.

Sien was admitted for her confinement while he was still in hospital himself. Her general condition was so weak that he had arranged for the doctors to take special care of her, financially assisted as usual by Theo. Still not completely recovered, he got busy preparing for her return. The apartment next door was still being renovated. When Sien came home they would take it. A large upper floor in their poor district only cost three guilders a week.

Sien's baby was safely delivered with forceps. Sien was in an exhausted doze when he went in with her small daughter and her mother. His description overflows with quiet joy. 'Theo, I was so happy when I saw her again. She was lying near a window overlooking a garden full of sunshine and green. Oh boy, she looked up and was so happy to see us. And she brightened up so much, and in a moment was wide awake, and asked about everything.'[47]

A few days after the birth she fell into a post-natal depression. He was bewildered by a miserable, incoherent note from her, questioning everything. He no longer cared about her, and would soon replace her with someone else, that is if he hadn't done so already. The poor woman had given way to a black mood and been swamped by her ugly past, he explained. When they were reunited, he and she and the baby, he would cherish her as never before.

Home again, and alone, he rhapsodised over the scene he had witnessed. Just to look at the cradle he had ready and waiting with its green cover there in the living room transported him, 'though it was only a hospital where she was lying and where I sat near her.'[48] In his imagination, though, it was a stable. Sien, the hard-bitten prostitute with the foul mouth, had become his star in the dark night, like the Virgin Mary with her newborn child. He tried to convey the power of the emotion which gripped a man at such a moment. Over the crib, in readiness for her homecoming, he had tacked up his most treasured prints. In pride of place was one of Rembrandt's great representations of the Holy Family, the two women by the cradle, one of whom reads a holy book by the frail light of a candle.

He moved in to the new, roomier accommodation. Sien's

mother had helped him sweep up the plaster littering the place. He scrubbed the floor, put white muslin curtains at the windows. Everything was spotless. He touched lovingly on all the details, the white deal working table, studies on the wall, in one corner a closet with their bottles and pots, and his books. Then there was the partitioned living area with a few kitchen chairs, an oilstove, a larger wicker easy chair for 'the woman' in the corner, near the window that overlooked the wharf and the meadows. He urged Theo to come and look for himself. The tone could not be more seductive; he could coo like a dove if it helped to get what he wanted. Right now, if he had his brother standing beside him, his happiness would be complete. As it was, he had been lifted out of the void in which he had barely existed, on to a plane that was *real* – he underlined it triumphantly. He had a new studio, a real home was about to swing into life, and, most wonderful of all, he had a studio with a *cradle* and a baby's pot in it.

He reiterated, with immense care and deliberation, why it was that Sien had come to mean so much to him. It was of paramount importance for Theo to understand that the feeling between Sien and him was *real*: 'it is no dream, it is reality.'[49] True, what he had felt for Kee was at the time a stronger passion, and so far as charm went they couldn't be compared. That didn't make his love for Sien any less true.

Still the reality he so urgently wanted to communicate seemed to escape him, as if he was distracted by a voice whispering in his ear of what might have been, if only Kee had said yes. His efforts to get it right, to tell the truth, are both painful and deeply moving. He was grappling to define love itself, in so far as he had experienced it and now understood it. The romantic agony that had bewitched him was a million miles from the conjugal love he was now determined to celebrate. What he had felt for Kee had left 'a large deep wound which is healed but is still sensitive.' Meeting Sien for the first time and getting to know her was like knowing 'a fellow creature as lonesome and unhappy as myself', no more and no less. By helping her he was able to help himself.

So how had this mutual aid, if that was all it was, slowly changed, so that their lives became interdependent, until one day it was love? All he could say was that it had to be called a great and profound change, and that it had happened. 'I have a feeling of being at home when I am with her, as though she gives me my own hearth, a feeling that our lives are interwoven.'[50] It was heartfelt and deep, but Theo should not run off with the idea that it was all laughter and light and the cooing of turtle doves. A shadow fell on them from time to time, from his own past as well as from hers, and it seemed then that they were threatened by some evil which could blot out their joy at a moment's notice.

In short, life could never be rosy for them. Her health was still uncertain. She experienced a lot of pain and perhaps always would; her privations may have damaged her health permanently. Her youth was over, and God knows it had been bitter and barren enough. Again one has the feeling that he speaks of himself when he speaks of her. The biggest threat, he predicted, was the presence of that 'gloomy shadow master: master Albrecht Dürer knew it well enough when he placed Death behind the young couple in that beautiful etching.'[51]

But enough of that: what he felt now was calm and brightness and an inexpressible gratitude. Up in the large attic was a large bed for them, with the bedding neatly arranged. The little girl would have his old one. If he happened to be out when Sien came home, the flowers in front of the window by the wicker chair would let her know he had thought of her. To save money he had stuffed the mattresses himself; bought straw, seaweed, bed-ticking. The love nest he had conjured out of so little would make up for all her pain.

He thought back to how it had been for him last winter. What was the reality then? 'Two great voids stared at me night and day. There was no wife, there was no child.' He put a direct question to Theo: did he ever experience moments when a groan or a sigh would be forced from him? Was living alone worth while? Wasn't it damaging for men like them, who 'often find it painful and difficult to mingle with people, to speak with them?'[52] It was marvellous how well Sien coped with his peculiarities of temper, as he called them. She had the knack of handling him if he got worked up about the posing, she knew how to quieten him down, and this ability to put up with his disagreeable side could only mean one thing, he reasoned. She understood him better than anyone else.

And he returned again to the article which symbolised so much,

Vincent aged thirteen.

Anna Cornelia van Gogh (Vincent's mother).

Theodorus van Gogh (Vincent's father).

Vincent aged about eighteen.

Theo van Gogh.

Kee Vos-Stricker.

Portrait of van Gogh by John P. Russell.

Jo van Gogh–Bonger with the baby Vincent.

on which he had begun to pin all his hopes. 'Do you think Father would remain indifferent and make objections – near a cradle? You see, a cradle is not like anything else – there is no fooling with it . . . .'.[53]

In the hospital, sitting up for the first time in several days, he had watched the doctor anointing an old man who would have made a superb St Jerome: 'a thin, long, sinewy brown wrinkled body with such very distinct and expressive joints that it makes one melancholy not to be able to have him for a model.' He thought of the old man, and he thought of Sien. His clean new home was about him like a blessing. The weakness still lived in his body but his urge to draw was reviving, he could feel it. Sien would come, the infant quivering in her arms. He would draw them both. Already he was inspired by the thought of their fusion. A profane woman, on whom he had committed profane acts; yet he could not help but see her with the child at her breast as holy. What was profane and what was sacred? Yes, that was how he would draw them: soldered together by a mother's love. This he would find touching beyond anything: Sien brought to rest, at peace in a thrilling silence. How could anyone repudiate her?

When he received the despairing note from Sien he hurried in to see her. The change in her was shocking. She looked as if she had withered from within, and she was obviously disturbed. The baby, born with jaundice, had an eye infection. It was like a blind kitten.

He decided to try to shake Sien out of her black mood by acting angrily, responding abnormally to what he saw as abnormality. She responded, he claimed afterwards, by emerging from her depression like a sleepwalker. He went again a week later to take her home, and sat in the hospital waiting room for her, full of trepidation. She came down with the baby in her arms, took one look at Vincent, and burst into tears. The crisis was over. He gazed again at the madonna he had sat beside when her child was just born. The baby looked at him brightly out of clear, wide-open eyes, as healthy as a young rabbit.

The family spent their first night in the large attic, in the bedroom that was completely timbered, reminding him of the hold of a ship. It wasn't strange, but perfectly natural to be in Sien's company, her and the children. She was still mortally weak, so he did everything, made the beds and cooked and cleaned. He had done the same for old and sick people when he lived in the Borinage, so it was nothing new. All in all, he was in his element. He had to watch her carefully, he said, and if she felt like pottering around, that was good medicine. Anything was that encouraged her to be cheerful. His protective instincts thoroughly aroused, he changed roles. Almost as good as being cared for, naturally and freely, was to care for someone else and imagine yourself the recipient.

The baby was now his delight. He soon set to work making drawings of the tiny fellow, and of the cradle. Albert Lubin remarks perceptively that the presence of babies 'relieved his sadness, and numerous drawings and paintings of babies attest to his fascination with recreating them.'[54] He depicted them with their mothers or alone, being held or rocked, or lying in cradles. He even painted their absences, painting empty cradles, or the mother attached to an unseen cradle by a cord which she is pulling, as he did when he painted Madame Roulin's portrait at Arles. Drawings done while at The Hague show infancy and old age in close proximity, sometimes hand in hand – the simplest, most natural representation of his death-and-rebirth theme. *Old Man with a Child* has a little girl facing a seated old man who holds her hands, and in *Old Man Holding an Infant* the tiny baby is being cradled by a bald old man with bushy white side-whiskers. Life is about to wriggle out of the arms of death itself.

The presence of a baby calmed his nerves and soothed his spirit, like drawing and painting. He thought one of the best places for meditation was 'by a rustic hearth and an old cradle with a baby in it, by a window overlooking a delicate green cornfield and the waving of alder bushes.'[55] Later he would say that fields of young wheat and orchards in bloom were delicate as babies. Young wheat especially, so pure and tender, woke in him the same emotion that he had when observing the face of a sleeping baby.[56]

If a gloomy mood descended on him, he could shake it off by taking a long walk in the direction of the most barren stretch of beach, out over the dunes. Looking at the greyish-green sea streaked with white waves was a good antidote, as indeed the grand and infinite was always. But there was no need now to go further than the baby in its cradle. 'I think I see something deeper, more infinite, more eternal than the ocean in the expression in the eyes of a little baby when it wakes in the morning, and coos and laughs because it sees the sun shining in its cradle.'[57]

The child, registered Willem, was already a miracle of vitality. The little girl too was much improved, no longer neglected, looking very pretty in the new shoes he had bought for her. Patiently occupied with his household tasks and with his sketching of Willem, it amused him to notice that 'already he seems to oppose himself to all social institutions and conventions.' That must be healthy. The infant spat out its porridge, and even without teeth enjoyed chewing on a piece of bread. The noises he came out with were amazing, laughing and cooing and gurgling, but he shut his mouth 'absolutely' against porridge. Vincent liked to have him sitting drowsily on the floor of his studio on a few sacks while he worked. He crowed suddenly up at the drawings tacked on the wall, then at other times was perfectly quiet and lovely, just looking at things, motes of light, bits of fluff, a pencil. He smiled broadly, clapped his tiny hands. 'Oh, he is such a sociable little fellow!'

An unexpected caller from the world outside rudely overturned this domestic contentment. It was Mr Tersteeg, never more detestable than in Vincent's account of the visit to Theo. Supercilious and bullying, he ignored Sien completely and told Vincent what an idiot he was making of himself. He would take steps to put a stop to it: write to his father, to Uncle Cent at Princenhage. Vincent barely managed to keep his temper in check in the blast of this 'raw north wind' that had come howling in through the front door. Afterwards, he was badly upset. He was most hurt and angered by Tersteeg's policeman-like dismissal of Sien as 'that woman and child,' and he worried that the scene might have affected her milk. He was strong enough now to attribute the man's parting shot about his drawings to sheer malice. Then he came to some characteristic conclusions.

If he *was* a nonentity, one of the lowest of the low, then he wanted his work to reveal what it was like to be such an unfortunate. That was his ambition. There was a calm harmony and a music inside him, underneath the misery. He intended to demonstrate that the two could coexist, and that from their coexistence could flow something unique and beautiful. 'I see drawings and pictures in the poorest huts, in the darkest corner. And my mind is drawn to these things by an irresistible force.'[58] It was a clear statement of his credo.

When was Theo coming to stay with them? He longed to see him again, to talk about a thousand things. It was no use expecting Sien to be able to understand books or art, but then their attachment was based on something else, on reality, of which books and art were only a part. If she had happened to be a woman out of touch with real life, that would have bored him. He looked for art in reality, and that was how he came to be with her.

Did Theo remember that mill on the road out of The Hague where they had once sat and pledged eternal friendship so passionately, over their glasses of milk? He had passed by the very spot only the other day, and it had brought tears to his eyes.

Then one day in August he made his momentous announcement: 'I have *launched my boat.*' He loved these allusions to river craft and the water, once describing himself approvingly as looking like a rough bargeman. He thought of his studio as a barge interior.

He means the boat of his creativity. He had launched himself into painting at last, into colour, and more specifically into painting with oils. Now he was a real painter with a real painter's studio. He thought oils would suit him. The medium had a robust quality. With it he could express the body, the mass and density of things. Rehabilitated by the partnership with Sien, refreshed by the gleams of baby life, confirmed by Theo's continuing supply of materials and basic finance, and by his unflagging moral support, he was ready to move in closer, as if to feel on his skin the buried heat of creation and experience its terrific energies. He was aware of dangers, but compelled by the promise of unimaginable rewards. His approach can be compared to that of a saint who risks everything when he bares his breast to the unknown. Though he began each day as before, in fear and trembling, he had found the courage to follow his own path.

Casting around for precedents for the next move forward, he seized on Michelet's improvisatory style, which he said put him in mind of the rough sketches of a painter. 'Michelet has strong emotions, and he smears what he feels on to paper without caring in the least how he does it, and without giving the slightest thought to technique or conventional forms – just shaping it into any form that can be understood by those who want to understand it.'[59] There was the rub. Who did want to understand it? But examples of this kind were pointing him in the direction he wanted to go.

As was so often the case, he sucked up nourishment from books he happened to be reading, finding parallels in the lives of characters to his own dilemmas and solutions. Pascal Rougon, in the series of novels by Zola, he thought a noble figure. 'In his profession he found a force stronger than the temperament he had inherited from his family; instead of surrendering to his natural instincts he followed a clear, straight path, and did not slide into the wretched muddle in which all the other Rougons perished.'[60] Zola's *Le Ventre de Paris* was one source of inspiration, and the theme of the fallen woman, which he kept coming across everywhere, another.

Sien was causing him a great deal of worry as the year wore on. She had begun to show signs of regression. He blamed her family, her appalling early life, anything but her. One of the finest drawings of this period shows only too clearly what he was up against. *Sien with a Cigar, sitting on the Ground by the Stove*, executed in mixed media, was as close to a painting as he could come without the use of colour: pencil, black chalk, pen, and brush with sepia and white applied over a wash. The hunched figure is such a picture of hopelessness that the heart sinks. One of the cheap cigars to which she was addicted burns ignored between her fingers, the skin of her face dragging down with indifference. Her big beaky nose gives her a masculine look.

The picture was done before the birth of Willem. Now she was sunk back in the same state, or perilously near to it. She smoked and drank, neglected the children, left the clothes unmended. Always seeking excuses for her, refusing to see her as bad – 'she has never seen what is good, how can she be good?' – Vincent quoted from Zola's *L'Assommoir* to back up his contention; or perhaps he had read it there in the first place and appropriated it. Zola had written: 'Yet these women are not bad, their errors and their disgrace are caused by the impossibility of living a straight life in the midst of the gossip and calumny of the Faubourgs.'

He knew all about gossip and calumny, having tried for months to cope with the shifty Hoornik family. Behind his back they were doing their utmost, he suspected, to turn Sien against him. As well as the nastiness being endlessly stirred up by her mother, who whispered lies about him, saying he only wanted Sien for the posing and would drop her back in the gutter when he was done, there was Sien's wretched pimp of a brother to contend with. He had put his wife on the streets, then divorced her. The scheme the mother and this brother were plotting entailed Sien somehow, and though he couldn't make head nor tail of it he feared the worst. If Sien went back with them, she would be driven back to her old life in no time. Why couldn't she see that?

There were moments of anguish, which tore him apart and made him sob along with her. He could scarcely bear it when she cried out, 'I don't know what's wrong with me!' like someone utterly lost. She was not alone, not lost, she had him, he told her, and implored her to persevere. He even castigated himself for not being a better example, more patient, gentler. Her slovenliness was a state of mind, the exteriorisation of her despair, and he saw all her faults as having the same root: bad company, bad education, bad conditions.

He was also learning the hard way what it was like to live with the 'changeability of women'. 'They vary, Theo, they vary like the weather.'[61] There was no point in trying to understand the weather: one had to submit to it. After all, there was something to be admired, something good and beautiful in every kind of weather. Thus he persuaded himself when writing to Theo, but not when he was face to face with a spitting hell-cat who abused him vilely, telling him to stop messing about with his stupid painting, scraping and altering it until her nerves were in shreds. He should get out and earn some decent money. Her mother was right, he was just using her, and one day he would be off. He was like all men, a liar and a cheat. An hour later she would ask to be forgiven. Her changes of mood were so bewildering that he had no idea what she was, angel or devil.

Unnerved and saddened by her bouts of instability, he tried to keep going, spending as much time as possible out of doors and away from her. In the winter he was driven back in again. What had gone wrong? How different things had been last spring, for all their difficulties. She had clung to him then, inordinately grateful for his food and shelter, and for the shelter of his body, which was stronger, more resolute than hers. They had been on the right road, he was certain of it.

Now, having regained a little strength of her own, she seemed cruelly intent on conquering him. A woman wants a man to be strong, and then some perversity in her enjoys seeing him brought to his knees – was that it? Certainly she seemed inclined to despise him for giving way to her. All the scenes she made out of nothing were part of another, more insidious pleasure she was experiencing: she wanted to see how much punishment he would take, how long he would go on bowing his head. But how could he help himself, when self-abasement was his deepest instinct at such moments? 'Don't you also think that if one meets someone in such a way – I mean, so weak and defenceless – something makes one surrender completely, so that one cannot imagine ever being able to desert such a person?'[62] That was how he was. Something at the core of him gave in to her.

The situation was Dostoevskian. Nerves were shrieking. He had taken up a woman's role, and in the most feminine way taken up the nursing of Sien when his own mental and physical health were at a low ebb. This forgiveness of her and of everyone had called up its opposite.

His total surrender had only earned her derision. His pity, to him the most selfless kind of love, had produced hatred. There is a type of woman who can forgive the man who hurts her, but not the sacrifices he makes for her. Vincent, the Eternal Husband, dreaming his wife.

He wondered, in his confusion, whether an encounter such as theirs was really some sort of apparition, not real at all. She was a phantom, a shadow of what he had longed for. He hung on to his memories, walking alone on the Geest, past the streets and houses and dark alleys where he had walked with her that winter. When he came in he said to Sien, 'It is still the same as last year.'[63] We don't hear the response. The best of her was preserved in his memory, 'the sea remains the sea', but that was no help to him now. She had joined forces with her shiftless family: they were ranged against him, and there was nothing he could do.

What was so horrible was the feeling of enmity, both inside and out. He could accept rejection, but to be actively disliked was to him a kind of living death. 'One is afraid of making friends, one is afraid of moving; like the old lepers, one would like to call

145

from afar to the people: 'Don't come too near me, for intercourse with me brings you sorrow and loss.'' '

His work faltered. Ugly tricks were played on him, set in motion by the mother. Sien confided in him for once, and the scheme to start another quarrel backfired. He took heart again, but not for long. Disgusted with everything, he tramped out beyond the town, near to where the public ash dump was situated, and soon found a scene accurately reflecting his inner state. 'I stood there a long time, looking at a row of the most twisted, gnarled, sorry-looking pollard willows I have ever seen. They bordered a path of vegetable garden – freshly dug up – and they were mirrored in a dirty little ditch – very dirty – but in which some blades of spring grass were already sparkling.'[64] The signs of rebirth, small enough to be overlooked, sprang up in the dirt for those who had eyes to see. His hope was hardly sparkling, but neither was it extinguished.

Theo came on a visit, alarmed by the growing despondence of his brother's letters. Cautious and practical, he took one look at the situation and advised Vincent to get out at once, while he still had a shirt on his back. Vincent agreed, too low-spirited to put up any resistance. He had had enough; the cause was a lost one. Time to move on.

Though he was not yet prepared to admit it, he had tried and failed to enter the realm of marriage. Theo distracted him from this gloomy conclusion by springing a surprise on him. He too had met a woman, in trouble as Sien had been, but educated, fine. She was ready to kill herself. She needed an operation on her foot, and he was taking care of that. And he had found her somewhere to live. No, he wasn't proposing to live with her. He called her his patient.

Completely forgetting his own mess, Vincent congratulated his brother. Well done! Wonderful! Theo answered dryly to the effect that it was not so wonderful for his finances. But Vincent was more touched by the news than he could say. Had he been an influence? Was he to blame? Didn't this bring them closer together, two brothers who were rescuers? We were together as two fools were together, Theo told him bluntly: a couple of foolish idealists. Vincent couldn't agree. No, such actions were wholly good, he maintained, whatever the consequences. It brought one in touch with the infinite.

After Theo had gone, Vincent waited for the right moment to break his own news to Sien. He would have to move out. The country was beckoning again, and his friend van Rappard had been telling him about Drenthe, a remote moorland region in the north of Holland which was starting to attract artists. For instance, it was rumoured that the German painter Liebermann had gone there to paint. The possibility that a colony of artists might form there revived his old dream of a brotherhood of kindred spirits.

None of this meant a thing to Sien. He showed her a map he had bought. He tried, perhaps not too hard, to persuade her to come with him. The last thing she wanted, she said, was to live with him in some godforsaken bog, cut off from relatives and shops.

He pressed her to agree that it was finished between them, but she merely shrugged. It drove him mad when she turned herself into a sphinx as a ruse to avoid facing the truth. But at least she made no objection. He felt that he had to move, before the stagnation killed him. He would have applauded the wisdom of Jung's 'Let things happen.'

Still reluctant to abandon her, he placed advertisements in the local paper in an effort to find her a job. It came to nothing. She pretended to keep appointments and went to the wine shop instead. Another trick of the mother's, now he was about to leave, was to delay his departure by various requests. Their source of money was about to disappear over the horizon.

He promised to keep in touch, to send monthly payments if he possibly could. Even this failed to penetrate Sien's listlessness. He feared for her, for 'my little boy', and for the girl too. Sien had taken to staring into the abyss with the kind of inherent fatality he dreaded in himself.

They came to the station to see him off. The little girl sat on his lap a moment, till the whistle blew. A few days later, from the bleak room of a grimy hotel, the rain pouring down outside the window, he surveyed his surroundings and wrote forlornly: 'Theo, I never suspected her, nor do I now, nor shall I ever suspect her of having had financial motives, more than is honest and just. People exaggerated. . . . Oh, when she came with the baby and the young girl to see me off at the station, I was unable to speak. The train came in and I got on. She stood there with the baby at her breast, holding the girl by the hand. For all that has happened, I couldn't stop watching for her figure as my train pulled out into the bright sunlight and the rails took me . . .'.

'And Theo,' he confided, 'when I pass on the heath here such a woman with a child on her arm, it pierces me right through, the melancholy, and my eyes get moist.'[65]

But it was over. He had known the reality of a home of sorts, with a cradle and a baby in it. From now on he would be on the outside of such domesticity, looking in. He was a man of thirty. Staring into the mirror he saw a man gazing back at him 'with wrinkles on my forehead and lines on my face as if I were forty.'[66] He repeatedly complained of being old beyond his years, and yet behind his words one senses at times an element of satisfaction. His youth had been a misery to him. And old people, like gnarled old trees, attracted him. The nearness of death always did.

8

ART OF DARKNESS

He took the train to Hoogeveen on Tuesday, 11 September, 1883. Probably he was already dressed for the part in a brown peat-carrier's suit: he had been anticipating the trip for at least a month. On the train he studied a map of Drenthe – not that there was much to see. He was heading for a desolate inland area in the north-east, a region without large cities and with few towns, a flat endless landscape of black earth, dotted with primitive cottages made of sods of turf and sticks. Inside, these dwellings were dark like caves. In the centre of his map was a large area, crossed by the Hoogeveen canal and empty of villages, labelled with the words 'Peat fields'. The canal petered out in the middle of it.

Only painters would find this featureless landscape interesting, but if Max Liebermann and Mauve – to name only two – had found it worthwhile, then he wanted to see it. He had stumbled on a reference to it in an English journal – a painter had once disappeared into the peat fields to escape civilisation. Tales like this inspired him to go and explore for himself; and apart from them he had another reason. Peasants, and only peasants, lived in Drenthe. He wanted to make a record of their hard life. He believed that reality was best approached through work or its cessation, whether in the shape of miners in the Borinàge, labourers digging streets in The Hague, the poor waiting submissively in long lines in soup kitchens, or old men in broken top hats walking through the gates of almshouses.

Here it would be the peasants. It was here that he first conceived the idea of being a peasant painter. Only the country, he believed, could solve his problems. Here he would be forced to work as hard as the people among whom he lived. Their example would shame him. Best of all, his work would take on a new virility once he rooted himself in the earth and responded to what he called its 'music', experiencing its moods as 'symphonic, dramatic'. A countryman by upbringing, he was always deeply uneasy in towns and cities. His simple habits were questioned, his clothes out of place. While in The Hague and anticipating Theo's visit, he had written humourously that he would have to change his Robinson Crusoe-like outfit when his brother arrived from Paris and they walked out together.

As soon as he reached Hoogeveen the weather deteriorated, and so did his spirits. He wandered around in a state of utter dejection, belonging nowhere. What did this place with its low houses and deserted air have to do with him? It was like being at the edge of the world. The vast heath stretched away like a sea, beyond this one wide street. It was unbearably lonely. Now he had no one to go to with his artistic problems, no hearth to sit at. Canals were everywhere, criss-crossing each other, more than he had ever seen. He would be out tramping aimlessly and come upon peat barges drawn by men, women, and children, and sometimes black and white horses. He was reminded of the Brabant, only this was wilder: it was immense. The heath shrank figures to mere dots. Sheepfolds were curious triangular structures, the shepherds impressive. Desolation could have its own beauty. The sun broke through, it stopped raining at last. Then the heath became menacing, like a hostile desert. 'Painting in that blazing light and rendering the planes vanishing into infinity makes one dizzy.'[1]

One day he wandered into a cemetery, no more than a patch of heath bounded by a hedge of conifers. The turpentine smell had 'something mystical about it'. It was one of the weirdest graveyards he had seen – and he was something of a connoisseur. The graves had to be searched for in what looked like a clearing in a pine wood, they were so thickly overgrown with grass and heather. Then he found the white posts marking each one, and could read some of the names. A few months later he would discover an abandoned graveyard in Nuenen, where his father now had a living, and paint a picture called *Peasant Cemetery*. In

Drenthe, feeling more than ever the despised outcast, he found consolation in a human resting place. At least everyone was equal in a cemetery. After painting the peculiar burial place in Nuenen, he felt so moved that he had to express his intentions in words. 'I wanted to express what a simple thing death and burial is, just as simple as the falling of a leaf – just a bit of earth dug up – a wooden cross . . . . And now those ruins tell me . . . how the life and the death of the peasants also remain forever the same, budding and withering regularly, like the grass and the flowers growing there in the graveyard.'[2]

Hoogeveen was a nondescript, cheerless place, and so was his room, with only a dirty skylight over his head for a window. He felt wretched, in fact at times so miserable that he wanted to laugh out loud. It was depressing to think of Sien and the children he had left to fend for themselves, depressing too to remember that Theo was having to bear the brunt of his trouble as always. 'Through one single glass pane the light falls on an empty colour box, and on a bundle of worn-out brushes . . .'[3] In short, he was on the point of hysteria, not knowing whether to laugh or cry.

He turned in sheer desperation to his parents and wrote them a letter, prompted by the news of the death of a cousin. Disguising his real feelings he wrote cheerfully, telling them that it was better here than The Hague, as if to say that nothing could be worse than the hell of being unloved. That kind of emptiness he associated with cities. City life was only too often a degradation, he thought. A simple farmer who worked intelligently was the truly civilised man, not the city dweller. 'Though they may cheat each other, it is not so bad as in the city.'[4] He told them not to concern themselves about him; his overcoat was all right, and the woollen undervest they had sent was comfortable, thank you.

They were no doubt relieved, as Theo definitely was, that he had escaped from the clutches of 'that woman'. And there was nothing in his present circumstances likely to ensnare him in sensuality. On the contrary, the women were beasts of burdens, strikingly sombre. 'A woman's breast, for instance, has that heaving movement which is quite the opposite of voluptuous.' The men wore leggings which revealed the shape of the calf and made their movements expressive – a distinct gain for an artist out to capture action. Feeling himself very much at a crossroads, he delivered himself of some reflections on the modern times they were living through. Society was increasingly corrupt, he declared, and values had been turned upside down. One had to return to grass roots.

He had certainly done that. While he was out painting a cottage, two sheep and a goat ambled up over the roof and grazed on its turf. The goat went on climbing and nibbling, until it was peering down the chimney.

When he came to employ the locals as models he hit bad luck. They just laughed at him. If they did consent, and accepted the money – it was good pay for this area – they wandered off before he had half finished, not wanting to be classed as figures of fun like him. He was driven to drawing them inside barns, where the light was too poor for painting.

Unable to stop worrying about the fate of his dependents in The Hague, he decided to go on a trip down the canal on a peat barge; anything to distract himself. He left just after noon and reached New Amsterdam at six. The snail's pace of the boat made it seem like an endless expedition into the interior. They passed other barges carrying heaps of peat, or bullrushes from the marshes. He was occupied with sketching whatever came into view; a mother with a baby that was draped in a purple shawl, lean cows of a delicate brown, meagre birches, scourged oaks, poplars.

The barge tied up at a quay. Overlooking the quay was a small hotel, the Scholte. Vincent went to enquire about a room. Hendrik Scholte eyed the stranger suspiciously – hotel-keepers invariably did – and was on the point of showing Vincent the door when his wife intervened. Scholte changed his tune when he heard that his customer was the son of a clergyman in Nuenen.

The room was a big improvement on the rat-hole he had crawled into at Hoogeveen. It was fairly large, with a stove – even a small balcony, from which he could see the heath, huts, and in the distance one of the lifting bridges typical of the region.

The Scholtes had three small daughters. One of them, Zowina, later remembered her fright when she encountered the strange red-haired man with the square forehead prowling along a dark passage at night. They liked him well enough, however, when they knew him better. He was quite harmless, and he had time for them. The youngest girl, only two, had her portrait painted by him. Better than that was riding on his back while he went down on hands and knees and neighed like a horse. The mother had to hold the child steady. He played trains with the older ones, sitting them inside upturned chairs and positioning himself in front, using a broom handle for the wheels' connecting rod. The child passengers gripped the broom while their arms pumped round in a rhythm, as their imaginary train gathered speed and went racing over the land.

As he walked further into the heart of the country, disappointed to find no painters with whom he could converse, he was struck by a desolation that matched his own worst moods. It was as poor here as anything he had experienced in the Borinage. Time had passed by this isolated district, with its peat bogs, and rain, its crudely thatched huts, the roofs nearly touching the ground, as dismal inside as stables – though sometimes the gloom would seem almost beautiful – and shared by people and beasts alike. It was dreary beyond belief, and at first it had the effect of offsetting his own emotional night.

Black-and-white art was still essential to him, as his inner war went on being fought, when it came to dramatising the reclamation of light from darkness. Diggers helped, so did graveyards with flowers, and a dark picture from Drenthe, *Landscape with Bog Trunks*, was another instalment in the story of his desired rebirth. He had discovered some decayed oak roots, locally called bog trunks, lying in a pool of black mud. They had been buried in the bog for perhaps a century, until unearthed by the peat diggers. Here was another burial ground, laid open under the light for resurrection. To signal the victory 'a little white path ran past it all'.[5]

The rainy weather came back. His temporarily revived spirits darkened again with the days. Autumn in Drenthe was often wet. When it poured down incessantly he saw only too clearly how he had got stuck, was at an impasse, handicapped as he was in so many respects. He was badly hampered and discouraged by the lack of a studio. Without one, how could he bring in models? They objected to posing for him out of doors. He thought wistfully of the studio he had created for himself so laboriously in The Hague, only to abandon it. Now he wished he had waited a year and a half and done the same thing here. He would have fitted up this room, only he couldn't afford it. He had left some of his belongings behind, which would mean a return journey to go and collect them. To tell the truth, he was too low for that. He lacked the will. Going back there would be walking straight into a trap. Irresolution made him turn and turn, like a beast sunk in a bog.

The atmosphere of this immensely still, stranded landscape, empty and waiting like an Eden, was beginning to affect him, in spite of all his doubts. Its dreariness was illusory. One was overwhelmed by its huge peace, opening to him little by little like the rose of peace in his own breast. He had found his kingdom, and though it filled him with Adamistic yearning, he was somehow powerless to enter and possess it. Why was this?

Simply, it was because, no matter how hard or how often he tried, he failed to get on too well with people. 'I take it so much to heart,' he mourned, 'that I do not get on better.' This was terrible, because the success or failure of his work depended on his coming to terms with his fellows. They were at the core of it, the focus of all his striving, the clue to everything. He had acted rashly in coming here, but now he *was* here he must forget himself in his work. He feared for his sanity otherwise. He would have a sensation of something malignant about to crush him.

He was exaggerating, of course. Baby cries appealing for comfort issued from him in letter after letter. He confessed frankly that he was 'overcome by a *je ne sais quoi* of discouragement and despair more than I can tell.'[6]

It was true that there were sights here not to be missed. For instance, yesterday he saw a funeral in a barge, fascinating – six women wrapped in coats in the boat, which the men were dragging along the canal through the heath, and the clergyman in his three-cornered hat and his breeches trailing them on the other side. There was poetry here, and he was bogged down in prose. If only he had some security, if only his art supplies were replenished. Why did his letters meet with an inexplicable silence?

Shortly after these outcries, he pulled out all the stops in an attempt to persuade Theo – who was embroiled in crises of his own and talking of emigrating to America – to join him and become an artist. One motive, of course, was his desperate need for some congenial company. As well as this, Vincent may have been influenced by Zola's theory that one could make oneself an artist by an act of will, providing one had the temperament – 'Art is nature seen through a temperament' – and although natural

talent was helpful, it was by no means essential. To think so was
to be conned by the art dealers. Theo had been confiding his
disappointment with the way his life was turning out, and Vincent
quickly swept in with an indictment: 'It seems to me that the
whole art business is rotten.'

His bid for Theo's conversion rose to a pitch of lyricism. Don't
wither on the sterile sidewalks of Paris, he exhorted, 'come and
paint with me on the heath, in the potato field, come and walk
with me behind the plough and the shepherd, come and sit with
me, looking into the fire – let the storm that blows across the
heath blow through you.'[7]

Theo knew his impulsive brother only too well. Disillusioned
at times he might be, but art dealing was what he was good at.
He couldn't have failed to note Vincent's other, contradictory
moods and feelings, such as, 'It doesn't matter in the least where
I am.' Throwing up his career like a Gauguin and turning his
back on civilisation would have meant the end of financial support
for both of them. And not only them. He was not only helping
Vincent but also his father and mother, his sisters, and the mystery
woman whose hospital expenses he had just settled. Worried that
his brother might be close to a nervous collapse, he refrained
from spelling it out bluntly, but what it amounted to was this:
Don't kick the bourgeois while they are still feeding you.

Vincent saw it differently – as a simple matter of courage. It
was a question of wanting an entirely new thing, of undertaking
a thoroughgoing renovation of yourself, 'in all simplicity, with
the fixed idea: ça ira.' He should just say straight out: 'I don't
want the city any longer, I want the country. I don't want an
office, I want to paint.'[8]

He had been reading some fine sentiments in a little book of
Carlyle's, his *Heroes and Hero-Worship*. It said there what he had
long believed, that one had a *duty* to be brave, a duty to one's
soul. It was possible, he warned Theo, to go against one's own
character. Self-knowledge was the thing. He tried one more time.
'Throughout the history of art one repeatedly finds the phenomenon of two brothers being painters.' His judgements take on
the *ex-cathedra* ring of a Lawrence: 'I *believe* in you as a painter.'
'Your soul is sick.' 'Don't go to America.' 'Get back to nature.'
'Give yourself up to the fixed idea: to become a painter.'[9] Behind

them lay the poignantly admitted longing for him to be there, so that he could 'have a comrade'.

Gradually his rhapsodies left off. In a sense he was singing siren songs to that part of himself which had got stuck in the old, dead forms, where the artist mattered more than the content. He would soon argue for a Whitmanesque, democratic art, drawn from the people and distributed to them in popular editions, accessible to all and finding its way into 'workmen's houses and farms'.

Before that could happen the sick spirit had to get well, in a time that – he was convinced – was poisoned at the root, shaky and tottering. 'One is ill because one doesn't live properly – can't,' says Birkin in *Women in Love*. 'It's the failure to love that makes one ill, and humiliates one.' Vincent would have agreed absolutely.

In Drenthe, with his unerring instinct for bringing old and new together, he took note of a gnarled old apple tree, how 'at certain moments (it) bears blossoms that are among the most delicate and virginal things under the sun.'[10] How did he, a rough-barked man, break into flower? Before the pangs of birth there had to come death throes, infinitely more painful, and whatever still chained him to deadness and the abyss had to perish. Perhaps the decaying, deathly process would be hastened here, in this black mud, on this brackish marsh land, where life and decay were somehow united.

He kept faltering badly, despite some initial optimism, and was soon more urgently dependent on Theo's letters than ever. If one failed to arrive in response to his appeals he felt 'bitterly, bitterly sad', alone like someone shipwrecked, 'absolutely cut off from the outer world'.[11] In a philosophical mood he would describe his loneliness as an occupational hazard. Painters had to accept that they were likely to be ignored, shunned, set on by dogs like tramps, under suspicion like wandering lunatics and criminals.

He was saved from sinking even lower by the balm of a journey he made in an open cart to Zweeloo with his landlord, who had to go to the market in Assen. Liebermann, so Vincent had heard, had once established his base there for quite a while. He was curious to see the village.

It was a momentous trip. He set off while it was still night, at three in the morning. Bearing in mind his liking for nocturnal walks, one can imagine his excitement. They travelled along a road banked up with mud, called a 'diek' in these parts. It was even better than going by barge. As the dawn slowly broke and the cocks began to crow in unison outside the cottages scattered over the heath, a sensation of rapt stillness cast its spell on him. How silent it was when the cocks had stopped! They were passing thin poplars in a quiet so intense that you could hear the yellow poplar leaves dropping to the ground, on past an old stumpy church and a graveyard, with earthen walls and a beech hedge around it. 'It all, all, all became exactly like the most beautiful Corots. A quietness, a mystery, a peace, as only he has painted it.'[12]

They reached Zweeloo at six in the morning, and still it was not properly light. Entering the village was like passing under an invisible triumphal arch, quite splendid. Enormous mossy roofs of houses awaited them, and stables, sheepfolds, barns.

The broad-fronted houses stood between oak trees that were dressed in all the splendour of autumn bronze. He was stunned by the absolute purity on all sides, on the wet trunks, tones of black contrasting dramatically with the showers of leaves, hung in suspension like clouds of golden rain, in loose tufts as if blown there by a wind. The sky glimmered through them, and through the poplars, birches, the limes, and apple trees.

He was at a loss to describe the sky, its lilac whiteness, so ineffable above him that it was like a secret waiting to be deciphered, reflecting everything and seeping into the thin mist on the ground. All was soft, wet, newly born. One went on tiptoe so as not to disturb the hush.

There were no painters around. Villagers said that none ever came at this time of year. Vincent decided not to hang about for the landlord, but head back on foot the way they had come. He did locate the apple orchard from which Liebermann had composed a large picture, and he made a sketch of it. He began to retrace his tracks, drawing as he went, back over that country around Zweeloo that was entirely covered, as far as the eye could see, 'with young corn, the very, very tenderest green I know.'[13] Imagine, he urged Theo, a vast expanse of black earth, planted with corn and now sprouting, so that the ground looked almost mouldy with fresh life. The haze in which all this fertility was bathed reminded him of Brion's *The Last Day of Creation*. Now the meaning of that picture was being revealed to him.

He left the fertile area behind and was soon lost in the midst of enormous tracts of poor soil, black as soot. He missed the lilac-black of the furrows, then grew accustomed to the ever-rotting heather and peat. He had left behind as well the massive structures of farms and sheepfolds, with their strange irregular shapes, their gigantic mossy roofs, and little low walls. Walking and walking until he lost track of time, he felt that this was the entire world, it was comprised of nothing else, just the infinite earth and infinite sky. 'Horses and men seem no larger than fleas.' As the specks came nearer and enlarged, one saw in each one the germ of a Millet.

He re-entered the domain of ploughed land, far off and spreading endlessly like a sea, with furrows instead of waves. He encountered people who were all busy – ploughmen, a shepherd, roadmenders, drivers with dung carts. He stopped at a little roadside inn and found inside an old woman at work with a spinning wheel, like 'a dark silhouette out of a fairy tale', and beyond her, through the window, the clear sky and a path through the delicate green, and geese pecking in the grass. He sketched the woman at her wheel. He ate a piece of brown bread and drank a cup of coffee, the only food he consumed all day.

Twilight descended, his favourite of all times. He was engulfed once more in an indescribable peace, and knew again, as he had known at dawn on the outskirts of Zweeloo, that he belonged to life, that the primal desire of man is to come into being, to achieve this peace. He trudged on down a wide muddy road, past the weird triangular shapes of sod-built huts, glimpsing through the smoky windows the red light of a fire, and outside the pools of yellowish water with the bits of sky that had fallen into them, and bog trunks lying half rotten. Everywhere the drama of black and white. He was on a road that led through a swamp, and then coming towards him was the rough figure of a shepherd, the jostling oval shapes of the animals. The flock divided around him, in the hoary biblical silence.

He was confronted by one rearing sheepfold that loomed in silhouette, a black triangle. The door was flung wide, and inside lay a dark cave. Boards let in chinks of dying light from the sky's embers. He stood humbled, with his heart, that had been so tortured, at peace. On his head the twilight rained down like something palpable, as the ancient biblical ritual took place before him. 'The whole caravan of masses of wool and mud disappear into that cave – the shepherd and a woman with a lantern shut the doors behind them.' He went on down the road. 'The day was over, and from dawn to twilight, or rather from one night to another, I had lost myself in that symphony.'[14]

If certain aspects of Vincent's personality repel us, it is perhaps because he is never full face. He is always half turned to darkness and death, a part of him inarticulate, caught up in gloomy, speechless passion. He draws and paints from his flayed nerves as much as from his baulked emotions. His plight affects us like the unwilling martyrdom of a saint who wants to be like other men. He is on the road to a conversion he would rather not have. His flesh is the modern flesh of the world-weary modern, the benumbed, faithless man who comprehends what he has lost, and prefers the sensations of torture to no sensation at all. Destructiveness and self-doubt are preferable to the enfeebled body politic and the parasitic Church. The natural world mocks him; it is quick, it encompasses death and blossoms forth in abundance.

The secret of its flowering, he thinks, is not the light and warmth of the sun but the rotting flood of corruption underneath, on which it feeds. His instinct is to nourish the corruption where it lives in the dark places of himself. He crawls, in a shame of abasement, when he longs to leap like a flung wave, like a cloud of starlings. He finds the surge of earth more beautiful than the sea because it waits for man to inhabit it, when man comes into his own and finds his true home. The laughable forerunner, he hangs his head and averts his face, while over his head runs the sky like a great river of peace.

What then must he do? His passage through darkness, marked by the 'woman in black', burdened women, the bent heads of sorrowing men, convulsed roots and empty chairs, leads from death to the growth that one frosty crisis after another nips in the bud – in fact to the *Baby in Cradle* he had pictured while in The Hague and been unable to keep faith with.

Dutch chiaroscuro, dark and sombre, would hold him for a while yet, until he freed himself from Rembrandt, Millet, and Israëls and turned to Delacroix's symphonies of colour.

Psychologically, the darkness had not done with him. Brightness tempted him, and yet many bright pictures he saw were insipid, cold lies that left him unsatisfied. 'I hate more and more those pictures which are light all over,'[15] he wrote. One senses his repugnance. In The Hague with Sien he had given himself over to light, like a Myshkin who was all love, meek as a lamb, becoming the woman's servant and in this roundabout fashion returning himself to infancy. It solved, or seemed to, the ghastly problems of adulthood. The baby in its cradle confirmed him in his desire for infantile carefree experiences. Gratification opened to him like a regained paradise. The joys denied him as a man he would forgo for those of a child-man. But there was still a murderous and suicidal Rogozhin inside him to appease, presiding over his disintegration. Reduced by that process he fell back into the void, the shrieking loneliness of the proud ego. He had gone to the limit as a babbling idiot, wringing his hands and begging for reasonableness from a woman who loathed his mother-worshipping love. Running out, he was back in a dark antagonistic Holland with a saviour he had forgotten, who said, 'I am the Light.' Somehow the wave of darkness and the wave of light were personified in his parents.

He wanted the refuge of his home again. Suddenly his will to endure alone collapsed. Living utterly without family ties on the moors of Drenthe was insupportable. Abandoning the isolation he had sought so avidly in September, he went back so as to be at home for Christmas, always a precarious time for him. His journey began with a six-hour walk in the rain and snow across the heath to Hoovegeen. Stormy conditions against which he had to battle seemed to put new heart into him.

Though loath to admit it, he was relieved at first to be back, among the familiar sights and sounds. He justified the return to Theo on economic grounds, while stifling a feeling of failure that was liable to erupt in displays of growling boorishness. His parents welcomed him, assuming he was back for an indefinite stay and perhaps interpreting this as a change of heart. This was even harder to bear than his own self-criticism. And to treat him like the prodigal son was stupid. Morose and angry, he now saw his parents as unhappy, telling his brother that 'the light within them is black and spreads obscurity around them.'[16]

Within a fortnight he was back in open conflict with his father.

It was hardly an equal contest. His father was ageing, unsure, falling back on old prejudices to defend his position. It must have seemed to him that Vincent had gained immeasurably in strength and confidence since their last confrontation. Reading between the lines, one sees the father quailing before the rude questions of his son, with his big, overwhelming needs. His very stance could be intimidating, standing with his head lowered, bull-like. One marvels at the weird contrast between the chastened, helpless child he had become with Sien and this rebel, flushed and combative, thirsting for battle, only disappointed because the fight could not be more prolonged and violent. Struggle, opposition aroused his animal vitality.

He protested to Theo at one point that he was trying hard to keep the peace – but how hard? He seemed more concerned to break than maintain the shaky truce existing between him and his father. How much of this savage attack was for Theo's ears only and how much of it was actually voiced is not clear. The Reverend Theodorus, anxious about the spell this demon artist might be casting on his younger son, wrote mildly to Theo advising him 'not to let yourself be influenced into doing things which are not practical, for alas, that certainly is his foible.'

'The line between God the Father, and Father the God, blurred to begin with, and increasingly fuzzy with time, produced a split image of troubling contradictions,' writes Ernst Pawels in his life of Kafka.[17] The parallel is striking. Vincent was fired as never before by the poetry of Christ's poverty. As he darkened his palette in Drenthe, this had been the thrust of his art of darkness. What had Christ's gospel of renunciation to do with his parents' comfortable parsonage? The fact that he was now sheltering within it does not seem to have occurred to him. In any case the struggle in his mind was an ideological one.

He had not yet abandoned Christianity, and he would never abandon Christ, but the dogmas preached by his father were to him false. Through his painting he would reach the kernel of moral truth 'they' had mislaid, and make it new. He had come home, it was beginning to seem, in order to finally wrench himself away from all his father represented, and not only him but the even more hateful world of the van Goghs; the art dealers, the bourgeoisie, polite society, 'them'. From this point on he would aim his life in a new direction.

Possibly too he aspired to this final showdown with his father in order to needle Theo, penetrate his tidy exterior and force him into the open. As if looking for a quarrel he went on to exaggerate the uncompromising nature of his position. He aligned himself with the workers, the rebels at the barricades, with Zola and Michelet and the students of 1848. And what he demanded to know was: where did Theo stand? He knew of course that Theo would equivocate. Vincent's utterances were now briefly, startlingly, those of a political animal. 'My sneers are bullets, not aimed at you who are my brother, but in general at the party to which you belong once and for all. Nor do I consider *your* sneers (a reference to Theo's occasional sarcasm) aimed expressly at me . . . . You fire at the barricade and think to gain merit by it . . . . Neither you nor I meddle in politics, but we live in the world, in society, and involuntarily ranks of people group themselves.'[18]

Out to provoke Theo into a declaration of loyalty, and at the same time sting him for continuing to belong to a hated class, he charged him with hypocrisy and self-righteousness in refusing to belong to either side. That was 'a dear little van Goghish trick.'[19] He spat out more venom at his father (to Theo), calling him narrow-minded, emitting rays of darkness from his breast – against him, the angel of fiery light – and by his clergyman's vanity creating error and confusion in the house. Then he laid down his challenge: essentially, he announced, 'I am *not* a van Gogh.' What about Theo, what was he? 'I have always looked upon you as "Theo".'[20]

It was to cut his ties that he had begun, from the earliest days, to sign his work 'Vincent', following the practice of his adored Rembrandt, and making the excuse then that foreigners would have difficulty pronouncing his surname. Here was his real reason. Even stronger than the need to disentangle himself from his father was his desire to break free from any association with those money-grubbing relatives of his, 'Messrs Van Gogh and Co'.

The real life Theodorus, whatever his limitations as a parent, was no monster. Theo was swift to point this out, at the same time rebuking Vincent for his bullying and insensitivity, hurting an old man who was in no condition to hit back. Vincent took this in his masochistic stride. To be branded an unfeeling brute reinforced the image he had made for himself of a man who was dog-rough, 'a foul beast', unfit for human company, not to be tolerated in civilised drawing rooms. Resorting to a dog-like whine, he complained to Theo: 'The dog feels that if they keep him, it will only mean putting up with him and tolerating him in the house, so he will try and find another kennel.'[21]

His father, retreating when accosted to his study, his church, his old age, was no longer a match for Vincent's increasingly vociferous rebellion. Why, we might ask, all the shot and shell? Partly it was fire directed at the father he carried in his heart, whom he still loved and admired despite everything, and who, after all, had been his benefactor and model for so long. 'Did I ever tell you,' wrote Kafka to Felice, 'that I admire my father? You know he is my enemy, just as I am his enemy, an enmity determined by our respective natures. Yet aside from that, my admiration for him as a person is perhaps as great as my fear of him. I can get around him at a pinch, but roll over him, never.'[22]

It was after Vincent went back to The Hague to collect some belongings that his correspondence with his brother became really acrimonious. For a time it was almost open warfare between them. Theo did not provoke easily, but he could defend himself. Vincent accused his brother of caring more about his career (a constant source of jealousy) than for him, and doing next to nothing to promote his work. So far he hadn't sold a single thing. Was that because Theo didn't want to risk his precious name in the Paris art world?

But the hostility had another root. Vincent had looked up Sien and been dismayed to find her and the children in poor health and deplorable conditions. She had not gone back to whoring, but eked out a miserable living as a washerwoman, for which she lacked the stamina. It was Theo and their father in unholy alliance who had talked him into abandoning Sien when she was on the mend, he now alleged. They were both cruel and worldly. Upset by what he had seen and casting around for someone to blame, he translated his guilt into aggression and resurrected the threat of marriage to Sien as a supposed solution. It would save her, and be doing the honourable, Christian thing. He was having a last vicious swipe at his father and his father's religion. A wild urge to uproot himself, coupled with unhappy years of accumulated bitterness, threw him into one assault after another. In love with Kee, he had taunted Theo with being no more than a 'man of business'. Years before, he had suddenly exclaimed with bitter irony, 'You are quite the plush gentleman and I am the black sheep.' He did simmer down at times, enough to recognise his tendency to pour oil on the fire, and catch glimpses of himself as a 'half-strange, half-tiresome person.'[23]

Should he go or stay? The atmosphere remained fraught, and though he may have secretly relished the animation it gave to things, he needed to settle into a quiet routine if he was going to produce good work. The unconscious blackmail threat levelled at his parents – he would marry Sien unless they accepted him as he was – hadn't resulted in his expulsion, but nor had it improved matters. He thought more than once of Antwerp as a possible bolt-hole. At least there he would find painters, and perhaps a market for his paintings. His friend van Rappard joined the fray, urging him to stay put, as he was doing. However, *his* family was extremely tolerant, unlike Vincent's – even though Rappard hadn't yet earned a cent from his art.

Then, towards the end of January something happened which, temporarily at least, put a stop to hostilities. His mother had a fall, hurting her leg as she alighted from a train at Helmond. Vincent was out painting at a farm when he was called. The doctor diagnosed a broken thighbone, and set it successfully.

Emergencies brought out the best in Vincent. So did tending the sick and injured. He was transformed, changing overnight into an endlessly considerate and patient nurse. He fetched and carried without a word of complaint, and painted little 'trifles' for his mother's amusement. He painted a picture of the rather dilapidated parsonage from the front garden, and the little octagonal church nearby where his father preached. His picture of the church, with people emerging after a service, demonstrated that he was now willing to alter nature if it suited his purpose. The church with its belfry is somehow spikier than in its photograph, the trees surrounding it elongated. Another photograph shows us his mother convalescing, a broad-faced, seated woman in black with a stick beside her, hands in her lap, wearing a black bonnet.

He decided to stay on at Nuenen after all, for a number of reasons. He liked the locals better than those at Etten. As spring approached, easing the mid-winter gloom with which he was always afflicted, he woke up to the beauty of Brabant, the country of his dreams, steeped in memories of his childhood. He was about ready to proceed, in Jung's words, 'from the dream outwards'. Precautions had to be taken to prevent his mother suffering from bedsores, and he helped construct a special stretcher to help move her around the house. There was plenty to occupy him and he was glad to feel useful.

There was another factor. His work was at last really starting to flow here. Soon he would refuse to budge while his luck held. An old washhouse at the rear of the house was cleared out and its mangle removed to make a studio for him. He took pleasure in telling Theo that – unlike the snug weavers' cottages he was visiting – his studio was located next to the coal-hole and the dung pit.

Weavers were to be both pitied and envied. They lived at home, as he did, and they managed to live from their toil. He then proposed a business deal with Theo. He would consign his entire monthly production to Theo from now on, for him to regard as his property, in exchange for 150 francs as a kind of retainer. This would make him feel better about both of them. It removed the stigma of charity from Theo's allowance. Gradually his morbid sensitivity on the subject of money began to occupy less space in his letters.

He drew and painted the weavers at their looms until they seemed like an obsession. Often seeing himself as a prisoner, he found analogies galore in weavers, men who were condemned to spend 'whole seasons alone'. When he came to paint his picture *The Loom*, he filled the space monumentally with vertical and horizontal forms, like the bars of a cage. The figure behind the bars works away in sad resignation, confined in 'a monstrous black thing of grimed oak'. If it had been possible he would have included the sigh or lament that he thought 'must issue now and then from that contraption of sticks.'[24]

Sometimes he saw the weavers as tragic victims. They had surrendered their humanity and become goblins or spooks. He completed one drawing of a loom in great detail and then had to add the 'spook' in order to make the picture more authentically haunted. He had an affinity for ghosts. He himself was a ghost of what he might have been if he could have been freed from his cage of loneliness, warmed by love, and he was accompanied through life by his double, the sometimes magical but often chilling ghost of his namesake, who refused to lie still in the Zundert graveyard.

Weavers were forced to work long hours for low wages, unable to compete with modern industry, of little more use to society than he was. Only their endurance and a phantom quality saved them from being gobbled up by the bars and beams which activated their arms and legs. Painting their portraits made these apparitions live again, conferred on them the immortality he wished for himself, together with the solemnity and power they deserved as workers but which had been denied them.

Nuenen was for Vincent a two-year period of consolidation, during which he began to forge for himself the language of modernity, 'marbled and veined in verdigris' as Gautier put it, but above all a language of movement, of nerves, charged with dreams and saturated with the earth. He had longed to be human and had succeeded in becoming monstrous. He was poised for flight and about to run amuck inside himself, to paint swiftly, freely, throwing caution to the winds as perhaps no one had done until now. Yet here he was, tormented by these workers who were caged by their own efforts, at the mercy of their own lives. It was a moment of irony. What prevented him from sharing their fate was the vision he had of man born for happiness. What kept his work dark and rigid was a fear of what might happen if he unchained himself. Would he go mad, commit murders, kill himself? Many commentators have blamed defective technique when explaining the stiff figures of Vincent's earlier work. The 'fault' was more probably the stiffness of a cramped spirit not yet able to free itself.

The path to his future liberation lay, he fervently believed, out of doors. Working outside in all weathers was also a way of making himself indistinguishable from other humble workers. Sending Theo a group of four landscapes, he explained in a covering letter that painting rural life entailed living in peasant cottages day by day, being in the fields like them, in summer in the heat of the sun and in winter suffering from snow and frost, not just taking a walk in it but day after day enduring its blows like the peasants themselves. 'As far as I know,' he added proudly, 'there isn't a single academy where one learns to draw and paint a digger, a sower, a woman putting the kettle over the fire, or a seamstress.'[25]

He was finding it essential now to work rapidly, without tinker-ing too much afterwards: not because of the changing light effects but because a painting attacked swiftly was more likely to capture the artist's feelings. In this sense he was anticipating Lawrence's belief that the work should be allowed to grow organically, as in the flung-down emotional roughhouse of a poem by Ted Hughes. He saw evidence of a similar approach in Courbet, and was encouraged by the gestural element in the work of Franz Hals. On an excursion to Antwerp with a friend, he went into a museum and stopped to admire Hals' portrait of a fisherboy. Hals, he said excitedly, was happy to leave a brush stroke where it was once it had landed, and he dismissed the rest of the room's exhibits as belonging to 'the periwig and pigtail period'.

There was even virtue sometimes in mistakes, accidents. And changes in reality were necessary – 'yes, lies if you like' – in order to get at the truth.

He was no longer terrorised by the blank accusing glare of an empty canvas about to be sullied by his 'muddy paws'. Mallarmé had spoken of the paralysis induced by a blank sheet of paper. 'The canvas,' Vincent wrote, 'stared at you like an idiot, and it hypnotised some painters, so that they themselves became idiots.' His answer was typical of the new, assertive Vincent: you should challenge, attack with daring and passion, invite ruin. He likened the canvas's stare to the stare of life itself, vacant, discouraging, hopeless, and perhaps was thinking of the cold white gaze of those women who had rejected him.

Margot Begemann, a lonely spinster in her mid forties who lived next door, was different. One look and she knew she had found a soul-mate. The truth was, she chased after him. At first he didn't mind. The lame affair, which culminated in a tragic incident, and even then didn't stop, began like this.

Margot came round to help Vincent's mother through her long convalescence. It was in her nature to serve others. She was the youngest of three sisters, and there was also a brother, Louis. Her father, a widower who was something of a family despot, had a business and she assisted him, as well as carrying the main burden of running the household. Her passive, soft-hearted disposition made her easy game when there were tasks to be off-loaded. She and Vincent were mutually attracted, but sex seems to have had little to do with it. The peculiar son next door would not have been much of a proposition for any woman – coming in out of the rain on Sundays in his fur cap and shaggy ulster he looked like a drowned tomcat – but perhaps for Margot he represented her last chance. The woman was without experience, plain, lacking in confidence, unhappy.

They went for long walks in the countryside. He took her with him on visits to his father's sick parishioners. She was a woman damaged by life, he reported gloomily. She reminded him of a misused Cremona violin, bungling repairers having done their worst. These were hardly the words of a man aflame with passion.[26]

Often drawn to older women, he listened to her patiently and tried to console her when she said, as she frequently did, that she would like to kill herself. If she told him this to arouse his pity, she succeeded. Walking through the fields with her in a dismal silence was like accompanying someone who was already dead. He told her about his own unhappy youth, which had crushed him with its disappointments as hers had done. But he had fought back, and she should do the same. As far as she was concerned this could mean only one thing: she had found an ally, and, who knows, maybe a husband.

If the sexual element had been stronger the outcome might have been different. Margot was intimidated by her father and her jealous sisters, who saw a maid-of-all-work about to get away from them. The sisters were soon pouring out their disapproval of Vincent, adding to Margot's emotional difficulties almost daily. Vincent too was apparently hanging back from a woman who represented a past he had done his best to shed. He used to be like her, he told Theo later. 'I'm not any more.'[27] She was sadness personified, an image of himself which he wanted to save her from. He also wanted to flee.

He could have had her sexually, he intimated to Theo in roundabout language, but that would have besmirched her name and he was determined to act responsibly. He discussed marriage with her, but was so alarmed by her disturbed state, which changed love into hate at a moment's notice, that he went off to see her doctor. He also had a talk with her brother. Their advice was to postpone any idea of marriage for at least two years. He disagreed.

It had to be very soon or not at all, he thought – if thought is the word for his fusion of rash energy and indignation. Margot's extreme fear of her father's anger had cast Vincent once more in the role of rescuer, and this time the situation was not an imaginary one, spun out of his infatuation, but only too real. It was Zolaesque; and so was its climax.

Out in the fields one afternoon, she suddenly slipped to the ground and cried out. She writhed about, unable to speak, jerking and twisting her body in horrible convulsions. 'Have you swallowed something?' he shouted, and she screamed, 'Yes.'[28] It was a dose of strychnine. He made her stuff her fingers down her throat until she threw up some of the poison. Then he rushed to her brother for help and between them they got her to the hospital at Utrecht. When he visited her there, she was more triumphant than wretched. 'I too have loved at last,' she told him. He was too moved and shamed to speak. Once again he had acted as he thought for the best and the result was calamitous.

All kinds of gossip circulated about him. The van Goghs' neighbours shunned the house because Vincent was inside. His mother, with only half the story, was baffled and distressed. When Margot did come home, she made one final bid for Vincent's love, getting an acquaintance to buy one of his drawings. He found out who was behind it, but he wasn't angry. Instead he blamed 'that damned icy coldness which . . . almost *killed* her, many years ago'. He meant Christianity, the new deadly enemy. 'That icy coldness hypnotised even me in my youth, but I have taken revenge since . . .'. He had become an unashamedly sexual being, living with a whore 'and *not* respecting many would-be respectable pious ladies.'[29]

Unable to settle at home, and no doubt wishing to distance himself now from Margot and her sad manias, he moved into two rooms belonging to the Catholic priest's sexton. You could call this more unconscious revenge on the father, camouflaged as expediency. Earlier he had met three amateur painters who lived in nearby Eindhoven, hearing of them first of all in the art supplies shop there. Hermans was a goldsmith of sixty. Kerssemakers, a forty-year old tanner, seemed to possess real talent, and there was a post-office worker, van der Wakker. Perhaps feeling a renewed appetite for male company, and still dreaming of a possible artists' cooperative, he volunteered to give instruction to all three. Either he visited his pupils at their homes or they called on him at his studio, which he said was open to them whenever they felt like it.

He was now turning out work at a tremendous rate, and with more and more conviction. A later pupil, Dimmen Gestel, entering Vincent's studio for the first time, was astounded to see a pile of drawings on the floor reaching as high as the table. They were in lithographic chalk, and were all of peasant heads, peasant implements, peasant interiors. Vincent's speed was now awesome. He told Gestel what he had told the others, that his studio door was wide open but 'it's no good asking me to entertain you, I haven't the time.'

The biographer M E Tralbaut has recorded an interview with an old man, Piet van Hoorn, who was a boy of ten living at the mill at Opwetten on the outskirts of Nuenen when Vincent was installed in his two rooms behind the sexton's house. Piet remembered first setting eyes on the funny red-bearded man with the paints as he sat by the roadside near the mill, ignoring everybody and everything. The strange man's pipe was stuck permanently in his mouth. He wore a straw hat and a farmer's blue smock. If Piet had his schoolmates with him he would pluck up courage and ask Vincent questions, but he didn't receive many answers. Van Hoorn told Tralbaut the bird's nest story he had probably related to a dozen other researchers. Vincent asked him to search for the nest of a golden oriole and bring it to him. Piet trotted off: he knew exactly where to look. He had seen orioles nesting high up in an oak tree.[30]

He turned up at Vincent's studio carrying the nest in its forked branch as one ensemble. The red-beard was hard at work and ignored the boy completely for ten minutes, or more likely didn't even see him – his concentration was extraordinary. He looked as crazy a sight as everyone had said. He wore only his long woollen underwear. On his head was the same straw hat; clenched between his teeth the same blackened pipe. He was painting trees. He painted rapid strokes, backed away, sat down, muttered angrily, scrambled up and stabbed at the canvas again. Suddenly he became aware of the boy standing there. His eyes opened wide. He said, 'Well done, lad,' and gave Piet fifty cents. This became the standard rate for a nest. The boy ran off like a hare to find some more.

Kerssemakers later recalled his impressions of the same scene: 'One was amazed at the way all the available hanging or standing room was filled with paintings, drawings in watercolour and in crayon: the heads of men and women whose clownish turned-up noses, protruding cheekbones and large ears were strongly accentuated, the rough paws calloused and furrowed; weavers and weaving looms, women spooling yarn, potato planters, women weeding, still-lives, certainly as many as ten studies in oils of the little old chapel at Nuenen that was being pulled down. A great heap of ashes around the stove, a number of chairs with frayed cane bottoms, and a cupboard with at least thirty birds' nests, all kinds of mosses and plants brought along from the moor, some stuffed birds, a spool, a spinning wheel, a complete set of farm tools, old caps and hats, coarse bonnets and hoods, wooden shoes, etc.'[31]

As far as food and shelter were concerned, Vincent's monkish tendencies remained unchanged. Although he had another room which was fairly spacious and could have made comfortable living quarters, he preferred to sleep on a bed in the empty attic. Asked to dinner by van der Wakker's mother, he accepted graciously, then refused anything but bread and cheese, his staple diet. Anything more he regarded as 'coddling'. But he was never without his tobacco, and carried a flask of brandy on his treks into the fields.

He was moving steadily nearer to the masterpiece of his Dutch period, *The Potato Eaters*. Not that he made any such claims for it. Clearly though he was deeply satisfied by what he had accomplished, and took offence when it was derided by van Rappard, a man he thought understood his intentions. All those tenacious studies of heads and hands seen by the astonished Kerssemakers had gone into its creation. Ian Dunlop calls the painting 'one of those works which is easier to admire than to like, to explain than to welcome. It is Vincent incarnate, an ugly, ill-mannered painting, dark, gloomy, awkward, passionate.' It is, says Dunlop, 'less a meal than a consumption of fodder. It is unrepentant realism, as unrepentant as the realism of Zola's *Germinal*.'[32] A better comparison would be with Zola's *La Terre*, published two years later in 1887. Whatever the verdict, one thing is certain: the rough dog with wet paws had come into his own.

Although he spent less than two years in Nuenen, Vincent

171

would never be more prolific than this. Part of his output while there was afterwards abandoned when his mother found traces of woodworm in some packing cases of his after he had gone: '60 paintings on stretchers, 150 loose canvases, two portfolios containing 90 pen drawings, and between 100 and 200 crayon drawings.' Most of this collection was handed over to a junk dealer, who sold some items for pennies from a pushcart and threw out the rest. Nevertheless, 225 drawings, 25 watercolours, and 185 oils survived with Theo, nearly a quarter of his total production.[33]

Why was Vincent so interested in birds' nests? The question is not necessarily a naive one. Psychoanalysts have had a field day with the symbols embedded in van Gogh's art, and they are not finished yet. Their interpretations are sometimes illuminating, while others make one suspect that the symbols were planted there by hands other than the artist's. We shouldn't be put off. Vincent loved symbols, and he allowed them to seduce him, deploying them continually in his letters and more subtly in his work, where he would play the game of simultaneously revealing and hiding himself. His language was the language of symbols, and it was one he used like a poet, allowing the symbols to arise naturally, nurturing them in the knowledge that through them he could speak more profoundly. Sometimes they spoke for him, laid waste to him with the savagery and beauty of images from a country where nothing is held sacred – the country of dreams. Hand in hand with this went his effort to 'salvage' reality – to use John Berger's apt word in his essay on van Gogh. He was a man totally dedicated to realism who saw everything he looked at symbolically.

Recovering after his first seizure in Arles, he saw in his mind's eye the house of his childhood at Zundert, the rooms, the paths, plants in the garden, the church, 'as far as a magpie's nest in a tall acacia in the graveyard.' Birds and their nests fascinated him. He must often have wished himself high up in a tree out of it all, and he did the next best thing, sinking back into his soul and slitting his eyes. He spoke of himself more than once as a caged bird. Holding a bird's nest in his hand and knowing its perfect shape was like being given a piece of freedom, like soaring with the birds. Soaring birds figure in dozens of his landscapes. Birds were also winged messengers, linking earth and heaven. He had lost his faith and had no belief in a literal heaven any more, but the nostalgia for a heavenly refuge still lingered.

Heaven, in all its forms, was a potent symbol. When he was able to discover in himself the power to be a medium for people and their sufferings, he discovered at the same time a way back to nature, to the earth, to that mother from whose side he had strayed. Ecstasy, the state of being suffused with empathy for everything that moves and flies and swims, he called heaven. 'Existence falters,' wrote Viktor Frankl, 'unless it is lived in terms of transcendence towards something beyond itself.'[34] Vincent's perspectives, conventionally drawn to begin with, were soon tilting him dizzily in the direction of heaven.

The light of heaven shone on a daylight earth. It rose as the consummation of light and darkness, and he loved to walk through the night and see the sun rise, out of the womb of night which had nourished it. Heaven was also the vast beyond. It waited with its eternal promise. Like death it was not to be understood. The earth was a splendour and a sorrow which gave us up, and we were in transit like birds between two eternities. The dead were not dead, they were the stars. They were the body of night covered in open eyes, in a rapture of sublime love. The light of heaven was as real to him as the singing of birds.

He loved the idea of birds in their nests as he did of babies in their cribs. He thought of them with a melting tenderness, and they joined his other devices for conveying his feelings about mothers, warm homes, welcoming hearths, and loving embraces. Peasant cottages around Nuenen with their thatched mossy roofs in a compact rounded mass were like wrens' nests, he told Theo.

He was spending so much time in one such nest, the grimy cottage of the de Groot family, that it must have begun to seem like a second home to him. The de Groots were his models for the innumerable studies he made in preparation for his big painting of them assembled for their evening meal. He paid them with money if they requested it, otherwise with packets of coffee. He took no payments from his own pupils, preferring them to replenish his stock of colours from time to time.

He attacked his composition with great deliberation, more so than with any other work. As well as the proliferating studies of heads and hands he executed a rough sketch in March 1885, following this with a preliminary oil in April and then the final version in May. This last version was painted from memory and imagination in his studio. His artistic models were Rembrandt and Hals: he was after the former's chiaroscuro, and endeavouring to combine it with Franz Hal's panache. He had set himself the incredibly difficult task of trying to make darkness visible.

As with any major work by van Gogh, we are confronted by supernatural and magical elements in a setting of utter realism. Rembrandt's *Christ in Emmaus*, where the risen Christ sits at the head of a table like 'a soul in a body', tenderly gazing at the others, was an abiding influence throughout his life. Its 'deeply mysterious' atmosphere and its tenderness were qualities he hoped would permeate his own painting.

Did he succeed? Without doubt the picture is religious in intention. The peasant family who seem united around their simple meal are in fact curiously isolated from one another. Whether because the heads were assembled from separate studies, or as a deliberate commentary on these people's lives, the figures do not coalesce. As if to emphasise their cruel fate, a wall juts out between the two figures, a man and a woman, at the right. The intimate space, over which the rays of a hanging lamp spills light, is a scene of five people unable to reach each other. Meyer Shapiro has noticed that 'each figure retains a thought of its own and two of them seem on the brink of an unspoken loneliness'.[35]

In the foreground, a child figure with its back to us is haloed in steam and murky light. Above the animal-like man on the left is a crucifix. His wife gazes at him from under her bonnet as if spellbound. For nearly sixty years the picture was thought to be unsigned, until someone deciphered the name 'Vincent' indistinctly written along the top strut of the man's chair. If Vincent did identify himself with the ugly man, as some biographers have suggested, then the older woman with a downcast expression pouring coffee opposite and ignoring him could by the same token be a representation of his mother.

For all that has been said, the picture is indisputably and mysteriously a celebration of the group's humanity and closeness. Their harsh toil has welded them, even though they are struck dumb. They eat what they have produced, and their colour and modelling are indistinguishable from the food that keeps them alive. They have potato heads, potato noses, potato ears, potato hands. Speech has given way to the contemplation of what they are about to share, as they sit like celebrants at an altar to taste the sacrament. It is, after all, and despite the grim reality of their lives, a communion we are witnessing. Shortly after completing it, Vincent wrote, 'I like so much better to paint the eyes of people than to paint cathedrals.'[36]

He was prepared to defend this painting if necessary, and almost looked forward to adverse reactions. He got behind the work in a letter sent on Theo's birthday, explaining how tenaciously he had laboured at its composition. He saw it as a slow growth that had come to fruition after years of sweat and blood. What he had aimed at he had achieved – a picture that spoke nakedly of *manual labour* (he underlined the words). It had not come easily, but he had kept faith in it. 'All winter long I have had the threads of this tissue in my hands, and have searched for the ultimate pattern.'[37] Here was the ugly duckling, his victory: the first real peasant picture.

His father, a marathon walker like his son, suddenly collapsed on the doorstep of the parsonage, on his way in from a long walk across the heath. It was a heart attack. He died almost at once. Only two days before he had written in a conciliatory mood to Theo: 'This morning I talked things over with Vincent; he was in a kind mood and said there was no particular reason for his being depressed. May he meet with success anyhow.'

For someone who had been so vituperative on the subject of his father when alive, Vincent's near silence after the death is strange. He even forgot – or omitted – to mention the event to his friend van Rappard. His feelings have to be read in his painted memorial, a vase of honesty beside his father's tobacco pouch and pipe, and guessed at in his more ambiguous *Still Life with Open Bible, Extinguished Candle and Zola's 'La Joie de Vivre'*, painted five months later.

Heavy irony has been suggested. The Bible was his father's. Opened at Isaiah, it contains the words Vincent would not have missed: 'One who grew up like a root out of dry ground. . . . He was despised and rejected by men, a man of sorrows, acquainted with grief.' The heavy black book of his Calvinist parents has snuffed out the light. The lemon yellow covers of the novel and its title proclaim a defiant joy that can never be extinguished. To place it prominently in the foreground was to mock his father, who hated and feared the 'damned French literature' and its devilish influence. But there is more ambiguity, more irony. Zola's novel is joyless. Only the Bible expresses hope, and that revolutionary new doctrine preached by Christ, called love.

His father's death weakened his ties with Holland, releasing him into the sensuousness of a world of colour. And there were other events over the next few months, all pressing him to bring his time at Nuenen to a close. The unmarried daughter of the de Groots, Gordina, had become pregnant while Vincent was working there. Vindictive gossip ran round against him once more. The Catholic priest issued an edict from the pulpit forbidding people to pose for him, so it was now virtually impossible for him to obtain models. The accusation of paternity, though Vincent denied it – even tracking down the father, a member of the Catholic congregation – went on circulating with the rest of the gossip about him. If he wasn't guilty, then he should have been.

Gordina had been one of his favourite models. He began to think seriously of leaving. It was autumn, the cold weather about to descend. Soon he would have to curtail his out-of-door activities.

Then some nastiness blew up over his late father's estate, which convinced him that he was as unwanted at home as ever. His mother seemingly wanted the whole inheritance – it was only modest – transferred to herself and her three daughters. Vincent's sisters agreed. It was their solid front against him that hurt, not the money. He protested to Theo that his mother and 'those at home were very far from sincere'. His mother, he alleged bitterly, was so involved in her own complex thoughts and feelings that they were strangers, and he complained outright that 'she had neglected him for a long time.'[38] Soon afterwards he posted off a curious poem, a love-hate song addressed to women:

> All evil has come from woman – Obscured reason, appetite for
>   lucre, treachery . . .
> Golden cups in which the wine is mixed with lees,
> Every crime, every happy lie, every folly
> Comes from her. Yet adore her, as the gods
> Made her . . . and it is still the best thing they did.[39]

Enough was enough. In Nuenen he completed a few landscapes and still-lives and then ground to a halt. He wanted to slake his thirst on models, and, if he told the truth, he was starved for 'available' female company. Deep in the country he was up against a familiar problem. Isolation cut him off from contemporary developments and the opportunity to discuss them with fellow artists. Bewilderingly, he felt a ravenous appetite building up in him for the teeming life of a city. The complete contrast would, he thought, stimulate him to new work and force up new ideas.

Antwerp would be his next destination. After that, Paris. By Antwerp he meant Rubens, whose example would teach him what he wanted to know next: how to paint portraits, how to enliven flesh. He would stand in front of Rubens in the museums until the master's technical superiority flowed into him by a kind of symbiosis.

Exciting rumours were reaching him about the ferment of artistic experiment in Paris. It made him terribly restless. Ian Dunlop has remarked perceptively that 'In a curious way he remained both behind and in front of the times.' Through Theo he was well acquainted with the work of Manet, of course, and there was a curmudgeonly fellow he had read about in articles by Zola, by the name of Cézanne. What could Theo tell him about Cézanne? He and Zola had met as youngsters in Aix, Provence, was that right?

Once in Antwerp he was determined to consolidate the gains he had made so far, and go on to make further progress in the direction of more freedom. How did he free himself from the static, give himself up to the flux of life? One solution was to paint rapidly. He wrote again and again in praise of painting in a rush, 'as much as possible in one rush', and asserted that the old Dutch pictures he most admired were painted like that, quickly, with next to no retouching afterwards. It was the one great lesson he had learned recently, thanks to the example of men like Hals and 'that splendid devil', Latour – 'in one stroke – but with absolutely complete exertion of one's whole spirit and attention.'[40]

Gradually he was detaching himself from his beloved Rembrandt in favour of a new source of inspiration, Delacroix. In other words, he was hungry for colour. Rembrandt, he had to admit, was more a harmonist than a colourist. On a note of elation he declared that his palette was at last (like him?) beginning to thaw out. The act of painting could have a savage aspect. It was like bringing an ice axe to himself.

Something dark and inconsolable was giving way to brightness, to the south. Rubens, the great painter of nude women, would help him – he didn't care for his religious pictures. As for Delacroix, he unfurled in a blaze of colour in his imagination like a banner, his very name synonymous with colour. Between the two he would establish his own impetuous, colourful style, using bold strokes and throwing into his art all the muscular energy of his short stocky body.

Before he left the Brabant, trying to explain why he had gone home in the first place, he said, 'I was sick of the boredom of civilisation.' He had fled The Hague for health reasons – and as usual he meant spiritual health. 'One may sleep on straw, eat black bread, well, one will only be the healthier for it.' He had made himself fit again by going out under a big sky and living among the mowers and diggers and the peasant girls, where nothing changed, and one felt 'that it has always been and always will be so.'[41] Now it was time to plunge back into the *fin de siècle* life of his century, and taste the sub-world of a culture that was in a process of dissolution. It was part of life, just as the timeless peasants were part, and he was not outside; he was up to his neck in modernity.

A man of his time, how could he fail to be aware of the Darwinian flood sweeping away everything that had once been rock-like, leaving only the ephemeral? He had to stand in that river, not pretend to ignore it.

Aware that by leaving he was once again making himself a homeless wanderer, he opposed to his old feelings of homesickness a new concept of the place of painting in his life. What he felt in his bones may have originally been consolation, but it was also a truth in its own right. He could only communicate it by saying simply: 'I mean that painting is a *home* . . .'.[42]

John Berger, in a pertinent essay written in 1982, helps us to understand what Vincent meant – though without mentioning van Gogh specifically. He argues that a painting is a shelter, and came about in response to a basic human need. The universe in which we live with its limitless space is a world in which we can get lost. A painting depicts this boundless world and brings it within its rectangular form, and inside its frame. Still-lives are brought in through its door, as is everything else: landscapes, seas, skies, animals, flowers, gods, darkness and light, the fire and the cold. Pictures provide us with a home that is both a comfort and a defence against what lies outside. Once inside the shelter of a painting, we are included with the rest of creation. We are at home when we look at it, just as a child feels safe when looking at the body of his mother.[43] Vincent was at pains to stress that, for all its attendant miseries, painting gave serenity, 'especially the painting of rural life'. One of his favourite words was 'homely'. His own true home was this one he erected time and again for himself, by the act of painting.

He was protean, an unpredictable personality. As far as he was concerned, the reality that lay beyond appearances was just as likely to be found in the streets and dance halls and along the waterfront in Antwerp as anywhere else. Sometimes painting had all the excitement of a hunt, he once said. Towards the end of November 1885 he arrived to hunt reality down.

9

THE HARLOT'S SMILE

In Antwerp he rented a little room at 194 Rue des Images. Appropriately enough it was above a paint-dealer's shop. It must have seemed a good omen. He soon pinned a collection of prints on the walls, only this time with a difference. They were neither biblical scenes nor photogravure clippings from the illustrated magazines but Japanese prints, no doubt supplied by Theo but in plentiful supply here. In Paris they were all the rage, and Vincent took to them enthusiastically. To discover this is a surprise: it was as if his very character was changing.

He loved these brightly coloured woodcuts, the ones of Hokusai and Hiroshige especially. He liked them for the same reason that he liked popular English prints – their popularity. They were cheap, within reach of everyone, and their subject matter – nature, domestic scenes, intimate and commonplace interiors – was bound to appeal to him. Their simplified designs, the use of large flat areas of pure colour, the elimination of shadows, were features he had seen in peasant art. He was impressed too by their refreshing clarity. What a wonderful antidote they were to the North and to his guilt-laden past, the dead father, the mother 'chary of speech' in her rusty black dress, with whom he now refused to correspond. Japanese art, he thought later, made him picture a very bright, quite bare room, open to the country. It was an interior place he liked to imagine was inside himself like a clean slate, swept clear of all encumbrances.

Above all the bright little pictures amused him, lightening his dark moods when he gazed at 'those little women's figures in

181

gardens, or on the beach, horsemen, flowers, knotty thorn branches.' And he came to another highly significant conclusion: 'Colour expresses something in itself.' It was an entirely new dimension. He did not know how else to put it. Back in Nuenen he had suddenly wanted to play the piano, so he went to Eindhoven and took lessons. His friend Kerssemakers says in his memoir that he was more interested in finding correspondences between the notes and colours such as Prussian blue, dark green, and ochre, than in mastering the piano keyboard. The teacher, of course, thought his unlikely pupil was unhinged. In France, a decade or so earlier, a boy poet, Rimbaud, had been experimenting along similar lines with vowels and colours.

Vincent went out in the pouring rain to explore Rubens' city. Ignoring guide books, he just followed his nose. His long sojourn in the heart of the country now seemed over-spiritual. The desire to render human bodies in terms of the spirit had broken down in him. A violent swing took him the other way, on to the lush flood of woman as she was, richly streaked in the red of sex like a Rubens nude. That was what he wanted. The other thing was ghoulish, the living body wrapped in cerements. His craving for a sensuality that was extreme had brought him here. He half dreaded it even though his feet took him towards it, the flesh he wanted to wallow in, the death of it. There was no father or mother to disapprove of him, no furtively watching villagers. He loved the anonymity of a large city.

Looking could be like possessing. His eye was voracious, though he often neglected to eat. One imagines him covering the docks and alleys with narrowed, predatory eyes. Physically, on the run from his spiritual excesses, he was in the mood to enjoy Antwerp. Suddenly women of all types crowd the pages of his letters.

Walking down a long dank street he came out on the quays. He stared at a white horse that was standing stockstill in the mud, where heaps of merchandise lay stacked under oilcloth against the black smoky walls of a warehouse. He passed through narrow streets, under rearing, tremendously high houses, warehouses, sheds. The tempo was exciting, the life raw, exposed to broad daylight. A sailor was being thrown out of a bordello by the girls – he went scrambling over a pile of sacks and dived through a warehouse window. Yet if you stepped back from the mêlée just

a little you took in a vista of Harwich and Havre steamers docked
at the ends of piers, with beyond them a dreary wet expanse
stretching away, flat inundated fields, dry rushes, mud, the widening river, and a single black boat. A desert of silence lay out
there.

Near at hand, so many sights caught his eye that he got dizzy
from such a tumult of impressions, so many painterly subjects.
Exotic sailors strolled by, and Flemish sailors, some of them
looking absurdly fit, swaggering their broad shoulders. In the
cafés, among the movement and din, people sat eating mussels
and swilling beer. The sheer gusto made him drunk. He suddenly
spotted a Chinese girl slipping by against the grey wall, a tiny
figure in black, her small hands pressed against her body. She
went by noiselessly like a thief, a tiny bug-like creature impossible
to comprehend. The Flemish mussel eaters stared past her impass-
ively. Vincent's eye registered the contrast between 'the dirtiest
mire' and this mysterious delicate thing with raven-black hair
framing a small oval face.[1]

Girls of all types came and went. In a number of cafés he struck
up conversations with them, talking cheerfully to disarm them.
He was delighted to find himself mistaken for a sailor. He saw
girls who looked splendidly healthy, simple and jolly like peasant
girls in the Brabant, only these were more open and direct,
quicker. Then the female faces that made one shudder, sly and
false, like hyenas. He couldn't wait to engage models. Meanwhile
he sat and stared, and went on walking everywhere tirelessly. He
stumbled one day on a quiet park, and sat and drew there all
morning.

Soon he was economising on food again to pay for models,
just as he had done in the Brabant and The Hague. He half starved
his body, perhaps in expiation of some blame he felt for his
father's death. Hadn't his father cried out, 'You're murdering
me?' He had also wished unconsciously for his mother's death,
telling Theo he felt sure she was about to die when he was on
the point of leaving Holland for good. A man as sensitive as
Vincent must have had remorseful thoughts on his mind. It was
no use pretending either that he wished to be back home. He
admitted frankly that it was a relief to be out of Holland, and
added a bitter note: 'I haven't the slightest inclination to write to

them at home, I think of them extremely little and I do not desire them to think of me . . .'.[2]

He was spending so much on paints, canvases, and models that his food and lodging money had to be reduced. He owed rent. Eating was cut back to a breakfast roll, augmented in the evening by bread and coffee. He smoked incessantly, which played havoc with his empty stomach. He provided Theo with morbid details of his privations in an attempt to extract more francs from his overburdened brother, who retaliated once by exclaiming that he didn't expect anything in return but 'stinking ingratitude'. Usually, however, he submitted with hardly a murmur. Vincent's demands on his parents had now been transferred wholesale to him.

In February Vincent complained that he was running a fever and experiencing spells of faintness, saying he could only remember eating six hot dinners since the previous May. It was a bitter winter. His teeth were loosening. He had lost or was about to lose ten of them. Because of the pain of masticating his food he had to bolt it down, which of course aggravated his digestive troubles. He would have to seek out a dentist; more expense. His face looked sunken, haggard. As always, one senses an element of masochistic satisfaction.

Theo rushed off another fifty francs and Vincent promptly engaged a model he had spied out, 'a girl from a café chantant'. He seemed to favour younger models now, rather than the worn-out prostitutes he had sought out perversely in The Hague. He would have liked a blonde model 'just because of Rubens', but this one had black hair, tied up with a scarlet ribbon, and flushed cheeks. She had apparently been 'busy' for the past few nights, informing him casually that champagne failed to cheer her up; in fact it only made her feel sad. He wrote later that when he painted harlots he wanted a harlot-like expression, and in this portrait he was trying to express something voluptuous and at the same time cruelly tormented.[3] A M Hammacher has pointed out that the head combines the features of Kee and Sien. When the girl had finished posing she delighted him by asking for a portrait of herself to keep, like the one he had just done. Here was the sort of approval he appreciated. As for critics, 'I feel quite obstinate, and I no longer care what people say about me or my work.'[4]

The Flemish women here had robust figures, and the urge to

paint them and possess them in the same impulse gave him no rest. His *Female Nude, Standing* has the unflinching realism of all his Antwerp and Paris nudes. This one radiates a bestial power. Her belly and buttocks jut, her smallpoxed face is shrimp-coloured in patches. Two or three months gone, she stands like a plant, squat, brutally indifferent, as if her toes were roots. The word ugly is somehow rendered meaningless by this artist who said that beauty could be found anywhere, 'in a single teardrop'.

In his room Vincent had begun reading serialised instalments from Zola's latest novel *L'Oeuvre*, the lurid melodrama of a painter who is being destroyed by his inability to match the emotional experience with a form 'that has been conceived but not created'. Claude Lanier is the herald of a new art and yet cannot produce anything worthwhile out of himself. The Zola character, a journalist called Sandoz, advises Lanier to abandon the romantic notion of woman as Devourer, grinding down his heart and eating out his brain, and to get married. Marriage, he tells him, is an essential stabilising condition for an artist. Lanier, unable to come to terms with either woman or his art, kills himself in front of his abortive masterpiece.

Vincent consulted a doctor about his health. The doctor's name, not mentioned in the letters, crops up as a note in one of his Antwerp sketchbooks: 'A Cavenaille. Rue de Hollande, 2 consult-ations'. Other notes refer to the medication he received: castor oil, alum, and a sitz bath treatment which the out-patients' depart-ment of a large hospital at the end of Rue des Images probably administered. Tralbaut ran Dr Cavenaille's grandson to earth in Antwerp in the course of his researches. Like his father and grand-father, this Cavenaille too was a doctor. According to him, his family discussed the 'queer dauber' dressed like a vagrant, who came for a consultation and said straight out that he was broke, but would paint Cavenaille senior's portrait. The doctor agreed, though the painting has since vanished.

Cavenaille's surgery was close to the waterfront, and the grand-son thinks Vincent may have been sent there by one of the dock-side models. Two scrupulous van Gogh scholars part company at this point. Family hearsay has it that Vincent had contracted syphilis. Tralbaut accepts the supposition, but Albert Lubin is clearly doubtful, noting that the symptoms and medication are not suggestive of syphilis, and that in any case it would have been impossible in those days, before the introduction of the Wasserman test in 1906, to give a reliable diagnosis.[5]

With no money for models, Vincent fell back on 'free' looking, gazing hungrily for hours in cheap dance halls at sailors and soldiers and their women. The entrance fee was only 20 to 30 centimes. A glass of beer in his hand, he could sit undisturbed for the whole evening and gratify this pleasure. In particular he studied the harlot-like expression, that inscrutable smile floating on the surface of hard experience, that still eluded him when he tried to capture it in paint. 'Manet has done it, and Courbet, damn it, and I have the same ambition.'[6]

He seemed to have decided against forming further anxiety-based attachments, thus forestalling the feared grief and rejection he had known before. Instead he prowled, cold and intent, like a wolf. Desperate for models, he enrolled at the Antwerp Academy and submitted to the irksome discipline of correct methods. He had heard that nude models were available in the evenings, but these turned out to be male wrestlers, to his intense disappointment. Nevertheless, he applied himself with tremendous energy. If we can accept the testimony of one eye-witness, Richard Baseleer, the Dutch newcomer rushed in 'like a bull in a china shop', gathered a crowd of students around him, and began unrolling canvases with all the aplomb of a travelling oilcloth salesman. He wasn't aware, it seems, of the spectacle he was making of himself: until the roars of laughter, that is. People were dropping in from other parts of the complex to have a look at this weatherbeaten, nervy savage, dressed, according to another classmate, in a blue blouse of the sort worn by Flemish cattle dealers. On his head was jammed his frowsty old fur cap. Instead of the regulation palette he wielded a lump of board torn from a packing case.[7]

Verlat, the director, came in to investigate the cause of the uproar. There was Vincent painting 'feverishly, furiously, with a rapidity that stupified his fellow students. He laid his paint on so thickly that his colours literally dripped from his canvas on to the floor.'

In order to gain access to female nudes he joined two private sketching clubs and attended their night sessions. Life classes using women models hardly ever occurred at the Academy.

Curiously, in view of his row with Mauve at The Hague, Vincent knuckled down to the necessity of drawing from plaster casts; until, suddenly, he was faced with a cast of the Venus de Milo to copy. He promptly transformed the serenely beautiful Greek goddess into the thickset figure of a swelling Flemish matron. Criticised for enlarging the breadth of the hips, he lost his temper and bawled, 'God damn you! A woman must have hips and buttocks and a pelvis in which she can hold a child!'[8]

Though he usually managed to restrain himself during classes, he was vociferous with his criticisms among the students thronging the corridors. Since something had to be done about this roughneck who since his admission had done nothing but undermine the school's authority, the Academy board voted to drop him down to a more suitable class. 'Thus at the age of thirty-three, when he had already created such masterpieces as *The Potato Eaters,*' writes Tralbaut, 'Vincent was sent back to the class for beginners between thirteen and fifteen years!' By that time, however, the beginner was on his way to Paris.

It goes without saying that he would never have jettisoned the painting style he had evolved by trial and error at Nuenen, one that was intuitive and emotional, allowing the thick strokes to remain as evidence of his labour and preserving the earthiness he loved, giving him results he found fascinating without knowing why. At mealtimes he had upset his family with unsocial behaviour, making use of two chairs, one to sit at the table and one to prop up his latest 'daub'. He would stare fixedly at his painting all through the meal without uttering a word.

Jacob Spanjaard has drawn A J Lubin's attention to a similarity between his painting 'language' and the awkward and jagged prose of the Letters, coming through even in translation as we receive the clumsy surge of his thought. Spanjaard proposes that an influence on both his literary and artistic style may have been the 'tachtigers', a group of Dutch writers who were experimenting at the time with syntax to overcome the limitations of correct usage.[9]

He had begun to sculpt in paint. Lubin suggests that with his liberal pigments he was in fact reproducing the juicy Dutch mud which came in on his boots and sullied the clean vicarage rooms so disgracefully. 'And when, later on, he gave up his dark browns and greys for brilliant yellows and blues, he would transform the repulsive dross with a heavenly glory.'

By increasing to the maximum the tactile, moulded quality of his surfaces he was inviting the spectator to reach out and touch them, and so make contact with worthier extensions of himself. Convinced that he was in some sense disembodied, he compensated with a throbbingly alive sensual art that would impinge physically on others and be impossible to ignore. Feeling his personality to be a wavering one, he emphasised realism and rejected fantasy in art. By insisting on the practice of starting at the centre and modelling outwards, rather than from outlines as taught at the Academy, he attacked the illusion of art itself and felt that 'the figures have backs even when one sees them from the front, there is airiness around the figures – *outside the paint.*' He fell foul of his teachers, but stood his ground: 'How flat, how dead and how dry-balled the results of that system are. . . . It is correct, it is correct, it is whatever you like, but it is *dead.*'[10] Drawing an outline around nothing encircled the very emptiness he feared. To plant himself at the living heart of a subject was to deny the void he fell into whenever his spirits plummeted and he existed again in a past time, denied human contact and wandering desolately, a non-person.

Unhappiness that has no obvious cause can sometimes well up from a sense of bereavement. Something inexplicable has orphaned us. When we use the word orphan we call up another word, 'family'. 'All happy families are alike,' runs Tolstoy's famous sentence at the start of *Anna Karenina*, 'but an unhappy family is unhappy after its own fashion.'

John Russell writes in *The Meaning of Modern Art* that during the nineteenth century, after political upheavals and the triumph of Darwinism, 'whole sections of humanity felt themselves orphaned.' Holland, like the United States, had become renowned 300 years ago as a refuge for emotional orphans. Persecuted peoples flocked there and were taken in. A Dutch family, and especially a clergyman's, would be familiar with the pathos of uprooted immigrants. Strangers were by definition sad persons.

Strictly speaking, Vincent was never an orphan. His mother outlived all three of her sons. Psychically, he was one. Though outwardly strong, he displayed signs from his earliest years of that 'failure to thrive' attributed by medical practitioners to a lack of parental love. Spending long periods away from home in his youth and young manhood and living a bleak, precarious exist-ence had made him a numbed, downcast, strangely moody character, striving and self-critical and totally lacking in confid-ence. His endless search for love and affection bears all the marks of orphanhood. His sadness at times was so profound that it could have led to death – a condition known in foundling homes as being given 'to the angels' – had it not been for the solace of art.

The worst thing that can befall an unhappy child, so we are told, is solitude. Vincent inhabited a world of intense solitude from an early age, finding it intolerable until he managed to change a secret agony into an inexhaustible resource. Even then he was forever being betrayed back to the most painful times of his life. When his father suddenly appeared in the school yard, Vincent flew sobbing into his arms. Abandonment can be felt as piercingly as this by a vulnerable child lost for a few minutes in a crowded store, or waiting hopelessly to be claimed in a 'lost and found' tent at a carnival.

One Sunday, walking alone down the boulevards, he felt the touch of spring. It was early March. As passionate an identifier as Whitman, he could soar with the lark in the spring air and in the next sentence of his letter despair with the young consumptive of twenty he had seen in the street, 'a girl . . . who will perhaps drown herself.'[11]

Bad times had arrived for Theo in Paris. No one wanted to buy pictures. A slump was depressing the whole of Europe; strikes were breaking out; thousands of the poor were on the move, homeless and starving. It may have been the need to share these common miseries which impelled Vincent to put his own health in danger. Or it may have been more personal, a discovery that the pains from an empty belly acted on his brain like the anodyne wished for by Hennebeau in Zola's *Germinal*, to kill 'the eternal pain' that visited him without reason. He was a ruin, he told Theo mournfully, old before his time, though his core was still sound. A turn in events could still save him, and Theo too. What did he mean? Well, Delacroix would have died an early death if he had not been cared for by a devoted mistress. It wasn't too late for them to find wives. Women were central to art, they taught one so much. So he had still not entirely given up hope of changing the course of his life through marriage. In the end it would happen vicariously, thanks to Theo, and be a very mixed blessing indeed.

10

PARIS IS PARIS

E ver an impulsive man, when Vincent set his heart on something he had to act. He was the kind of lover who must know
the truth, and he had fallen in love with his vision of Paris. It fed
his dreams, made his heart hot. He had to hurry to it and find
out if he was loved back. He would be free there, he could draw
and paint figures to his heart's content. The important studios
were there. An artistic revolution was simmering, a new one,
now that the Impressionist uprising had spent itself. He heard
rumours, he was tantalised by the mention of new names; he
couldn't wait. At the Academy he had met a couple of English
painters, Livens and Pimm, both of whom spoke rapturously of
the famous studios in Paris, Gerôme's, Cabanel's, Cormon's. If
he spruced himself up a bit, Theo would pull strings and get him
admitted to one of them.

This was a metamorphosed Paris, not the one he had actually
lived in as a young lovesick man thirteen years ago, where he
had stayed with his friend Gladwell in a garret, kept his nose
firmly stuck in the Bible, and ignored the scandal stirred up by
Claude Monet and his associates. Now he was 'longing terribly'
to immerse himself in the treasures of the Louvre and to catch up
with everything, walk the same streets as Zola, and inhale the
French air which, he was convinced, cleared the brain and did
you a world of good. 'Paris is Paris.'

First of all, though, he had to overcome Theo's resistance.
Helping Vincent from a distance was one thing, but having him
like a fizzing bomb in your own sitting room, disrupting your

191

career and antagonising your guests, was quite another. He made all manner of excuses, tried to re-route his brother back to Holland, harped on the financial difficulties. It was like trying to divert the course of a river. In his last fifteen letters from Antwerp Vincent bombarded him with the subject mercilessly. He brought it up forty times. He begged, cajoled, explained, reprimanded. It all boiled down to the same thing in the end: 'I have to go back one of these days.' Why not now?

'Be honest enough to let me go my own way,' he wrote impatiently, 'for I tell you that I do not want to quarrel, and I will not quarrel, but I will not be hampered in my career. And what can I do in the country? There is no chance, absolutely none, of making money with my work in the country, and there is such a chance in the city.'[1]

For Vincent, Antwerp was only a detour and an interlude on the road to Paris, his finishing school. Why all these obstacles, and what was the point, when his mind was made up? He had turned his back on Holland, its darkness, rigidity, taboos, and wanted what France epitomised: every kind of freedom and daring. It was feminine. It was the land of revolution. For years he had been saturated in the French writers, he adored Millet, and now Delacroix was his hero. Although his father was dead and relations with his mother were strained, nevertheless their values were planted inside him. His efforts to release himself into some greater reality would continue to the end of his days. Just to think of his parents' stories of a great uncle who had been 'infected' with French ideas and become an alcoholic was enough to make him react angrily in favour of France. Paris opened her arms, a sweet-smelling Magdalene. He stepped closer. His heart was light as a convert's; he had had his fill of *dolorosa*s. From 1886 he would drop the use of Dutch and write only in French.

He suddenly did the unforgiveable: landed one day on Theo's doorstep and so presented him with a *fait accompli*. Early in March a note was delivered to the smaller branch of Goupil's which Theo ran in the Boulevard Montmartre. Scrawled hastily in black crayon, it said: 'Do not be cross with me for having come all at once like this; I have thought about it so much. . . . Shall be at the Louvre from midday on or sooner. We'll fix things up, you'll see.'[2]

Unable to contain himself any longer, he had just arrived.

Lubin sees this as an act of spiteful resentment, but it is equally likely that he had simply lost patience with his brother's endless delaying tactics.

Although Theo had wanted Vincent to stay put until June, he did at least appreciate the gains. They would have each other's company, and by sharing Theo's modest apartment in the rue Laval, south of the boulevard de Clichy and the Place Pigalle, there would be only one rent to pay.

As soon as Vincent joined him, the tiny quarters seemed hopelessly cramped. The strain and claustrophobia were eased somewhat when Vincent took himself off every day to the studio of Fernand Cormon, where he had immediately enrolled. He spent four hours each morning there, and afternoons busied himself at the Louvre – called by Cézanne 'a book in which we learned to read' – studying and copying the masterpieces there and at the Luxembourg Palace.

He was in Paris, that was all that mattered. Nietzsche, another cruelly fettered man, had declared that it was every artist's true home, while Emerson compared a visit to Paris with a dose of morphine that would relieve any pain. Vincent sank into its brightly sparkling water and felt his dark world under crouching grey skies slip away from him. He loved the relief, but he was here to learn, to grow.

Cormon's studio, on the boulevard Clichy, was no distance from the apartment. Fernand Cormon was an academic painter specialising in history subjects, a good teacher and a tolerant man. He was a dark, sharp-featured, alarmingly thin fellow, his movements quick and nervy like a bird's. Toulouse Lautrec went there, as did Emile Bernard, later to be Vincent's friend. The following year Gauguin turned up. Vincent was older than most of the others, and the rowdy horseplay of the students grated on his nerves. Newcomers would be subjected to humiliating initiation rites, but the dour little man from the north was left alone, presumably because something violent in his demeanour worried them. Artistic discussion raged to and fro, Seurat's colour theories dividing them into two camps. When the excitable Vincent became worked up he was an awesome sight, almost frothing at the mouth and trembling with emotion.

A fellow pupil, A S Hartrick, draws a vivid word picture of him at this period. 'Van Gogh was a rather weedy man with pinched features, red hair and beard, and a light blue eye. He had an extraordinary way of pouring out sentences if he got started, in Dutch, English, and French, then glancing back at you over his shoulder and hissing through his teeth.'[3] In Hartrick's opinion the French students had no great liking for him, staying civil with him in the hope of selling their pictures to his brother, who had begun to collect work by the younger generation in the upper rooms of his gallery. To put it bluntly, they thought he was 'cracked', his work too messy and personal to appeal to them. All the same he seemed harmless enough. They had to admit he worked like a demon, hurling himself into things and completing three studies to their one. He stayed three months.

Later, Lautrec would sketch one of the finest likenesses of Vincent. The portrait, in pastel and watercolour, is alive with tension. Vincent sits leaning forward on his forearms at a café table, listening intently. His head bristles fiercely. The face is in profile, the hunched shoulders about to propel him forward. The impression puts one in mind of Ottoline Morrell's initial response to D H Lawrence. She remarked on his flame-like being and thought how much he resembled the portraits of van Gogh she had seen. After reading a life of the painter, Lawrence told her: 'He couldn't get out of the trap, poor man, so he went mad.'

Vincent's extraordinary series of self-portraits, twenty-five in all, more than in any other period, show him changing his appearance in Paris and even his physiognomy to suit the image he had of himself at different times and in different moods. 'In some he appears small and retiring,' Lubin writes, 'in others strong and audacious; in some contemplative, in others a man of action. Sometimes he is coarse and ugly, only to be refined and dignified at other times.'[4] In the earliest of them, painted between April and June of his first year in Paris, he is got up to look like a man-about-town. The ill-cut beard of Antwerp is now soft and washed, the face has a scholar's pallor. On his head is a dark homburg, probably borrowed from Theo. His shoulders are draped in an expensive winter coat. Another gentlemanly portrait from the following year reveals Vincent acting the part of a man of substance in his fine coat, high white collar, and grey felt hat, but struck dumb by his impersonation in the mirror, his eyes sliding fearfully sideways, his cheeks sunken. The full face is an illusion, about to vanish when we look away or blink. Here he is dressed up for his mother to admire, not him. Going to a doctor in Antwerp he had been relieved and flattered when the man saw nothing intellectual in the cast of his features and thought he might be dealing with a manual worker.

In Paris he went to see Theo's doctor. By then his health was recovering from the punishment he had dealt out in Antwerp. He had his bad teeth extracted and a dental plate fitted. Theo wrote a dutiful report to their mother, telling her about Vincent's dental work, and how much fitter and in better spirits he was now. Curiously, Vincent's health improved as Theo's deteriorated, as if they were physically joined, so that when one of them flourished the other was made to weaken. Vincent's was by far the stronger will, and his black rages, irate comments, and multiplying grievances wore the younger man down when he came home tired from a long day at the gallery. It was no good either escaping to bed; Vincent would trail after him, draw up a chair, and continue into the small hours.

With only seven letters surviving from Vincent's stay in Paris it is difficult to know for certain just what was going on. By not returning to Cormon's he was in effect admitting once again to an inability to get on with people. Distancing himself from unwelcome influences enabled him to continue along the 'dog's path' he had chosen for himself. Theo's wail of despair to his sister Wil only tells us what we know already, that Vincent was extremely hard to cope with. 'No one wants to come and see me any more because it always ends in quarrels, and besides, he is so untidy that the room looks far from attractive. I wish he would go and live by himself. He sometimes mentions it, but if I were to tell him to go away, it would just give him a reason to stay.' He was bewildered by the 'two persons in one' living inside his brother. One was marvellously gifted, tender, sensitive, and the other a merciless egotist with no heart at all. His sister thought he should give up on Vincent, but for Theo the bond was too strong to break. 'It is such a peculiar case,' he replied. 'If only he had another profession I would long ago have done what you advise me.'[5]

Behind the protestations lies the fact that Vincent's love for his brother was a jealous love. If Theo could have only given himself

195

up to illness instead of fighting it, then it would have been a different story. Vincent would no doubt have cared for him as selflessly as he did his mother after her fall. Everything had gone swimmingly in his relations with Sien while she was a sick person in obvious need of his love. Theo was a charming, kindly, and considerate man, but his puritanical Dutch industriousness kept his nose firmly to the grindstone. Vincent was prepared to exhibitionistically bare his weaknesses but Theo kept his well hidden. One of Vincent's most repeated complaints was that his brother withheld things from him. Often this took the form of accusations of stinginess, of a concern for his own career at the expense of Vincent's. Money was easier to talk about than a less easily grasped emotional currency.

Vincent's behaviour when at close quarters with Theo is strikingly similar in character to the boorish manners he displayed at home with his parents. He left paints around in Theo's apartment for people to tread in. He picked up one of Theo's socks and absent-mindedly cleaned off a painting with it. He littered the place with his dirty underwear. He invented grudges where no grounds for them existed. He rebelled, provoked, reproached. In short, he became the adolescent rebel without a cause.

Theo was as solicitous and responsible and as infuriatingly virtuous as any parent. Vincent both wanted and did not want this younger brother for a father, who passed judgement on him by falling silent, opposing him by refusing to be ill. Theo for his part must have asked himself a hundred times what he had done to deserve this thankless brother who was liable to glare furiously at him like a reprimanded child for no reason.

Madly irritable though he could be, Vincent was never more prolific than during his time in Paris. For the first time he produced more oils than drawings. Colour had gained the ascendency over graphic work. Deprived of the models at Cormon's, he painted flowers as if they were women. *Fritillarias in a Copper Vase* could be a study of a gold, glowing woman, announcing her hips brassily in a fat glisten of circles, raising green fronds of arms, laughing joyously in peach clouds of blossom. He painted Montmartre scenes, walking down the twisty cobbled slope of the Rue Lepic to the old village of Montmartre. The stunted little garden plots behind railings and the parks where nameless people sat intrigued and charmed him. He painted from different viewpoints the Moulin de la Galette, just as his beloved Corot had done many years ago. It was Corot who, according to Picasso, 'discovered the morning'.

He felt part of a French Renaissance. With every day that passed he felt freer, more French, adoring Paris with an expatriate's grateful passion. He wanted France to be his real motherland. Setting out with a large canvas slung on his back he would divide the space into boxes and fill each box with its own subject: boats, islets, neat restaurants with their pretty blinds under oleanders, derelict houses with their paint peeling, neglected corners. Whether he painted a person or a slice of park, he rendered it 'with the same utter lack of prejudice', wrote Rilke. A bench waiting for its occupant would express the tiredness and simplicity of the man or woman yet to arrive. Objects and human beings had the ordinary look about them that their life in the world without resistance and without pretensions had left them with.

One of his first paintings of Montmartre shows that he had already, with incredible speed, begun to assimilate the secrets of French art and adapt them for his own purposes. The delicacy of atmosphere has an indefinable emotional glow; the pearly greys of Paris, oyster grey, dove grey, seep down from the sky and pervade every element of the picture, fences and lamp-posts, gardens and trees, and wash them back to the blurred ocean of the distant city. Fences and posts tilt gently. The very irregularities and tiltings are from the heart, as exquisitely tender as the barely suggested stirring of the leafless trees.

His flower pieces gained in luminosity from his study of the work of Adolphe Monticelli, discovered and collected by Theo. Monticelli's rich colours, glowing like jewels on dark velvety backgrounds, stimulated him to seek out the few facts he gleaned about his life. The artist's life was a sad one. Saddled with the reputation of a drunkard and harassed by poverty, he died in Marseilles, possibly by his own hand, 'dreaming of the sun and of love and gaiety.'[6]

Besides painting flowers and Montmartre street scenes and the windmills of the Butte he went further afield, painting views of the outskirts, bridges, boats on the Seine, cafés, wheatfields, small factories, open roads. His excursions took him as far as nearby towns like Asnières, where Emile Bernard lived with his parents. Bernard's father thought a career in art was no career at all, and Vincent quarrelled hotly with him. Emile, a young man of twenty-three, had found a champion.

In Asnières he struck up a friendship with a woman one would not have associated with him, the Countess de la Boisière. He was attracted to her, suggests Lubin, just as he was to Eugenia's mother, by the obvious affection the countess and her daughter had for each other. All the same it was a strange liaison for a man to make who had created a furore at Cormon's with his compassionate painting of two battered boots, hoping to convey what he called *les petites misères de la vie humaine*. Post-mortem experts have been confounded by this picture, which appears to be of a pair but is in fact two left boots! What does it symbolise, if anything? It is anyone's guess.

Theo hit on a solution to the problem of living with Vincent. In June, the two brothers moved into a bigger apartment on the third floor of a building at 54 Rue Lepic, on the hill north of the Place Pigalle. Things immediately looked more hopeful. They had a grand view of Paris spreading far and wide below them. There was a large living room with a fireplace, a bedroom for each of them and a room which would serve as a studio for Vincent, though not very satisfactorily. Sometimes he would work in the basement of the house, or at the house of a friend he had made at Cormon's. One of their neighbours, Fourmentin, said later that he knew the two gentlemen upstairs must be brothers because they looked so much alike. At this time Theo had a goatee. From a photograph that has survived of him the resemblance is indeed marked. Trudging in from the suburbs, Vincent would have had the disreputable appearance of those painters who habitually dabbed their brushes on their sleeves. Someone called him a walking example of Pointillism. The neighbours would have had no trouble deciding which of these two foreigners was the artist.

The ménage at Rue Lepic soon included Andries Bonger, a friend of Theo's and the brother of his future wife. He moved in with them that summer as he needed somewhere to sleep. Perhaps by his presence he defused the situation somewhat. Then Theo decided to give shelter to one of his mysterious females in distress, a woman known to us only as 'S'. She was so unbalanced that Theo soon lost his nerve, telling the others, 'either she gets out or I get out'. Vincent advised against ejecting her, though he admitted that she was 'seriously deranged'. This is confirmed by Andries Bonger.

Vincent, however, was of the opinion that Theo would suffer remorse and worse if by his action he drove the woman to suicide. It could leave him a 'broken man'. He came up with an amazing proposal, which was that he would take her off somewhere and if necessary marry her. It repeated the pattern of his previous offers of marriage, to Sien and to Margot. In both cases he was motivated by pity. But this was more an impulse than an idea. Andries, it seemed, talked him out of it.

Gauguin tells the story, in his *Intimate Journals*, of another impulse. Vincent had just pocketed five francs for a picture sold to a shopkeeper. A sad-looking whore gave him a wan smile in passing and Vincent promptly handed her his five francs, then ran off 'as though ashamed of his generosity'. Another time he caught sight of Vincent in winter hurrying towards the outer boulevards in a sheepskin coat and a cap made of rabbit fur, looking like a cattle drover.

However fraught Vincent's relations were with some people, he had no reservations about Père Tanguy, who had a colour shop where artists like Monet, Renoir, and Cézanne met and talked. He was soon fond of the friendly little man, who gave him paints on credit and put his work, along with the unwanted canvases of other artists, in the 'little mortuary chapel' of his shop window. Vincent, it is rumoured, met Cézanne here. If he did, it was their only meeting.

Tanguy, a gentle radical of sixty, had served time on a prison ship for subversive activity. Vincent called into his shop frequently and painted three portraits of the owner. In the most famous, Tanguy is posed self-consciously, like a combination of primitive photograph and medieval icon, absolutely frontal and against a backdrop of Japanese prints. The effect is at the same time Buddha-like in its serenity and warm like an embrace. The tightly clasped hands are workman's hands. The eyes and homely features reflect back Vincent's love for the man and for the oasis of bright and deep colour where he lives.

Tanguy actually sold one of Vincent's pictures for twenty francs. This must have helped their friendship, which flourished until it was marred by Madame Tanguy objecting to the amount of credit he was being allowed. Tanguy was forced to ask for his account to be settled, because his 'old witch of a wife got wind of what was going on and opposed it.'

He also became intimate for a time with a café proprietress, Agostina Segatori, the owner of 'Le Tambourin'. Vincent left paintings with her. His *Woman at 'Le Tambourin'* is assumed to be her. The eyes are set asymmetrically to accentuate her sadness. She sits wistfully at a round table alone, a cigarette burning between her fingers. Before her is a glass of beer.

Segatori's café went into bankruptcy and Vincent trundled off his paintings in a wheelbarrow. This seems to have concluded the affair, and Vincent commented: 'Just now she is in a bad way; she is neither a free agent nor a mistress in her own house, and worst of all she is ill and in pain.' It was enough to excuse any differences they might have had, for he added, 'I still have some affection for her and I hope she still has for me, too.'[7] Sickness, and ill-treatment by others, as with Sien and Margot, activated the pity which for him was the most genuine love.

He was on sufficiently friendly terms with Lautrec to call on him, and Suzanne Valadon, a model to many artists before becoming an artist in her own right, spoke of meeting a Dutchman named van Gogh at Lautrec's studio. Nesto Jacommetti, in her life of Valadon, describes how the red-headed Dutchman – who insisted on being called Vincent – arrived every Sunday and unwrapped a roll of wrapped canvases. No one took the slightest notice; no one said anything; nor did Vincent. His face grim, he watched the cocktail drinkers (Lautrec was one of the first Frenchmen to mix cocktails), then packed up his pictures without a word and marched off. Valadon was furious and ashamed at her friends' indifference. All painters are swine, she muttered once, then shouted it aloud. She could be quite rowdy when in a temper. Her own work shows how impressed and influenced she had been by the paintings she had seen laid out on the studio floor.

After Vincent's death Emile Bernard wrote an article giving his first impressions of the man he would soon befriend: 'Red-haired, with a goatee, rough moustache, shaven skull, eagle eye, incisive mouth as if he were about to speak; medium height, stocky without being in the least fat, lively gestures, jerky step, such was van Gogh, with his everlasting pipe. . . . And what dreams he had: gigantic exhibitions, philanthropic communities of artists, colonies to be founded in the south, and the conquest of public media to re-educate the masses – who used to understand art in the past . . .'. When Bernard visited the Rue Lepic he was shown a mass of work spilling out of boxes from Holland, and finally *The Potato Eaters*. He was dumbfounded by the 'fearful canvas of remarkable ugliness and yet with a disturbing life. . . . Poor folk at a meal in a primitive hovel, under a dreary lamplight, with astonishing labourers' faces with enormous noses, thick lips, and with vacuous and wild expressions.'[8]

An inside story only becomes available when Theo takes himself off to Holland for the summer and the correspondence briefly resumes. This was when his affair with La Segatori ended, prompting further philosophical ruminations on the subject of women and art. His disaffected friend had procured an abortion – unless, that is, she had had a miscarriage. Uncertain as to the fate of his pictures, he thought she would treat him fairly and not let the receivers get their hands on them. She wasn't a bad person, as people said, and if she trampled on his toes a bit, well, he probably deserved it. At least she didn't trample on his heart. 'As for me – I feel I am losing the desire for marriage and children, and now and then it saddens me that I should be feeling like that at thirty-five just when it should be the opposite.'[9]

It gave him a grudge against this rotten painting which was devouring him like a greedy lover, and he quoted Richepin: 'The love of art means loss of real love.' Reversed, it was equally true, he observed. Real love made you disgusted with art.

Now he felt thoroughly sorry for himself. 'I feel already old and broken at times, yet still enough of a lover to be a real enthusiast for painting. One must have ambition in order to succeed, and ambition seems to me absurd.'[10] The truth was that he was becoming disgusted with Paris, by its din and racket and bad air, above all sickened by the swarms of ambitious artists infesting it like fleas.

In a similar mood about this time he explained to his sister Wil half jokingly that he was 'making swift progress towards growing into a little old man, you know, with wrinkles and a tough beard and a number of false teeth, and so on. But what does it matter? I have a dirty and hard profession – painting.' His own youth had gone, but he hoped to replace it with pictures full of youth and freshness, his 'babies'.

He was still prone, as ever, to sudden plunges into desolation. These could afflict him anywhere, at any time. 'Old cab horses have large beautiful eyes,' he said once, 'as heartbroken as Christians sometimes have.'[11] To Wil, the one sister who was dear to him, he recommended the French naturalists, Zola, Flaubert, Maupassant, Daudet, Huysmans, and then reprimanded himself for sounding despondent. 'In these days, I believe, Jesus himself would say to those who sit down in a state of melancholy, It is not here, get up and go forth. Why do you seek the living among the dead?'[12] And he ended his letter to Theo with an insouciant flourish: 'It's better to have a gay life of it than commit suicide. Remember me to all at home.'

More and more restless, he would soon be ready to 'get up and go forth'. He spoke vaguely of taking himself off somewhere down south, but for the moment this was purely negative; he simply wanted to get away from 'the sight of so many painters who disgust me as men.'

One painter who didn't repel him was Pissarro, an understanding, hospitable, and patient fellow. It was Camille Pissarro who told him that painters 'must boldly exaggerate the effects of either harmony or discord which colour produces.' Much older than Vincent, with a venerable grey beard flowing down over his throat, he dressed like a countryman and treated him like a father his son – a father he would have preferred to his own. There had been 'Father' Millet the peasant painter, 'Father' Michelet, 'Father' Corot, and here at last, instead of a wise old man plucked from the annals of art, was a real flesh-and-blood stand-in.

Like Vincent, Pissarro admired Millet, and followed his example, drawing and painting peasants at work. He had been one of the few artists to extend a helping hand to Cézanne, another extremely awkward customer. He favoured mutual aid and communes for painters, topics dear to Vincent's heart. It was through Pissarro, who had painted at Auvers near Paris in the 1870s and knew Dr Gachet there, that Vincent came to go there himself in the last months of his life. After his death, Pissarro said, 'I always knew he would either surpass us all or end up a madman. I never thought he would do both.'[13]

11

CLOSER TO THE SUN

Vincent, a man of violent extremes, now loathed the city he had once likened to a softly welcoming woman. Paris had the 'tainted air of a hospital', and the exhibitions, private galleries, 'everything, everything, are in the clutches of fellows who intercept all the money.' It went much deeper than that. No matter what one did or what efforts one made, it all came to nothing. Paris represented nullity, everything that was diseased and debauched. The French had cold little minds, they were rotters. Living there meant becoming like them, incapable of doing anything worthwhile, stupefied, only half alive.

Most of all he loathed the deplorable state he was in. He was drinking heavily, red wine and 'quantities' of absinthe, and for some mysterious reason he was banned, so Theo asserted, from painting in the streets. His irascible temper caused one unpleasant scene after another. Models refused to pose for him.

He departed as abruptly as he had arrived. Like all his apparently sudden moves, this one was long premeditated. When he had got right away he wrote telling his sister of a series of 'not very seemly love affairs, from which I emerge as a rule damaged and shamed and little else.' Not that he regretted any of it, because 'in the years gone by, when I should have been in love, I gave myself up to religious and socialistic devotions, and considered art a holier thing than I do now. . . . Why is religion or justice or art so very holy?'[1]

His 'rising fury' had nearly brought on a stroke, he told Gauguin several months later, and he was well on the way to being an alcoholic. Paris, which had taught him so much about colour, had paradoxically sapped his strength. 'And sometimes you lack all desire to throw yourself heart and soul into art, and to get well. You know you are a cab horse and that it's the same old cab you'll be hitched up to again: that you'd rather live in a meadow with the sun, a river and other horses for company, likewise free, and the act of procreation.'[2]

Often swayed in his decisions by literature, he may have settled on Arles after reading Daudet's *Tartarin of Tarascon*. The romantic descriptions of the region were alluring. Long before this, however, he had been attracted to the idea of a milder climate and a stronger sun. With Monticelli in mind he talked of Marseilles as a possible destination. He hoped to be rejuvenated, his faith restored. His idol Millet he saw as a true believer, with a 'miner's faith'. There was little genuine faith in Paris. You were dragged down by an insidious enervation of the spirit and before long were fit for nothing but meaningless promiscuity, which only drained you further. It was absurd, degrading. The root of the evil, he concluded obscurely, lay in the 'fatal weakening of families from generation to generation.' And the replacing of all forms of physical sympathy with money-intercourse. Only a vast revolution would sweep it away.

Nearly forty years on, D H Lawrence was in Paris and reaching a remarkably similar conclusion, declaring that he would have no peace until he reached the Mediterranean; 'all the rest can go to hell. I can't help feeling that the north has gone evil . . . morally, ethically. It's anti-life now.' The world was a lovely place if one avoided man, and especially man close-packed in cities. One shouldn't blame God for this world, thought Vincent – 'it's just a study that didn't come off . . . slapped together in a hurry on one of his bad days.'[3]

Another work having a bearing on his choice of country may have been Multatuli's Dutch classic *Max Havelaar*, a book published when Vincent was seven but which influenced his youth in the same way that *Uncle Tom's Cabin* did. 'I don't say: there I saw a woman who was as beautiful as this or that,' wrote Multatuli of the women of Arles. 'No, they were all so beautiful, and so it was impossible to fall in love there for good and all, because the very next woman always put the previous one right out of your mind.' What could be more enticing?

The author of *Max Havelaar* was E D Dekker, who chose a pseudonym for himself which meant: I suffered much, or I endured much. Supposedly a tract written to expose the treatment of the Javanese by their Dutch rulers, it was in reality a satire, and a biting one, mounted against the Dutch bourgeois and Dutch officialdom at home as well as abroad. Issued in an English translation early in this century, it has a preface by Lawrence, who pounced on it with evident relish. For him it had 'a passionate, honourable hate' under its missionary guise. Multatuli hates the powers-that-be with a passionate intensity. Even when he harps away on pity for the oppressed, 'the chick of pity comes out of the egg of hate'.[4]

What does this tell us about van Gogh? Towards the end of his stay in Paris he fell into a hatred which sounds as venomous as Multatuli's, and without a mask to disguise it. His growing revulsion for civilised society was never more virulent, so much so that it threatened his very sanity. His misanthropy equals that of Lawrence in Cornwall, dreaming of a flit gun that would exterminate humanity. Vincent's urge to go south had more than one motive. In part it issued from a repudiation of his class, his grisly experience of Christianity, the compromises of Parisian artists, and his brother's unavoidable compromise. He had a hankering to go south and to keep on going, until he had left the white races behind. Perhaps he imagined too that he would leave behind his own shameful connections. He would have liked to do what Gauguin wished to do, and soon did, sail away from it all, leaving it to rot.

Unlike Gauguin, he had no delusions about his own worth. He suffered, as we have seen, from a deep sense of personal unworthiness. If there was a paradise waiting beyond the horizon, he had no passport for it. He would only foul it up. He had caught the germ which lurked in all moderns and there was no help for him; he had to live with the consequences of his neurosis like everyone else. Love, even love, was no more than a microbe, or so he had been told.

Vincent's deep-seated hatred has been somewhat played down by those biographers and art historians eager to canonise him as a saint of art. His sainthood was of a different order. Like everything else about him it was modern. He was on his way to being a saint who did not believe in God, but in ecstasy, the kind of ecstasy we associate with sex, or the extension of sex, if that were possible. He dreamed of happiness for himself in his day, and one day for us all. He really thought that it was the only thing worth having. 'Compared with happiness,' writes J C Powys, 'fame is nothing, ambition is nothing, work is nothing, progress is nothing. But this happiness which the (modern) saint sets about to evoke is not the same thing as excitement or pleasure. It is a calm, deep-flowing satisfaction, mounting up at intervals into tidal waves of quivering ecstasy.'[5] And leading, Vincent believed, to the shores of a great peace, declared by Paul to be that peace which passes all understanding. Sometimes he saw it as lying on the other side of death, and asked once: 'Is the whole of life visible to us, or isn't it rather that this side of death we see only one hemisphere?'[6]

Theo had begun to acknowledge that his brother was an extraordinary being. Once separated from him, he at once missed him acutely. Despite all their differences, he now freely admitted what would soon be impossible to deny, that he had been in the presence of someone who may one day be great. How did one replace a person like Vincent? Theo's flat seemed emptier than ever. Painters he knew confirmed what he increasingly felt, that 'his knowledge and clear perception of the world are incredible. . . . He is one of the champions of new ideas – or rather, as there is nothing new under the sun, of the regeneration of old ideas which have been corrupted by routine and have lost their colour. Furthermore, he has such a great heart that he is always trying to do something for others.'[7]

Vincent's imminent departure brought the two brothers back together again. Theo took Vincent along to Seurat's studio, where the artist was at work on his big experimental painting, *Parade*. The van Gogh brothers also went to some Wagner concerts. Vincent was impressed by Wagner's bold use of an immense canvas to produce astonishingly intimate effects.

Before leaving, Vincent enacted a little ritual that was meant to communicate his love for his brother. He asked Emile Bernard around to the flat and between them they 'composed' Vincent's room to give the impression that he was still installed there. They put up fresh Japanese woodcuts, leaned a canvas against the easel and others against the walls. Theo would still have him for a companion when he came home, even though only in spirit. Interiors, like chairs, were for him palpable reminders of the person who had used them. Then Vincent embraced his friend and extracted a firm promise from him. He must join him before long, 'for it is in the South that we must create the studio of the future.' Shabby, worn-out, jaded, he couldn't wait to get away from those streets where 'nothing is fresh'.

He left Paris on 20 February, 1888, a Sunday. As usual, winter found him at his lowest ebb. He arrived in Arles the same day. Homeless again and alone, knowing absolutely no one, he saw himself as an adventurer who had no wish to be one, but without choice in the matter. All the same it was better, less bitter, to be a stranger in a strange land than outcast in one's own family and country.

Lautrec was apparently one person who had suggested Arles to him. This could have been in order to get the Dutchman out of his hair. Vincent had been wondering whether Lautrec, with his wealthy background, could be persuaded to sponsor one of his plans for an artists' colony. Alas, the very word community was anathema to Lautrec. An apocryphal story has it that he dreamed up Arles as the ideally remote place to send this wild painter who plagued him, thereby putting plenty of distance between them with tact and benevolence.

Approaching Arles, Vincent looked out of the carriage window and imagined he had reached Japan. 'Childish, isn't it?' he wrote to Gauguin. There was about two feet of snow everywhere, and more was falling. On the journey he had noticed rows of small round trees with grey-green leaves which he thought were lemon trees. Looking across the huge plain to the mountains in the distance, and at a sky as luminous as the snow, it struck him as being exactly like a Japanese print.

He got out at the station and made his way into the town down an avenue of plane trees and crossed the public gardens with its three clumps of trees. Three weeks later he returned to paint a picture of the scene, showing the planes, a weeping willow, stretches of grass and bushes. The gardens no longer exist.

He passed between the red stone towers of the Porte de la Cavalerie and found himself in the centre of the town. Bombing destroyed this gateway in World War Two, and also the building where he lodged, the Hôtel-Restaurant Carrel. It was no more than a hostel. He took a small attic room. From the window he could see the ancient Roman arena.

Ironically, he had landed in an area which had enormous stretches of flat land and reminded him at once of Holland. Like his native country it was a huge delta land, and in this respect unlike any other part of Provence. Vincent was pleased to be in a country similar to his own but without its dull darkness and its perpetual rain.

Something else he could have hardly anticipated was the decadent squalor of the South, becoming more evident as the weather got warmer. Lawrence was another northern traveller who objected to the squalid conditions he encountered in Sardinia. Less fastidious than the Englishman, Vincent was nevertheless still a basically clean-living Dutchman in principle, if not always in practice. Somehow one's own squalor seems less objectionable than other people's. Prosper Merimee wrote that the Provence of the Rhone Valley was a sad and dirty place. Stendhal called Arles 'a hole'. When Gauguin arrived towards the end of the year he had no hesitation in calling it 'the dirtiest hole in the south'.

One building that has remained unchanged, although the shop façade is modernised, is opposite a café where he positioned himself to paint a pork butcher's that first February. In *The Charcuterie*, a section of pavement, the shop front itself, a passer-by, all in the frame of café window, are drawn freely with the brush, without charcoal or any preliminaries. This scintillating little picture, in blues, greens, and ochres, has all the verve and freshness of a Matisse. Like a gaily waving flag it signals the onset of Vincent's greatest period. His long years of preparation and study were about to bear fruit; the longed-for breakthrough was at hand.

In May he painted, with the same facility, dispensing with props as before, a still-life comprising a blue enamel iron coffee pot, a royal blue cup and saucer, a milk jug with blue and white checks, arranged on a blue tablecloth against a yellow background. Among the crockery lie two oranges and three lemons. Victories like this must have sent his spirits soaring, and some fabulous weather had arrived. He rushed out to execute a view of Arles itself, moving to the edge of town where he had discovered an immense sea of buttercups. These meadows are divided in his composition by a ditch full of violet irises, his emblematic flower before the sunflower displaced it. Behind, one could glimpse only some red roofs and a tower belonging to the town, the rest of it hidden by the green foliage of fig trees. Think of it, he wrote jubilantly to his friend Bernard, 'that sea of yellow with the band of violet irises, and in the background that coquettish little town of pretty women!'[8]

Clearly the ominous inner storms of his Paris days had abated. Letters to Theo stopped griping; lugubrious reflections on his premature old age were soon being elbowed aside by happy accounts of work done, discourses on technique, busily drawn up plans for future projects. The identity-seeking crises which had driven him to the 'mirror-test' of those relentlessly probing self-portraits, psychoanalysing his own condition as doctor and patient, were for the time being no longer dominant.

Antiquities and ruins in the district held no interest for him. He was looking for something else – the undiscovered, the neglected. As Dunlop remarks, 'Vincent had the ability to find subjects which others might have ignored,'[9] and he soon found himself swamped by ideas. Some instinct kept telling him that he had the chance here to do unheard-of things. He did make at least fifty trips to the Abbey at Montmajour, an ancient ruin perched on a hill above the plains, but only as a vantage point from which to survey the flat landscape. When the vigorous sun shone on it all, 'sometimes it is as enormously gay as Holland is gloomy.' The Gothic cathedral of St Trophime and its portal were admittedly beautiful, though the grandeur chilled him; it was somehow cruel and monstrous 'like a Chinese nightmare'.

He was more at home observing the Zouave soldiers, the brothels, 'the adorable little Arlesiennes going to their first Communion, the priest in his surplice, who looks like a dangerous rhinocerous, the people drinking absinthe.'[10] It was so different from the world he had known at home. Avid for inner change, he altered his attitudes if not his character, and was soon urging these changes on his sister Wil, who had sent him a piece of writing and wondered if she should aim for a literary career. Whatever you do, he told her emphatically, don't think you have to grind away at studies in order to produce literature. 'No, my dear sister, learn how to dance, or fall in love – play any number of pranks rather than take up study in Holland. It serves no other purpose than to make one dull-witted, and so I don't want to hear it mentioned.'[11]

His new geographical location gave him a taste for the kind of psychological freedom he had never enjoyed, one he thought was possessed by the working-class society of Arles. 'I profoundly despise regulations, institutions, etc,' he wrote, 'in short, what I am looking for is different from dogma.'[12]

However, his admiration for the apparently careless, happy-go-lucky customs of these people was soon being adjusted. For one thing, their lethargy exasperated him. It was preposterous; even the simplest things were hard to get. And the same with food in the little restaurants he frequented. Could he get a baked potato? Impossible. Rice, then, or macaroni? 'None left, or else it's messed up in grease, or else they aren't cooking it today, and they'll explain that it's tomorrow's dish, there's no room on the stove, and so on.' Gradually he delved under the surface to a darker, more sinister reality that was harsh and fierce, full of devilry and contradiction, alternately marvellous and monstrous like the weather. They were capable of immense warmth, and they could be violent and cruel. He soon concluded that they were on the verge of madness, a sickly lot on the whole; everything 'has a sick and battered look about it.' All the same, he asserted, it suited him because he was by instinct a low-brow. He would have been like a fish out of water if he had gone to Antibes, Nice, or Menton – like Monet, for instance. The Arlesien might leave plenty to be desired, with their fever, hallucinations, lunacy, but was he any better? 'I am thinking of frankly accepting my role of madman, the way Degas accepted the part of a notary.' At least he wasn't made to feel inferior here. 'We understand each other like members of the same family.'[13]

Soon after arriving at Arles he was given a taste of their dark side. In a brawl outside a local brothel, two Italians killed a couple of Zouaves. The Zouaves belonged to a French infantry regiment stationed in Algeria. Their military costume was flamboyant: a red fez, dark blue jacket, and fiery red billowing trousers. A Provençal mob gathered and was intent on lynching the killers, but were so excited and disorganised that the Italians got clean away.

In May, Vincent quarrelled with the innkeeper at his lodgings.

For once he was justified. He moved to somewhere cheaper. Then the swindler demanded money he said he was owed, hanging on to Vincent's belongings in order to get it. Vincent approached the local court. The verdict went in his favour.

The investigation maddened him, for he was up to his eyes in work. For two months the orchards had been in blossom. Soon he was clamouring for more canvases, paints, brushes, and he begged Theo to send them quickly, for he had to make haste, nature wouldn't wait. Anyway, he must look on these things as sound investments.

Although a reclusive man, he was not short of company. In the first month he acquired an odd collection of friends; a grocer who sold painting materials, a justice of the peace, a Danish artist by the name of Petersen who had a nervous disorder, and Boch, a Belgian artist of thirty whom he eventually dispatched to the Borinage to explore its artistic possibilities. There was also Milliet, a Zouave second lieutenant, befriended in August at the brothel used by the soldiers. Milliet was good-looking, 'only twenty-five, God damn it', an easy-going youngster who would, he thought, suit him very well for the portrait of a lover he had in mind.

He set to work and immediately ran into difficulties. Milliet posed badly, had little free time, and couldn't seem to keep his legs still. Any day now, Vincent reported, he would have to return 'to his fucking garrison, as he says'. That meant saying a tender farewell to the 'hussies and tarts' who were all so fond of him. The man made so light of lovemaking, Vincent remarked, that he nearly despised love itself. As for his own sexual powers, he felt they were on the wane. He looked forward to the relief of being impotent. He had once regarded sex as essential for one's health, but now, deeply immersed in his creative work, he thought continence was better for the committed artist: he agreed with Balzac. He told his friend Bernard in plain language: 'Painting and fucking are not compatible; it weakens the brain, which is a bloody nuisance.'

Nevertheless, he was far from dead to the erotic ambience of certain motifs. Declaring himself to be a different creature from when he first came south, he explained that he was writing his letter in a public garden, quite close to 'the street of the kind girls', and the comings and goings he witnessed gave a touch of Boccaccio to the spot.

When spring broke and a deluge of blossom drowned him, the strain of working so fast made him reach out in the evenings for some release and some outlet for his excited thoughts. It was 'the mental labour of balancing six essential colours' that wore him out. But that was a small price to pay for the ability he now had to realise himself fully in paint. He wrote about the day's work to his brother, now and then to friends, and he resorted to drink. He drank the local raw red wine and the cheapest absinthe. Red, blue, yellow, orange, lilac, green – the colours buzzed madly in his head. The sheer effort of calculation went on incessantly, 'with one's mind strained to the utmost, like an actor on the stage in a difficult part.'[14]

He often thought of Monticelli, 'that excellent painter' who drank heavily and went off his head. At the back of his mind he still regarded Arles as a temporary halt on the way to Marseilles, where Monticelli had lived and worked. Meanwhile, for ease and distraction, it seemed the only solution was 'to stun oneself with a lot of drinking or heavy smoking.'[15]

Why did he maintain such a killing pace? Nature here was such an enticement, he said. He was continually ravaged by its extraordinary beauty. Strange to say, he was not referring to 'the scorched, trivial scenery' of his part of Provence, but to the light, the marvellous blue heaven, the sun shedding a pale sulphur radiance that was so soft, 'as lovely as the combination of heavenly blues and yellows in a Van der Meer of Delft.' If only he could equal that!

A late van Gogh combines fearful haste with foetal growth, his perspectives thrusting us deep into the canvas as if we had boarded a nineteenth-century train. And the deep country we penetrate is stirring with the morphogenesis of its plants and trees and geology. Topographically accurate it might be, but its realism is elsewhere, in its sensations, prophesies, idealism. The Fauves who came after him, taking their cue from him, present us with a frontality which is all energy and surface boldness but has little to do with his battle to break through to air, more air – or, as Lawrence would say, *more life* – and to take us with him. We board his train with a mixture of elation and trepidation, knowing that at any moment his mental torment can derail us, just as our own hyperconscious states have been derailing us since then; though without leaving us any precious freight of intimacy, and without the discovery of any hope that we may become reunited with the universe. Only too often we are left standing in the midst of rubble.

Vincent's diet was still the staple one of bread and cheese, except that he had replaced milk and water with red wine. And for two months he was permanently drunk on orchards. From the end of January onwards the almond trees – planted out of reach of the strong winds – had been in leaf. From the beginning of March he was in a country of flowering orchards, broad masses of whiteness and pinkness suspended under the sky so discreetly and yet exuberantly that he thought he must be in Pierre Loti's Far East. The intoxicating blossom kept coming, on almond trees, cherries, peaches, plums, apricots, pears, and apples. By 20 April he had completed ten pictures of orchards and was still working furiously, so as not to miss such a glorious opportunity.

These white and pink ecstasies are the evidence of his debt to the Impressionists, showing beyond doubt what he had learned from them, the pointillism of Seurat in particular, and how he was able to exploit it for his own ends. For he had a very different end in view: not to dissolve everything and escape into *le grand néant*, the great nowhere, deliciously tempting though that was, but on the contrary to re-establish things as they had once been, to rehabilitate them – to present the world as a feast of blossom. Like Cézanne he dreamed of painting the world's virginity.

The clouds drifting on a delicate spotting of white and blue in his paintings are exquisite feathery blossoms. The blend of warm blue and lilac and light yellow tones spotting the ground causes the earth to blossom magically like the sky, part of the same transparent substance. All is arboreal, belonging to some enormous phantom of a tree. Whole orchards are about to float off. We see the tiny vibrating lung-particles of which the earth and sky and the fence – painted in long parallel striding strokes – are made. Above the leaning trunks, among branchings and leafage as precise as veins in an X-ray, the fragrance and drunkenness explodes, then spreads, then radiates, overwhelming the space.

We are meant to lose ourselves in the palpitations of this lover-like blossom.

On leaving Paris Vincent's instinct was to unlearn everything and return to the ideas he had had in his country wilderness before he encountered the Impressionists. His 'orchard' technique was Impressionism but with a vital difference. His dots and dabs were like personal exclamation marks, arbitrary, not in the least systematic. He projected himself through them, subjectively. But no matter how strenuously he later withdrew from the Impressionist camp, as he recoiled from all schools and systems, insisting that the 'suggestive' colour used by Delacroix and Monticelli meant more to him, the truth is that it was his first dip into Impressionism which really opened his eyes to light and colour.

Renoir was another Impressionist who didn't fit the pattern. Cézanne certainly didn't: he reacted, like Vincent. Lawrence, in his trenchant essay, *Introduction to These Paintings*, asserts that the movement's attempts to get rid of solidity were in essence an escape 'from the dark procreative body which so haunts a man.' Renoir, who said in his jolly fashion that he painted 'with my penis, and be damned', was an exception. Degas another. 'Courbet, Daumier, Degas, they all painted the human body. But Daumier satirised it, Courbet saw it as a toiling thing, Degas saw it as a wonderful instrument. They all of them deny it its finest qualities, its deepest instincts, its purest intuitions. They prefer, as it were, to industrialise it.'[16]

Renoir didn't. He liked to shock, and said that if a woman didn't have buttocks and breasts she wouldn't be paintable. Vincent, it will be remembered, demanded a Venus with broad hips and a pelvis wide enough for child-bearing. When he was confronted by a naked model he saw a womb, and the earth to him was an enormous womb.

It is true that until Provence he repeatedly portrayed the human body as a tool, a spade. That was out of defiance, and it was meant to challenge. No one else had included the everyday labour of man in art. It was a way of taking leave of the elect, the chosen few of art. So the charge of industrialising does stick, but only as mud sticks. As soon as he got to Arles he was baptised, washed clean of the dross of Holland by a light and a sun that took the place of the god he had lost. The 'good sun' was now his great visual god. He remained eternally grateful for this wonderful gift he had discovered, this open secret, freely available to all. He worshipped it. He put its halo around countless objects, and around the heads of his sowers, whose heads glow like the Christs in church windows. 'Oh! those who don't believe in the sun are the real infidels,'[17] he cried out, a cry Lawrence was to echo forty years later. 'Start with the sun,' runs the concluding sentence of *Apocalypse*, 'and the rest will slowly, slowly happen.'

Vincent followed a tradition, that of the Dutch masters of light. As a colourist he broke new ground. Yet when he sent work to people at home he did so hesitantly, unsure of its reception. Hearing that his old teacher, Mauve, had died, he was moved to send his latest and best orchard – of two peach trees, one directly behind the other, a reed fence, a blue and white sky – to the painter's widow. He inscribed the picture, 'Souvenir de Mauve – Vincent', although he had told his brother he would sign it 'Vincent-Theo'. Biographers have speculated as to the significance or otherwise of this omission.

He was traditional also in another respect. It was Impressionism, and not the rise of photography as has been supposed, that had virtually put an end to portraiture. Meyer Shapiro makes clear that 'The Impressionist vision of the world could hardly allow the portrait to survive; the human face was subject to the same evanescent play of colour as the sky and sea: for the Impressionist it became increasingly a phenomenon of surface, with little or no interior life, at most a charming appearance vested in the quality of a smile or a carefree glance.'[18] If this momentary face put in an appearance at all, it was one wiped clear of strain and devoid of will; the outdoor summer holiday face.

Vincent was now a passionate portraitist. In his one year at Arles he painted 46 portraits of 23 people, if we include self-portraits. One of his projects while in Nuenen had been to paint 50 peasant heads. He told Theo more than once that he believed the future of art lay in portraiture. Undeterred by the revolutionary overthrow of substance into the bath of sunlight, the triumph of the ephemeral, and the delight of the grand escape, he hung on to the portrait and reinvigorated it. His reasons were subjective as well as social. For a long time he had nourished an ambition to paint memorials of humble anonymous people for future generations to see. As well as this, portraits were bridges to the love and affection he could not otherwise gain. When he painted a person, that person became accessible to him, since their humanity was given up to him involuntarily for the duration of the session. There were no demands, no fears of rejection or loss. Shapiro points out that these pictures of plain people in their working clothes, neither formal as of old nor dressed up, with manners to match, do not occur in past art. They are original by virtue of their anonymity, unique as blades of grass in a meadow are unique. They exhibit on their faces for the first time the distressing wear and tear of life. These are the first democratic portraits, and would have pleased Whitman especially, writes Shapiro.[19]

From blossom, a material emanation most akin to sunlight, he turned his attention to the sky. In his new aerial pantheon, the sun's equivalent in the cosmos was the night sky ablaze with stars. How could he paint this difficult subject? For the children of Arles, the street arabs and hooligans, he was somebody to look out for and yell after, a hurrying, hatless figure in the beating sun, a heavy easel slung on his back as he scuttled out of town; at other times wearing a huge straw hat spoked at the disintegrating brim edges like a broken cartwheel. The urchins and louts screamed 'Fou-rou' after the red-headed crazy man their parents ridiculed among themselves. Fame at last, Vincent commented wryly to his brother.

A vicious wind, the mistral, sprang up, throwing dust over his canvases and making him curse, then dying away as unexpectedly as it had appeared. He brought pictures back and next morning saw that he had painted the wind along with the landscape: everything was buckling and twisting. His own rage too, as he fought to anchor himself in the eye of the storm, and nature's blind rage at itself, were woven into the same picture. The nagging malice, the tormented trees.

He was living erratically again, overspending his budget to buy more paints and canvases and going short on food. For four days he existed on forty-three cups of coffee and crusts of bread. His moods fluctuated; he had dizzy spells. He did a week of night painting, sleeping by day. The hot weather had arrived. The night, he declared, 'is more alive and richly coloured than the day'. He meant, of course, that inner colour, analogous to an enthusiasm for life. The brilliant colours of his Arles canvases were from deep inside himself, as any visitor to Provence soon discovers.

He had embedded himself in Provence's earthbound world, painting its flowers and roads, his chair and pipe, cafés, streets, its river. Now he wanted to paint its upper zone with the same sense of its tangible substance. It frustrated him that he could not draw strong heavy lines around it and give it the conviction he wanted. The thick cobalt sky was as warm and solid to him as the earth under his feet, yet was eternal. He solved the technical problem of painting at night by sticking candles in a ring around the crumbling brim of his hat and along the top of his easel. In this way he painted a nightscape of the Rhone and the town's gaslight reflections in the water, cypresses under the moonlight, and a *Pavement Café at Night*, with its unstable yellow, orange, and green illuminated shape repeated in the silhouette of the piece of starry sky, just as the table top ellipses were matched by the scattered discs above.

At the end of May he consolidated his position, renting the right wing of a narrow two-storeyed house on the Place Lamartine. It took him until September to move into it, probably because it was in need of renovation. The outside was painted yellow – the Yellow House of his paintings – and the inside white-washed. He had taken it for 15 francs a month, and though there was a snag – its dirty lavatory was in an adjacent hotel – he saw the house in visionary terms as 'the studio and storehouse for the whole campaign, as long as it lasts in the south.'

In other words, the place was more than a dwelling. It enshrined a long-cherished ideal of Vincent's, one that Lautrec had found repugnant, namely the establishment of a base for a guild of artists who would collaborate – his key word – on fundamental issues. There was already a list of members forming in his head: Theo, who would be a sort of honorary member, and Gauguin and Emile Bernard. Others would feel the magnetic attraction and be drawn in. It was to be an opting in rather than an escape. Instead of living with the disease of ownership and the curse of money, the kind of group he envisaged would safeguard a painter's material welfare: 'By loving each other like comrades-in-arms instead of cutting each other's throats, painters would be happier . . .'.[20] As a vision it lived again in the dream of Rananim,

217

Lawrence's name for his unrealised colony in Florida's orange groves. He announced his intentions in similar ringing phrases: 'One must destroy the spirit of money, the blind spirit of possession. . . . I want so much that we should create a life in common, a new spirit . . . each of us free and producing in his separate fashion, but all of us together forming one spring, a unanimous blossoming.'[21]

Vincent's nucleus of the new life in the south would be a group of 'brothers' united for the common good and sharing all. It was important to strike now, because 'life drags us along so fast that we haven't time both to argue and to act.'[22] Were they living in a time of renaissance or decadence? In his opinion they were too close to events to judge. And what did it matter? 'What is needed,' he wrote, as far back as 1882, 'is courage and self-sacrifice.' He was attempting then to organise a group for the distribution of prints for the people. Now he proposed a society like that formed by the English Pre-Raphaelites. They were twelve, so he believed, and their Christ-orientation appealed to him. He purchased twelve chairs for his Yellow House, and dubbed Theo a 'dealer apostle'.

Just like Lawrence, he put himself forward as an example for others to follow, and in the same messianic spirit proclaimed: 'I shall urge every man who comes within my reach to produce . . .'. Both men suffered spectacular failures when in contact with others, yet seemed to crave the very intimacy they half feared and distrusted. Before long, Vincent's hero-worshipping nature and his eagerness to win recruits focused on Gauguin, a man he hardly knew, whose genius was being extolled in every letter by Bernard. They were both at Pont-Aven in Brittany, though Gauguin took care to distance himself from the colony there. A rather arrogant, powerfully built man, he was not in the least idealistic. Bernard went in awe of him.

As for Vincent, he was ambivalent towards the self-contained vain Frenchman from the start. He sent him seductive invitations; he wrote to Theo on his behalf to enlist help for him. The man had to be rescued from poor health and poverty, the Yellow House awaited him, it was being decorated most lovingly with him in mind, he informed Theo. Although Theo had been named the leader of his new society, Gauguin was later offered the role as a lure and a tribute. With mounting passion he longed for his arrival. It would mark the end of his years of isolation and loneliness. Would Gauguin like the region? Was he to be trusted? After all, he had connections with the world of bankers. He gladly acknowledged Gauguin's supremacy as a front-runner, denigrating his own work at one point to pay homage to him and sounding at times like someone expecting a persecutor he could not resist, or a man enslaved by an indifferent lover. As the reunion drew nearer, his reservations and his anxiety increased. What swayed him more than anything else was the news that Gauguin was unwell and penniless. Instead of Vincent being in Theo's debt, Gauguin would be in debt to him. He relished the reversal for the opportunity it gave him to take care of the ailing artist. Once recovered, his mercenary nature transformed, he would be their abbot, the head of their order of artist-monks.

For the time being Vincent was sleeping at the Café de l'Alcazar (the famous Night Café of the painting to come) and using the Yellow House as a studio only. Now and then he took meals at the Café de la Gare, run by the Ginoux family. Madame Ginoux would be the subject of another portrait. Painting the human figure and face moved him the most deeply, he said. We have to look at his still-lifes and landscapes with this in mind. Still-lifes are nearly always self-portraits; a sky coils and writhes its clouds in forms analogous to that of a woman in labour. Single figures are kept apart by pollard willows, a waiter is caught and held stiffly between a wall and a lamp-post. There is a multiplicity of couples: entwined pairs of lovers, two trees from one root, a pair of chairs, a pair of bottles. Cottages are found to share the one thatch, sprouting a double chimney. In the happiest paintings, pictures are audacious weddings of colours. In the saddest, snow-fields and empty roads dwindle a figure down to a mere single stroke.

Vincent painted nature when his nerve failed him in front of people. If a portrait succeeded it made him terribly happy and infused his work with fresh, generous attributes. Woefully cut off, he strove each time to get back into human sight, to be seen as he saw others. 'In a picture I want to say something comforting as music is comforting,' he wrote. What could be more consoling than to be recognised and accepted by men and women he trusted, who had no privileged status, and whose labour and simplicity gave them 'something of the eternal which the halo used to symbolise, and which we now seek to give by the actual radiance and vibrancy of our colourings.'[23]

He visited the coast at Saintes-Maries-de-la-Mer in June, and was given his first sight of the Mediterranean. He drew and painted boats drawn up by the fishing village, and the peasant cottages adorned with crosses. The flat sandy beach was 'like Holland without the dunes'.[24]

But human beings were now his prime concern. Some he knew personally and he was able to learn about them first and then paint their portraits. Others were glimpsed briefly and escaped, and he had to content himself with rapid word sketches. His preoccupation with the old and care-worn had waned temporarily in favour of the erotic and virginal. In the country on the outskirts of Arles he saw a girl with coffee-tinted skin, ash blond hair, grey eyes, a print bodice of pale rose 'under which you could see the breasts, shapely, firm, and small', a young woman as simple in her lines as the landscape in which she moved. What a detailed snapshot of a glance this was of her, against the emerald leaves of fig trees. Nor did he miss the mother, just as stunning a figure to him, dressed in dirty yellow and faded blue.[25] If circumstances forced him to stay indoors, then he could call up these visual images from his store for company, make compositions of them in his head, solve problems. He spoke of being 'ravished, ravished by what I see', and this gratification of his voracious eye made up for a great deal of physical and emotional impoverishment.

An even younger model sat for her portrait, one of his most delicate and sympathetic pictures. Of *La Mousme* he wrote to his brother: 'If you knew what a "mousme" is (you will know when you have read Loti's *Madame Chrysanthème*), I have just painted one. A "mousme" is a Japanese girl – Provençal in this case – 12 to 14 years old.'[26]

The little girl, her torso waspish in the trim striped bodice, is posed carefully in a curved cane chair. There are various subtle echoes and transitions in this painting of nuanced tones: the drooping right hand, elongated with a composer's instinct to follow the arch of the chair, the long curving row of buttons, the curving stripes themselves, with many delightful and light feminine touches in the modelling of the small wary face, the upper lip lifted slightly back. An ample blue skirt dotted with cool red spots forms an immensity from which the upper body grows like a stalk. In her stiff left hand she holds a spray of oleander that she has clearly forgotten, hypnotised perhaps by her inquisitor's queer intensity. Her hair is pulled back with red ribbon, a piece of it sticking out in brave silhouette against the pale green of a wall.

In moments of revulsion he would want to abolish art, or rather advance to a future where art was no longer necessary, when life itself was an art. Then a pretty woman would be what she was, a living marvel, 'whereas the pictures by da Vinci and Corregio only exist for other reasons. Why am I so little an artist that I always regret that the statue and the picture are not alive?'[27]

He was able to report that his 'bony carcase' was getting sunburnt, and that his digestion had improved, after living for three weeks on ships' biscuits with milk and eggs. He was having water and gas put in at the Yellow House. Gauguin, when he came – he *must* come – was an ex-sailor who would take charge of the cooking. Vincent could hardly believe that he had hit on the solution to his hateful loneliness. Plenty of artists found the question of lodgings a serious problem, he told Theo with touching naivety. His door would always be open.

It was so important to be settled, not shiftless and not decadent. Things would be put on a sound footing, everything clean and ship-shape – clean as a Japanese interior. This was what he was determined to achieve before anyone came to stay with him. How curious that he hardly mentioned Bernard, a close friend, whereas Gauguin was an unknown quantity. He was painting a 'poet's garden' to hang up in Gauguin's room, because that was what he was, a poet. A little later he bought country beds, big double ones made of pale wood instead of iron cots. The household should have a solid, durable look to it, an atmosphere of quiet and permanence. He was like someone preparing for a marriage. He intended to hand-paint his own bed, using as decorative themes perhaps a nude woman, or a child in a cradle – he hadn't yet decided.

All the time, as he advanced into the heat of high summer, his palette was getting brighter. Behind the heads of his portraits were hung daring backgrounds of radiant yellow and deepest blue. Vincent stated quite plainly that these backgrounds were symbolic colours, when he said: 'Beyond the head, instead of painting the banal wall of the mean room, I paint infinity, I

221

make a plain background of the richest, intensest blue that I can contrive, and by this simple combination of the bright head against the rich blue background I get a mysterious effect, like a star in the depths of an azure sky.'[28] When these amazing canvases began arriving at Theo's in Paris and he welcomed them timorously, seeing the 'glaring colours' as appropriate to the direct treatment, he paused to wonder whether the art world was at fault in automatically despising popular taste. Had they got it all wrong?

Vincent's colour was gathering steadily in intensity and boldness but it was never primitive; his responses were as civilised as they were sophisticated. As Meyer Shapiro explains, 'his most intense colours are elements in a scale of intensities. . . . The primitive does not appreciate yellow as a region of colour with a great span between opposite poles of brightness and pallor. He knows only one red, one yellow, one blue. Western art discovered the possibilities of colour as a set of dimensions only by eliminating the extreme saturated tones and dividing up the intervals of value and hue. What van Gogh did was to restore the absolute pole, in itself too crude and barbaric for civilised eyes, but to treat it as the final term in a series.'[29] It was at the same time a technical venture and a spiritual quest.

One day he sat writing to Theo in a restaurant that was 'very queer; it is grey all over.' The floor was grey like a pavement, the walls covered in grey paper, green blinds were always drawn, and a big green curtain flapping in the doorway stopped the dust coming in. It was a Velasquez, even to the fierce sunlight aiming rays through the blind slantingly. It was possible to look from this grey world through to the kitchen, clean as a Dutch kitchen, the floor of bright red bricks, the kitchen range shining with brass fittings, and with blue and white tiles. An old woman and a short fat servant could be seen: grey, black, and white figures. There it was; he sat in it and marvelled. It was pure Velasquez.

And as if to prove that his lust for colour had not unhinged him, he went on to describe a stable with four tobacco-coloured cows, a calf, in a bluish-white stable hung with spiders' webs, the cows very clean and beautiful. The green curtain in the doorway contributed to that grey composition again – 'Velasquez's grey'.

One morning he was near a communal washing place where there was a crowd of town women 'as big as Gauguin's negresses';

especially one, in white, black, and red. Another giantess was all in yellow. There were at least thirty of them altogether, old and young. The magnitude of the subject seems to have defeated him. The more he saw of life here, the more he was convinced that it would take a Maupassant of painting to do justice to the Midi, he said.

He woke up one day feeling extraordinarily good – it was most unusual. He thought he would stay in the country forever, it suited him so well. Suddenly his heart flowered, rejoicing. 'Oh, these farm gardens with their lovely big Provençal roses, and the vines and the fig trees! It is all a poem, and the eternal bright sunshine too, in spite of which the foliage remains very green.'[30] Something in the limpid air of the south was more lovely, happier than the north – like a bouquet by Monticelli.

Some of the little farms had no cows. There was a miniature system of canals at one spot, with a cistern which irrigated the land along trenches. An old white horse tethered to the machinery walked round in a circle and kept it in motion. Rilke, admiring a portfolio of van Gogh reproductions, came upon 'an old horse, a completely used-up old horse: and it is not pitiful and not at all reproachful: it simply *is* everything we have made of it and what it has allowed itself to become.'[31]

In August, Vincent found – to his delight – a whole family of models. Joseph Roulin, a postal official – Vincent called him a postman – in a splendid blue uniform and a cap bearing the legend 'Postes' in gold lettering, welcomed him into his home. So did his wife Augustine, later to figure in his painting, *La Berceuse*. They had an adolescent son, Armand, and a boy, Camille. Shortly after Vincent made their acquaintance the mother gave birth to a girl. Spending time with them and painting them all in turn must have had a calming effect, as well as boosting his morale. Evidently he was not such a fearful leper as he had supposed. Roulin was not quite old enough to be his father, he remarked wistfully. All the same his gravity and tenderness were like that of a war veteran for a young soldier. Vincent's pleasure irradiates the description.

Before finding a haven with the Roulins he had subjected himself to a baptism of fire out in the wheatfields. The sun was a burning eye even hungrier than his own. The heat fell on his head in savage blows. He came back with canvases covered in molten expanses and went back again and again for more. He painted haystacks, wide plains yellow with wheat, men reaping with enormous scythes, and the women following with sickles, cutting and binding sheaves. His *Wheatfield with Setting Sun* is of a country on fire, as he was, the foreground seething in a lava of savage yellow, the town strung out in a jagged line of black silhouettes, factory chimneys smoking, a bonfire of sun only half visible, huge behind it all.

He came back from the fields tottering, pieces of field stuck to him. He had walked all day swimming in it, in the thick blood of it. In the night he would go out again, as if against his will. Over him were the stars, a swarm of eyes. The skin of the earth, a faceless body under his feet, now had eyes all over it and was over his head, pricking him. One imagines it dragging him out like an unsatisfied woman, an African with a dark skin that changed to a blinding white by day, into violet, into straw yellow. He went hurrying back to it at dawn to satisfy a passion he could never quench. At the high point, at noon, he spoke of entering a mirage of lasting peace. On his return his eyes were bloodshot, his lips burnt, people in the street falling back aghast. The criminal fervour of his labour made him feel like a public menace.

The olive orchards and the Mediterranean sun transformed Provence into a biblical land. He was both drawn to religious subjects and repelled, nervous of them. A Gethsemane scene he did, painted in June, showing an olive garden, with Christ in orange and blue and an angel in yellow, was hastily scraped off again. Religious impulses were best expressed, he believed, 'realistically', that is to say by reverting to his old practice of using landscapes, in this case olive trees and the starry sky, as his models.

The tremendous heat and his own premonitions of instability were reminders of Monticelli, with whom he clearly identified. The man was a bit cracked, but strong, he told Theo. He had refined taste. Working as he did not far from Marseilles where Monticelli had died, Vincent felt his work carried on from where the other's left off, 'as if I were his son or his brother.'[32] Stories about Monticelli standing drunkenly before a canvas were, he thought, Jesuitical lies – no one could have painted as well as he had done in that condition. 'Perhaps Vincent did not know it,' writes Lubin, 'but Monticelli also fell in love and was turned down by his cousin, Emma Ricard, a refusal that caused him to withdraw from his work for a while and contemplate becoming a monk.'[33]

With the harvest gathered in, he slowly lost his frenzy and came to himself. He went about dazedly, a burnt-out case. The Roulin household took him in without reservation. His rate of work now was so rapid that he could knock off a portrait at a single sitting, and in any case his sitters were ordinary people who had no time to spend waiting around for long periods. He preferred it that way. His distrust of 'fine painting' had led him to a method of working straight on to the canvas, slashing out pictures at high speed, drawing with colours. He was able to spend time at the Roulins' because he did numerous versions of them all in turn. Between sittings they would press him to join them at their table and share simple meals with them. Roulin himself was a talker and he was prone to reminisce, slowly and with dignity.

Once he had lost faith in his father, Vincent sought to replace him with his opposite, revolutionaries in art like Rembrandt, heroes with revolutionary ideas like Michelet, and with living men, contemporaries, often men as ugly as his father was handsome, such as the little Republican Tanguy in Paris. The paint seller was childless, however. Roulin was a patriarch like his own father, but tolerant and expansive, with a huge Socratic beard. Like Socrates he was 'ugly as a satyr, until on the last day a god appeared in him that lit up the Parthenon.' No one would have been more surprised than the humble postal worker at this exalted comparison. In a more realistic mood, Vincent admired his new father for being such a good person, 'and so wise and so full of feeling and so trustful.'[34] His voice possessed a mournful quality, yet he was far from sad. When his brand new uniform arrived he put it on with pride. Marcelle, the tiny baby, was held on his knee, and he sang for her.

Above all, he loved the man's naturalness. Roulin was a drinker, spending a lot of time in cafés, which didn't mean he was in any sense a sot. He liked to talk politics, and when this happened Vincent heard 'the trumpet of revolutionary France' sounding again. He argued naturally, with a grand and simple sweep, in the style of Garibaldi. Vincent saw the Roulin marriage as an exemplary one, 'like that of our own parents', he added suddenly, as if weirdly justifying the transfer of his allegiance.

Telling Bernard he wanted to do 'figures, figures, and more figures', he announced 'a series of bipeds from the baby to Socrates, and from the woman with black hair and white skin to the woman with yellow hair and a sunburned brick-red face.'[35] Both women were Madame Roulin: as a nursing mother she underwent a metamorphosis and became sun-saturated, her yellow hair the colour of generous unselfish love.

The Postman Roulin depicts Joseph Roulin in his official capacity, resplendent in full uniform decorated with gold braid at the cuffs and forearms, eight gold buttons arrayed at the front. He looks like a Russian, sitting there as imperishable as 'a faraway bugle'. Totally modest, he stands for something big. He is the truth. One hand rests on a chair arm, the other on a table. His large beard parts and spreads its square magnificence above, and Shapiro compares it to a landscape, 'an inverted forest with a profusion of yellows, greens, and browns.'[36] The head is rigidly held to convey the solemnity of the occasion, the face is open like a book, fresh as a meadow. The blue of the uniform and cap seem at first to be swamping the man's character, until one sees the blue eyes, the buttons bright as eyes, the features quivering with character.

Armand, the Roulins' teenage son, is given a moodier, darker treatment. The self-absorbed youth wears his clothes without enthusiasm, in fact uneasily. A struggling dandy moustache follows the rather sullen upper lip. A pointed bit of hair leaking from under the brim of his blue hat adds to the sharp-featured shyness of his profile. *Camille Roulin*, an altogether brighter and more active portrait, seems to catch the boy with swift snatching strokes of tremendous circular vigour. He comes spinning straight at us, the sharp blue points of his eyes, his floppy blue cap which is as full of energy as his face, absorbed not in himself but in the world of his sensations, out of which he bobs up, a splinter of bright life in his grass-green coat caught at the neck with a single bright red button.

Whereas *Augustine Roulin with her Baby* portrays the mother at a curiously ambivalent moment. The mewling child in its white gown, white bonnet, ungainly, not in the least sweet, has power, for all its helplessness, over the blurred subordinate mother pushed to one side of the frame. She in turn half thrusts her child into the air away from her in a strange impulse. Shapiro draws our attention to 'the brilliant play of analogous silhouettes . . . the wavy outline of the child, into which the mother's profile could fit.'[37] Behind them both is the deep yellow mortar of a pounding sunlight, urging growth on this infant with its face drawn piecemeal, without spiritual identity, staring out pop-eyed from every scrap of its physical being.

In September, a momentous month, he moved into the Yellow House and wrote to inform Theo of a new ambition. If he could only do a figure in a few sure strokes then he would be happily occupied all winter, drawing and painting people walking the boulevards, along the streets, in the park. It sounded simple yet was complicated, 'because what I am after is that the figure of a man, a woman, a youngster, a horse, a dog, shall have head, body, legs, arms, all in keeping',[38] and in a matter of minutes. How he envied the Japanese this facility! They achieved it as simply as breathing; made it look as easy as buttoning your waistcoat.

At about this time he produced a self-portrait of terrifying beauty. Here was his self-styled Japanese look. His head shaved to the skull in self-abasement, beard hacked to a reddish stubble and his throat bared, he is neither the Samurai nor the Buddhist monk he perhaps intended to combine, though his eyes are slanted and he has clearly left the human world. His fanatic red eyes narrow like a wolf's, above the bestial cheeks and nose, and the saddest of drooping mouths. Around him in a swirl of colour behind his earthy jacket sings the unimaginable green of a lost paradise.

Though his letters to Theo maintained a consistent image of the suffering victim, epistles to his friend Bernard were often light-hearted, at times almost jocular. He remarked humorously that the terrific midsummer heat made everyone in these parts more than a little crazy, but what the hell, he was half crazy anyway. Think of that lovely man Delacroix, he exclaimed, who only found his true style of painting when he had lost his teeth and his breath! Someone who saw him at work said that when Delacroix painted it was like a lion devouring his piece of meat. And he went on to speak of another old lion, Rembrandt, with his toothless smile and the piece of white cloth wrapped around his head. In this same letter he mentioned for the first time that he was thinking of decorating the Yellow House with pictures of sunflowers. He wanted the raw or broken chrome yellows to blaze forth from a variety of blue backgrounds, 'from the palest malachite green to royal blue', so that the effect would be like those stained glass windows in Gothic churches.

It was to Bernard, not Theo, that he confided his most uninhibited reflections on sex. No doubt consoling himself he praised Degas for behaving like a small lawyer with a horror of going on a spree, in order that his painting would be more 'spermatic'. 'He looks on while the human animals, stronger than himself, get excited and fuck, and he paints them well, exactly because he doesn't have the pretension to get excited himself.'[39] This was all very well, but in the next breath he contradicts himself. How he envied, admired and would have liked a dark sensual nature, tender and phallic like Lawrence's wistfully created Mellors.

Take Rubens. 'Ah, that one! He was a handsome man and a good fucker, Courbet too. Their health permitted them to drink, eat, fuck.'[40] Unlike his own bitter fate, crucified into an individuality that gave him no rest, that he would have liked to disown. The Dutchmen of past times who were great artists were *married men* (his italics) and begot children, and were deeply rooted in nature. Wasn't his condition, and Bernard's, the inevitable consequence of belonging to the white Christian race? He cursed him, 'the horrible white man with his bottle of alcohol, his money, and his syphilis – when shall we see the end of him? The horrible white man with his hypocrisy, his greed and his sterility.'[41] Viewing the future with foreboding he prophesied disasters that would fall like terrible lightning on the modern world, 'through a revolution or a war, or the bankruptcy of worm-eaten states.'

These were thoughts prompted by a book about the Marquesas Islands he had been reading; not a well-written one but unutterably sad for all that in its exposure of a whole tribe's extinction by the all-conquering white man. He understood so well Gauguin's longing for the tropics and found the pictures he painted of negresses 'high poetry' – 'gentle, pitiful, astonishing'.[42]

This same month he completed paintings – in watercolour and oil – of the café where he ate now and then in the evenings. *The Night Café*, seen by commentators with the benefit of hindsight as predicting his collapse into insanity, is Dostoevskian, devilish, and according to Vincent's own testimony is of an ugliness comparable to that of his *Potato Eaters*. He intended no self-criticism. A clock high on the end wall gives the time as a quarter after midnight. The painting contains a wealth of symbols, some of them indicated by the artist, whose literary gift enabled him to illuminate the sources of so much of his art. Men – he called them 'sleeping hooligans' – are slumped at tables and in chairs. They are perhaps thieves, pimps, or just loveless roughs like himself. A green billiard table occupies the middle of the room, which to us looks lugubrious rather than sinister, but was for Vincent a place 'where one can ruin oneself, go mad, or commit a crime.' Even more explicit is his statement that he had tried to express 'the terrible passions of humanity by means of red and green.' Blood-red walls clash with the green of billiard table, ceiling, stove. The *patron* stands isolated, the one standing figure and therefore authoritative, in his significantly white coat.

Vincent has given us a 'devil's furnace' where absolutely nothing is happening and where anything might happen, as suspenseful as Hemingway's café in his short story 'The Killers'. The deep meaning is that none exists. We look at an unbearable nothingness, a paralysis in the entrails of hell. It is a dream picture. A man with carrot-coloured hair crouches at a table to the right. His face is bent to the table and thus obscured, his right hand covering part of his head. A J Lubin believes that Vincent has projected himself into the painting by means of this figure. For what reason? It is all him. Citron-yellow lamps hung overhead have whirling dervish-like halos of orange and green. The perspective sucks us forward and propels us headlong past the chairs and inmates and through a doorway in the end wall which has an opening shaped like a standing figure. Among the bottles on the end counter is a bouquet of flowers, painted in a flurry of furious strokes.

Vincent had begun working again at a frantic pace. 'I have a terrible lucidity at moments, these days when nature is so beautiful, I am not conscious of myself any more, and the picture comes to me as in a dream,' he confessed. He added a frightening observation: 'As a matter of fact I am again pretty nearly reduced to the madness of Hugo van der Goes in Emil Wauters' picture.'[43] It is a picture of the fifteenth-century Flemish artist, who entered a monastery and suffered fits of madness after worrying obsessively about the completion of a commissioned work. Vincent's anxiety was mounting as he anticipated Gauguin's visit. He saw Gauguin as an artist of great power, and before he came he hoped to complete new projects of his own so as to resist the man's influence. Either you created your own system, said William Blake, or you were enslaved by another man's. Vincent's passionate fight to stay clear of schools and strong personalities was bound up with his struggle to recreate himself as a free human being.

No sooner had he delivered his inferno-like painting than he opposed to it a scene of inviolable rest and safety. *Vincent's Bedroom*, a sunny, cheerful room in the Yellow House, is one of his best known and most popular pictures. He set out the colour scheme with obvious pleasure:

> The walls are pale violet. The floor is of red tiles.
> The wood of the bed and the chairs is the yellow of fresh butter, the sheet and pillows very light lemon-green.
> The coverlet scarlet. The window green.
> The toilet table orange, the basin blue.
> The doors lilac.[44]

The Night Café and this were polarities, and meant to be so, he told Theo. He was perhaps aiming to marry heaven and hell, as a way of calming his inner fears and putting his over-heated mind to rest. Indeed, this seems to have been his quite deliberate intention. 'In a word, looking at the picture ought to rest the brain, or rather the imagination.' *The Night Café* was an attempt to exorcise the powers of darkness. All the things in *Vincent's Bedroom*, the wooden bed, wooden table and chair, wooden frames around pictures and window, are meant to return us safely to the realm of growth, of the sun. How does such an area of rapid convergences, high colour, and abrupt angles, together with another rushing perspective, create peace? Shapiro's answer is a fascinating one. By projecting movement into things Vincent got rid of his tensions in a cathartic process which left him with a feeling of great repose. Mysteriously this moment of reprieve seems also to be ours. It affects us like a smile, and unites us with it like a prayer.

The Yellow House was at last ready and waiting for its guest. Hopefully this would be Gauguin. In addition to Vincent's bedroom, simple and plain as we have seen, with clean squarish furniture of yellow deal, there was a guest room upstairs with white walls and a decoration of great yellow sunflowers, and a pretty bed; like a boudoir in fact. And, after hesitating and stalling for months, Gauguin did come at the end of October. He landed at Arles in the early hours, too early to disturb his benefactor. He breakfasted at a café – by chance the Night Café. The scene painted by Vincent, where absolutely nothing was happening, now had its protagonist.

Paul Gauguin, five years older than Vincent, was born in Paris, the son of a Breton father and a Creole mother. His childhood had been a disturbed one: his father, Clovis, a Republican journalist, died on board ship while sailing to Peru as a political exile with his wife and son. Back in France, Gauguin boarded at a Jesuit seminary until he was fourteen, then entered a pre-naval college in Paris. He served five years at sea as a cabin boy and merchant seaman, then was able to take up stockbroking with the help of his guardian, a businessman called Arosa. Leading a comfortable domestic life he painted in his spare time and married a Danish girl, Mette. His artist friends thought him over-assertive, with a habit of smiling sarcasm and a sailor's restlessness. At home with his wife and bourgeois in-laws he was inclined to be sardonic, a malcontent. By the time Vincent came to meet him in Paris he had deserted his wife and children and had lived and painted for a year in Martinique.

Vincent in Paris was initially overcome with admiration for this travelled freebooter, whose work had a monumental, impressive gravity, and whose conversation was eloquent and ironical, in marked contrast to his own guttural speech, his uncontrolled bursts of enthusiasm, and his lapses into dumb silence. The man was mature, ambitious, sexually confident, of large physique. Vincent began to see him as the natural leader of his artists' colony, with himself chief disciple. Once in Arles he enlisted Theo's assistance in trying to persuade Gauguin to join him.

At last Gauguin agreed. Before coming he sent Vincent a self-portrait which he inscribed *Les Misérables*. This was a reference to Victor Hugo's novel, he explained: he saw himself as another Jean Valjean, the book's hero, emphasising that the portrait was

231

not simply of himself but of 'all of us, poor victims of society, who retaliate only by doing good'. The words were, of course, meant to appeal to Vincent's idealism. He passed on the letter to his brother reverentially as a document of 'extraordinary importance'.

The truth was that Gauguin had no particular desire to take up residence with the Dutchman, a man he had met only once or twice, briefly, and found somewhat uncouth and incomprehensible. However, it seemed expedient. It was Theo, in funds because of a legacy, who persuaded him with the bribe of a contract worth 150 francs a month, in exchange for which he had to deliver twelve paintings a year. Ever the boastful optimist, he bragged to cronies that a cautious Dutchman had made a deal with him that was all in his favour. It included free lodgings at the Yellow House.

Vincent, agog with excitement, anticipating wonderful things shortly to issue from their collaboration, had worked himself into the ground with his preparations, including the completion of new paintings to impress his friend, and was in a state of dangerous anxiety. The smooth-talking cynic from Paris who was all raillery, intellect, and superior silence was about to arrive, his mask firmly in place – he had called his self-portrait the mask of a powerful ruffian. As far as he was concerned Arles was no more than a stop-gap. He would escape from money worries for a while, then be on his way. Pont-Aven was preferable to Arles, which by all accounts was a frightful dump inhabited by clod-hoppers. He went there determined to exploit the situation to his advantage. Vincent, eager to cosset and nurture him, yet terribly unsure of himself now the hour had struck, was in fact in much poorer shape than the supposed convalescent. He had been drinking heavily again and forgetting to eat.

Later on that first day Gauguin went round to the Place Lamartine and Vincent welcomed him warmly. The other man was perhaps wondering what to expect – Vincent's letters had been so full of a curious appeal, like love letters. After a day or two he took over the domestic arrangements, which Vincent relinquished gladly. He had always been an untidy devil, whereas Gauguin liked order around him. He thought they could economise by self-catering, and he took over the cooking too. An epicure, he knew about such things. It was a tremendously promising start.

Vincent, however, was puzzled. He was no fool, and something about Gauguin puzzled him, a hidden weakness maybe, or a taste for self-destruction. Close-up, he wasn't so much strong as sensitive, with almost a woman's voluptuousness, his wide face a little puffy and feminine. In contrast, his big nose had a kink in it, like a boxer's that had been broken. He wore his hair long, nestling in the nape of his neck like a woman's. He was a strange bird, fastidious and secretive. When his fleshy mouth closed tight, it stayed closed. Now and then his eyes slid sideways and his face wore an expression like one of his negresses, making him look sullen, debauched. He belonged in a hot land. Here he had the appearance of an actor who had been given a wicked part.

It is significant that Vincent's love of portraiture didn't produce a portrait of Gauguin, though the famous portrait of Vincent by Gauguin, made in November, was done in spite of his preference for non-realist subjects. Here is a fine action painting of Vincent at work on a canvas of sunflowers, leaning back as if in a gale, his eyes small and heavy-lidded and his jaw exaggeratedly heavy. 'It is certainly me,' Vincent said when he saw it, 'but me gone mad.' Painting Gauguin may have been a project he contemplated but gave up on as perhaps too intimidating, finding the man's personality an altogether too baffling one.

At any rate, Gauguin complimented his friend on the painted sunflowers in his room and on other paintings, a sower for instance. He told Vincent marvellous tales of the tropics, and of his sea voyages. Soon his host had a real respect for him: but with reservations. Studying him closely for the first time he kept coming up against something he didn't trust at all. What was it? For one thing, his sexual prowess may have been hard to take. Gauguin was a compulsive womaniser, 'a virgin creature with savage instincts. With Gauguin blood and sex prevail over emotion.'[45] Here was an attempt to put in an idealistic light those traits that were soon to make him feel inadequate and threatened as a man. 'Gauguin interests me very much as a man' could be decoded to read: he creates agitation in me with his potency.

He was certainly popular with the Arlesiennes: another pill to be swallowed. By no stretch of the imagination could Vincent have ever been described as popular. Gauguin exuded charm, and a veiled contempt. Besides excursions to the brothels, called by Gauguin 'nocturnal promenades for reasons of hygiene', they went out painting together. They both painted Les Alyscamps, a tree-lined pathway leading to a church, but they were facing – ominously – in opposite directions. On another trip they painted the grape-pickers in a vineyard. Their differences as men are obvious from their differing approaches. Vincent's canvas, 'a red vineyard, all red like red wine . . . the earth after the rain violet, sparkling here and there', is a poem in praise of the pickers, deep-lined men and women like gnarled branches, with hard bony heads and static lives, knowing neither hope nor despair but just persisting, poor peasants rich with a splendour imparted by their labour, glorified by the light in spite of their stony souls. Gauguin's picture is a study in resignation, of lives limited and defeated, with a seated woman turning her back to us, entitled *Human Miseries*.

In his heart Vincent must have known the oscillation from elation to a sort of despair as his admiration for the man crumbled. Things seemed to go progressively against him and in favour of Gauguin during the two months they were together. There was no overt rivalry, but Gauguin was an overweening character who expected to succeed, in the field of art and with women. Vincent had sensed, before the other's arrival, that he would be forced into the position of having to prove himself. Slaving away at paintings in a hectic race against time, he wrote, 'I am vain enough to want to make a certain impression on Gauguin with my work.'

His self-esteem took a severe blow from the outside world as early as November. Gauguin heard from Theo that one of his Brittany paintings had fetched 500 francs. In the same month Theo arranged a small exhibition of his works, telling Gauguin shortly after it opened that Degas was considering the purchase of a Gauguin, and several other sales were in the offing. Vincent, as if to counter his fear of a contest in which he could easily be found inferior, told Theo that he wanted to complete thirty big canvases before exhibiting anything, and then 'only once in your apartment for our friends, and even then without exerting any pressure. And don't let's do anything else.'[46]

Before long Gauguin was confiding to Emile Bernard that 'I find everything here – the scenery, the people – so petty, so paltry.' Arguments soon broke out, with Vincent managing to suppress his anger at being flatly contradicted. Usually he shouted rudely and slammed his fist on the table and then went stamping off. Gauguin summed it up like this: 'Generally speaking, Vincent and I hardly ever see eye to eye, especially in regard to painting.' To Theo he wrote laconically, 'Your brother is indeed a bit jittery, but little by little I hope to quiet him down.' Many years later in his journals he spoke of seething volcanoes and storms brewing. The battle between line and colour, for that was part of it, kept breaking out. Gauguin would say brutally that he detested Daumier, Daubigny, Ziem, all artists Vincent admired. He preferred the 'line' painters, Ingres, Raphael, Degas. Hearing this Vincent would get terribly overwrought, swallowing down his feelings about the wrongness of Gauguin's view. Why did the man come out with such things? Did he enjoy trying to torture and annihilate him? On the wall of the room where they sat to eat and talk he wrote one day, 'I am of sound mind, I am the Holy Ghost.'

It wore him down horribly, listening to things which were a torture to him, and having to go on living in false harmony with a man who might well be the 'painter of the future', a man who was undeniably, swaggeringly male in the brothels but whom he had come to hate, with his sensual cruel smile and his insulting indifference. Yet somehow he still loved and revered him. He loved the man's physical presence, his animal indolence, his almost female inaccessibility, and yet loathed with all his being the cold mind and the schemer he kept seeing, though he tried not to see. His tall hero shrank at times to a little speculative Parisian with his eye on the main chance. He seemed to express grandeur in his work while denying any spark of it in himself. He saw himself as of a greater intelligence than Vincent, yet was cynically unheroic and without large humanity in his soul.

Vincent's life of heroic hope, like his fighting and suffering, was, he saw, perfectly absurd and crazy to Gauguin. He loved and hated the man. He had given up a part of his soul to Gauguin, and when they argued he was aware of his own idiocy, as he tried to retrieve the betrayed part of himself. Beneath the names they tossed to and fro, Delacroix, Rembrandt, Millet, ran the current of his violent opposition to this man who had seduced him, who seduced him still with his eyes fixed on him in cold amusement. 'Our arguments are *terribly electric*, we come out of them sometimes with our heads as exhausted as an electric battery after it has run down,'[47] he informed Theo with remarkable detachment. He had it seemed given his love to the wrong man, someone as alluring as the erotic mysteries of his art, who was also lewd, untrustworthy, amused.

They went together to visit the Fabre Museum in Montpellier, fifty miles from Arles. There Vincent was upset by a portrait of Alfred Bruyas by Delacroix. Bruyas had red hair and a red beard. Moreover, the portrait was done in 1853, the year of Vincent's birth. Its resemblance to him and Theo disturbed him, and he tried to explain it by writing that this 'gentleman . . . who's a dead ringer for you or me . . . made me think of those lines from Musset: "Wherever I set foot, a wretch garbed in black would come and sit by us and watch us like a brother".'

For much of what happened next we have to rely on Gauguin's memoirs, written much later and since called into question because of his subsequent actions. On 15 December he wrote to Theo saying he had to return to Paris. Living with Vincent was, he said, proving impossible. 'I respect him highly and regret leaving.' Whether or not Theo interceded at this point, begging him to stay on for his brother's sake, is far from clear. However, Gauguin did postpone his departure, asking Theo to treat his previous letter as 'a bad dream'. What Gauguin really felt was conveyed in a letter to his friend in Paris, Emile Schuffenecker: 'Remember the life of Edgar Poe who became an alcoholic as the result of grief and a nervous condition. Some day I shall explain all this to you. For the time being I shall stay here, but my departure will always be a possibility.'

Vincent was now faced with a situation that was a deep misery and dread to him. Gauguin was living with him on sufferance; he could leave at any moment. It was a new torture, to know he would be abandoned without knowing when. Any love he had felt was being murdered. He had treated Gauguin like a brother; his senses had been aroused by him. Now he recoiled in a loathing as callous as lust, that had hate and love inextricably mixed in it. Gauguin was about to thrust him off and flee and he would be alone again, crying out to Theo for comfort in a home that was in ruins.

The threat of Gauguin's imminent desertion was unintentionally compounded by Theo, who suddenly announced his engagement to Johanna Bonger, the sister of his friend Andries. Their son, Dr V W van Gogh, has said: 'The trouble with Gauguin in Arles started right after Vincent had heard from Theo that he intended to marry. . . . It must have passed through his mind that he would lose his support, though he never mentioned it and it never came about.'[48]

It was nearly Christmas, a poignant enough season for Vincent at the best of times, for he yearned then to be reunited with his family, usually compensating by getting together with Theo. Now Theo was off to Amsterdam for the holiday to visit Jo's family. Vincent undoubtedly wanted Theo to marry, projecting himself into the union vicariously, and he approved of Jo, yet the defection meant that he could no longer rely on Theo's undivided attention. The news threw him back on his doomed entanglement with Gauguin. Possibly a self-inflicted illness was his unconscious solution to the problem of how to get love from both Theo and Jo that Christmas. The following February, once the crisis was past, he reprimanded Gauguin half jokingly in a letter for passing on the news of his self-mutilation to Theo, said he needed a *papier mâché* ear, and asked whether his brother's journey had been really necessary.

To go back to the eve of the tragedy: Gauguin had grown cold as ice, uncommunicative, his surly silences more and more unendurable. Vincent drank hard. 'At times,' he wrote, 'driven by a certain mental voracity, I even read the newspapers with fury.' In *Le Petit Marseillais*, a daily circulating in Arles, articles describing the gory crimes of Jack the Ripper were appearing between September and the end of December. Vincent suffered from insomnia and was heard prowling about the house at night. Several times Gauguin woke to find Vincent peering in or coming towards him, as if to make sure he was still there. He told Bernard later that Vincent asked him one day if he really did intend to leave. He said, 'Yes.' Then Vincent tore out a sentence from a newpaper that said, 'The murderer has fled,'[49] and placed it in front of him without a word. Soon after this he flung a glass of absinthe in the Frenchman's face as they sat in a bar.

Gauguin's account of the events that followed is dramatically brief. On the evening of 23 December he left the house and took a stroll through the town. Vincent slipped out behind him and followed him like a shadow. One imagines him chained to the source of his torment, condemned to seek further degradation for himself. Hearing Vincent's thief-like steps, Gauguin whirled on his heels and faced Vincent, glaring him down. Then his pursuer had gone. There was no one to witness what happened afterwards. Vincent ran back to the Yellow House, took his razor, and slashed at the lobe of his left ear. The blood flew out. He pulled a large beret over his head and so covered the wound. He washed the piece of his ear, wrapped it in newspaper like butchers' meat, and rushed to the nearest brothel with it. Did he hope to find Gauguin there, so that he could present him with the bloody evidence of what he had been made to do? At any rate, he handed the parcel to a girl prostitute he knew, Rachel, and said to her, 'Keep this object carefully.' Gauguin later told Bernard that his actual words were, 'Verily I say unto you, you will remember me.' How could he have known? And if inventing, why the need to present a Vincent suffering from Christ mania?

There was a violent scene outside the brothel. Roulin is supposed to have helped Vincent back to the Yellow House. When the police called, apparently to find out whether Vincent had been attacked by his friend, they found him in a coma. He was removed to Arles Hospital. Gauguin, ignorant of these events until the next morning, had spent the night in a hotel. He sent a telegram to Theo suggesting that he come at once. Gauguin, who may have been held briefly for police questioning, reached Paris on 27 December and told Bernard that Vincent had said to him before the incident, either in the street or just before, 'You are taciturn, but I shall be likewise.'[50]

They are the words of a man forcing himself to retaliate against the cruel tactics of silence, and, who knows, by slicing off a piece of his ear he perhaps meant to protest by the bloodiest means possible, and with a deed impossible to ignore. If so, he certainly succeeded. The dream of brotherly love he had nurtured for so long had turned black. He ran red blood over the perverse self-sacrifice of it. Living for other people was a ghastly mistake.

12

ASYLUM

Christmas was often a crisis time for Vincent. It had an effect on him that he felt acutely. He desired gifts that were with-held – most of all the gift of a new self – and wished to rejoice like others at the hearth of his family, blessed by a crib with a child in it. All kinds of unacknowledged longings would rise up, intensified. The birth of Christ was a bitter reminder that his own rebirth still lay ahead as he struggled up out of darkness towards the light. 'I know that what I am struggling for is life, more life ahead, for myself and the men who will come after me,' wrote Lawrence: 'struggling against fixations and corruptions.'[1]

Vincent had broken with his father on Christmas Day, when he left the house at Nuenen and went to live at The Hague. Now crisis meant calamity. The same psychosis that struck him down so cruelly in 1888 would strike again the following Christmas. Unhappy people are said to fear Christmas, as they do the onset of spring.

He recovered rapidly; sufficiently at any rate to write in shaky pencil to Theo, saying how upset he was to have caused him such distress, and at such a time. Gauguin hurt him by not getting in touch. He felt remorse about him. 'Have I scared him? . . . Why doesn't he give me any sign of life? He must have left with you.' Perhaps, though, it was all for the best. Gauguin was better off, more at home in Paris. He pleaded with his brother to tell Gau-guin to write to him. 'I am always thinking about him.'[2]

On the back of this letter was a note from the hospital doctor, Dr Felix Rey: 'I am happy to inform you that my predictions

239

have been realised, and that the over-excitement has been only temporary. I am firmly convinced that he will be himself again in a few days.'

The optimism was misplaced but understandable. Vincent was fully conscious of his circumstances, and conversed rationally and with obvious intelligence. He was allowed to leave hospital on 7 January. He would call on Dr Rey at his office for a chat now and then, and was soon at work on the young doctor's portrait. The masterly self-portrait he completed at the same time is a famous one. He stares past the spectator unseeingly, his gaze inward, his ear bandaged, wearing a shaggy fur cap and a rough green coat buttoned at the neck. He is clean-shaven. He puffs at his pipe, which emits rising circles of smoke. A blood-red ground above the wounded ear divides his head in two symbolically.

He still fretted over Gauguin, wrote sweetly and sadly to him, and heard nothing back. A letter came at last to the Yellow House, saying briefly that he, Gauguin, had gone back to Paris out of concern for Vincent, rather than disturb him further with his presence. What Vincent saw as the duplicity of his words was proof that he had been right to distrust him all along. For a masochist, outright attacks are preferable to protestations of affection that ring false. At least they are meant, 'from the heart', and can be absorbed. Inflicted pain is a kind of love act. If your enemy refuses to give it, you have to give it yourself on his behalf. On 17 January he wrote a long rambling letter to Theo, picking up various topics and dropping them again abruptly, swinging back obsessively to Gauguin. Halfway through he broke off to say bitterly: 'How can Gauguin pretend that he was upsetting me by his presence, when . . . I kept asking for him continually?' He was particularly incensed by Gauguin's request for his fencing masks and gloves that he had left behind in a closet. 'I shall hasten to send him his toys by parcel post.'[3]

He was painting two studies of an unusual theme. One was a sturdy chair with a woven grass seat, of white deal. It was his chair. The still-life, with his pipe and tobacco pouch lying on the seat, is assembled to give the maximum amount of satisfaction, and is as much the work of a carpenter as a painter. The mystery of its presence has to do with its objects, 'like the attributes of saints in old pictures,' as Shapiro remarks. Also, the painting is one of a pair. He painted Gauguin's wooden armchair at the same time. On the seat of that one rests a burning candle and two books, like reminders of the man's inflammatory mind.

He painted a still-life, including in the composition objects that were a pathetic recipe for his future health – a health manual belonging to Dr Rey, an envelope linking him to more vital transfusions through the post from Theo, and his pipe, to ward off thoughts of suicide.

Equally restorative in intention was a beautiful picture, *Woman rocking the Cradle*, begun before his attack and using Madame Roulin for the model. Known to us as *La Berceuse*, it is a picture he intended to really sing and be a lullaby in colours. A woman in a green dress holds the cord of a cradle which is out of sight at her feet. Her hair is orange and in plaits. Her complexion is chrome yellow. At the lower part of the painting is a vermilion background – either a stone or tiled floor. Behind the buxom woman swirls a wallpaper of arresting gaiety, of bluish green with pink dahlias spotted with orange and ultramarine.

The picture was extremely important to him; so much so that he made a number of copies of it. After hearing Gauguin's tales about the fishermen of Iceland, mournfully isolated and 'alone on the sad sea', he conceived the idea of a picture of such simplicity, so maternal, that 'sailors, who are at once children and martyrs, seeing it in the cabin of their boat should feel the old sense of cradling come over them and remember their own lullabies'.[4]

There are five versions in all. To get this sentimental idea across, one that would have appealed instantly to Whitman, he utilised a seemingly primitive style that gave it the look of a chromo, to use his own word. The shapes fit together poster-like, outlined in black, the bosom is darkly swelling, the red wooden armchair firmly clasps the broad figure. Shadows are eliminated. The softly absorbed and dreamy expression can be read at a glance by an unlettered person, and speaks of calm, solace, and – now that we have Vincent's expressed aim – the sea. Whitman's great poem 'Out of the Cradle Endlessly Rocking' comes to mind. The canvas is meant to encompass that moment during which the intimate and the eternal merge, as for Vincent they surely did.

Although he had severed an artery his wound healed well. His great fear, insomnia, he was now treating himself by dosing his pillow with camphor. It seemed to work. He had dreaded going back into the house and sleeping alone. Now this fear ebbed away. He no longer cared what people thought, or whether he was half mad or not. He was even able to say equably, 'Old Gauguin and I understand each other basically, and if we are a bit mad, what of it? . . . . Perhaps some day everyone will have neurosis, St Vitus' Dance, or something else.'[5]

In complete contrast to *La Berceuse* he suddenly tackled a new canvas that he thought Theo might even call *chic*, a wicker basket with lemons and oranges, a cypress branch, and a pair of crumpled blue gloves. It was an odd assemblage of objects. As always with his still-lifes one expects to find a self-portrait there; but gloves? The fingers of the gloves branch organically, and there are nine visible – together with nine fruits. The hues are subdued, the tones broken. We are in a maze of overlapping forms, wicker and cypress, gloves and space, of great charm and subtlety, and a world away from the earth goddess he had made available to those in peril on life's sea.

A few days later he completed his *Portrait of Dr Rey*, a head and shoulders likeness every bit as accessible as Madame Roulin's, showing an alert and natty young house surgeon in a bright blue jacket, his sharp little black beard and spruce curly moustache setting off a rosy cupid's mouth. Only his eyes peck at you with the expertise of his profession. Vincent, grateful to the likeable doctor, asked Theo to send him an engraving of Rembrandt's *Anatomy Lesson* for the man's study.

On 2 February he paid a visit to the brothel where he had caused such a commotion on handing in his sinister present. They set his mind at rest by telling him that plenty of folks around here were sick in the head and did crazy things: he'd be surprised. He was glad to hear it. In the country he had heard strange tales of hallucinations and fevers, and once felt along his nerves the mass hysteria spreading through Arles when there were rumours of earth tremors. A mad negress he saw in the hospital made him think of Gauguin and his tropics. Really he had gone to call on the girl prostitute, Rachel, who had passed out, they told him, when she unwrapped his gift, but soon got over it. No one, it seemed, blamed him for anything.

Two days later he broke down again. Taken back to the hospital, he refused to utter a word. This time there had been no violent incident – he was just overcome by a terror of others. People were plotting to poison him. The Reverend Salles, a Protestant minister in the town, now became the intermediary between Vincent and Theo. On 13 February Theo wired Dr Rey and got the following reply: 'Vincent much better, keeping him here. Do not worry now.' Another five days and Vincent was back in touch, having discharged himself.

Though his persecution mania had subsided, he was nevertheless aware of rising hostility in Arles against him. This time he had grounds for his suspicions. Wherever he went he caused visible panic. The local people, who had always been nervous of painters, now had a mad painter loose among them. It was too much – something ought to be done about him. A youth of seventeen, M Jullian, eventually the municipal librarian of Arles, had this to say in his old age when he was interviewed by Marc Tralbaut: 'We were a gang of young people between sixteen and twenty, and like a lot of young imbeciles we used to amuse ourselves by shouting abuse at this man when he went past, alone and silent, in his long smock and wearing one of these cheap straw hats that you could buy everywhere. But he had decorated it with ribbons, blue, yellow. I remember – and I am bitterly ashamed of it now – how I threw cabbage stalks at him. What do you expect? We were young, and he was odd, going out to paint in the country, pipe between his teeth, his body a bit hunched, a mad look in his eye. He always looked as if he were running away, without daring to look at anyone. We only became afraid of him after he had maimed himself, because then we realised that he was really mad . . . .'.[6] These marauding teenagers would crowd round the house in a mob, climb up at the windows, and be thrilled by the fear they felt when the curious animal trapped inside screamed back at them.

The good people of Arles got up a petition and sent it to the mayor, requesting the painter's internment. Gendarmes came for him on 27 February. He put up no resistance.

From now till his death he would be assailed by the fear that he was losing control of his actions, his brain treacherous, flashing across with wild jolts of contradictory messages. For those of us spared the plunge into chaos his anguish of mind is beyond comprehension. One ceases to possess one's own life. Such a victim is torn open, then is unable to close the wound out of which his strength drains. It must be like losing grip on one's memory in the prime of life, only much, much worse. He might do anything, wander anywhere, become the prey of any vile thought. He might commit crimes, perhaps in his sleep. He was in a process of inner disintegration that he was forced to witness, isolated as never before. To be like this and to have to face nights of sleeplessness, in horrified consciousness of the vacuum which had closed around him, was more than Vincent could bear. He suffered a merciful relapse, a loss of violent super-consciousness.

An enormous sadness clouds our view of these days and weeks. Theo lost touch with him completely until 19 March, when he broke silence by saying: 'I write to you in the full possession of my faculties and not as a madman, but as the brother you know. ... . Here I am, shut up in a cell all the livelong day, under lock and key and with keepers, without my guilt being proved or even open to proof.'[7] He consoled himself with the thought that 'in the secret tribunal' of his soul he would have much to say, one day. He advised Theo to go along with things for the moment and not oppose anyone: it was the wisest course, since he was regarded here as a dangerous lunatic. He added a heart-rending note: 'In present-day society we artists are only the broken pitchers.'[8] His house had been closed by the police, and he had canvases in there he wanted to send. The one ray of light in this desperate state of affairs seems to have been that provided by the minister, Salles, who was 'very kind and very loyal, and a pleasant contrast to the others here.'

Near the end of March he was visited by a painter friend, Signac, who was travelling through the region and no doubt called at the suggestion of Theo. Vincent was cheered, and even managed to obtain leave to call at his house accompanied by Signac to collect books and paintings. Books in particular he craved, so as to have 'a few sound ideas in my head'. He wanted to get his hands on old friends such as Uncle Tom's Cabin, which he reread for the umpteenth time, and Dickens' Christmas books.

The outing had its ludicrous side. The police at first objected to their entry into the house – it had been sealed and the lock destroyed – but Signac was an insistent character, and they were finally allowed in. Vincent presented his friend with a still-life of two bloaters on a plate – a painting which had caused annoyance because 'the gendarmes are called that . . . . That's enough to show you how meddlesome and what idiots these people are.'[9]

Dr Rey had been telling him that the regime he had been following before Christmas – keeping himself going on coffee and alcohol – was just asking for trouble. Vincent readily agreed, but said he was after 'the high yellow note' that he had reached last summer, and to pursue that he had to stay well keyed up. If you stuck to the rules and nothing else, what could you achieve? The artist of the future would be 'a colourist such as has never yet been.' It was hard to imagine such a person living as he had done in little cafés, false teeth in his head, going to the Zouave brothels, and so on.

Now it seemed, the hospital staff were being most attentive to him. For some reason this upset and confused him. How did you distinguish between friends and enemies? Paranoia still hovered at his shoulder. The management was – 'how shall I say, Jesuit' – his word for the hypocrite. He feared their power, their cleverness, and their subtlety. If he lapsed into silence defensively, here was the reason. It was best to keep one's own counsel.

A painting he did of the hospital ward at Arles is like a scene from the Crimean war. A floor wide as a street tapers away to the door in the end wall with the crucifix above it. The foreground is filled with a crude iron stove, the stovepipe rising vertically and then shooting off at right angles and up through the ceiling boards. Around this focal point of warm life huddle patients who are like the figures in Vincent's pictures of almshouse men. There is a line of beds against either wall, some curtained off. Nuns in white and black habits and wearing wimples watch from the middle distance.

He was still incarcerated there when spring broke. Salles advised him – since the owner of the Yellow House was creating difficulties for his tenant – to find somewhere else to live and work. If Vincent wished, he would undertake to locate something suitable. But Vincent confessed that he lacked the courage at present to go back to the beginning and set up a new studio.

He sat in the hospital courtyard among the profusion of spring flowers, painting what he could see. His beliefs were terribly shaken, but reality had to be accepted on its own terms, and although he knew 'inner seizures of despair' from time to time, the urge to work was rising up again like a stubborn sap in him. Indeed, it always did. He went out in search of his great god, the sun, and sat in the garden worshipping it, his head bent 'like an old dog, the dog of this work that is calling him again and that beats him and lets him starve. And yet he's attached with his whole being to this incomprehensible master.'[10]

Roulin came to see him, and to say goodbye to him. He was being transferred to Marseilles, a hardship both for him and his family, yet he didn't think to complain. His was the unquestioning endurance and strong constitution of the peasant, wrote Vincent.

In his next letter to Theo he mentioned that Monsieur Salles had told him about another, more suitable institution at Saint-Rémy, fifteen miles from Arles. He thought he might like to go there at the end of April. The bitter truth was that he was afraid now of venturing out into the world and living alone, inciting people's aggression by actions he could not foresee. It was better if he remained shut up, for his own peace of mind as well as for that of others. He ended on a note of praise for Dr Rey, 'a nice fellow, a tremendous worker'. Theo and Jo had recently got married, and Vincent wished them every happiness.

Hearing that his attacks or fits were thought to be epileptic in origin, he passed on to Theo some information he had gleaned. There were 50,000 epileptics in France, and of those only 4000 were under restraint. So maybe his confinement would be short. Once at Saint-Rémy and on the mend, he thought he might like to make himself useful and be a hospital orderly. Then Salles came in to say that the cost of his stay at Saint-Rémy would be 100 francs a month. It was too much. How would it be if he joined the Foreign Legion for five years? This crazy idea was soon dropped, and was probably only mentioned in the first place to ease his conscience.

The asylum of Saint-Rémy, about a mile and a half outside the town, surrounded by olive groves, cornfields, and vineyards, had once been an Augustinian monastery. Early in the century it was converted into an asylum by adding two wings to the cloisters. One was for male and the other for female inmates. Theo had been in touch with the director, Dr Peyron, and arranged for Vincent to have two rooms, a bedroom and a studio. This sounded fine, though the rooms were in fact adjoining cells with bars at the windows.

Outside, the institution was not unattractive, with overgrown gardens, rough park-like grounds and a circular stone fountain, a number of stone benches, and some twisted conifers. Beyond, to the east, Vincent's window looked out on an irregular area of wheat bounded by a stone fence. Inside, however, it was dark and primitive, with long gloomy corridors and a communal room where the patients congregated on wet days, putting Vincent in mind of a 'third-class waiting room in a stagnant village'. Some of the more bizarre 'passengers' were rigged out in hats, spectacles, canes, and travelling cloaks, and seemed to think they were at a resort.[11]

The Reverend Salles accompanied him on the journey from Arles. He heard Vincent explain his own case calmly and clearly to the director. Leave-taking for Vincent was always a highly emotional affair, and when it was time for Salles to go he tried to express his thanks and his hopeful feelings for the future in this building soon to be his prison. So his friend left him to it. Vincent's last tie with the outer world was cut.

At first he spoke of his strange new home as a menagerie. Though his windows were barred he did have curtains, two of them, sea-green with a design of pale roses, probably left behind by some well-off patient who had since died. Also abandoned was a threadbare armchair upholstered with tapestry 'splashed over like a Diaz or a Monticelli, with brown, red, pink, white, cream, black, forget-me-not blue, and bottle green.' There were thirty empty cells in the place, and only ten male patients, which would explain the asylum's dilapidated condition. Theodore Peyron, once a physician in the navy, was kindly enough but he had no real interest in his job nor in Vincent. He wore thick glasses, a small gouty man who was a widower. In the hospital register, after an initial examination, he wrote a brief diagnosis confirming the one made at Arles: Vincent was subject to infrequent epileptic fits and acute mania, and should be kept under close observation.

The only treatment for mental disorders at Saint-Paul de Mausole seems to have been hydropathy. Twice a week for two hours at a stretch Vincent would lie soaking in a bath. He soon pitied his fellows for having absolutely nothing to do except for the odd game of checkers or bowls. He at least had the therapy of his work.

He had been so repelled by the antics of the mad when at Arles that he had shrunk from contact with anyone. The dangerous cases here were in a separate building, but even so he was among some who were seriously ill. His fear and horror of them lessened as he became familiar with their plight. You heard terrible cries and howls 'like beasts in a menagerie', and when these poor creatures' attacks came on you did your best to help and restrain them, so that they did no serious injury to themselves.

'For though there are some who howl or rave continually, there is much real friendship here,' he wrote on 25 May.[12] He felt no aversion to anyone. After a lifetime of failure in his dealings with people he found himself accepted by this sad collection of lunatics and was able to accept them in his turn. Sometimes he chatted as well as he could with a man who, though he could only utter incoherent noises, clearly wanted his company. The irony wouldn't have escaped him. He was less feared and fearful in here than he had been in the streets of Arles. It was sound reasoning, he remarked to Theo, to say that we must put up with others so that others will put up with us.

He complained of the food. It tasted mouldy, 'like in a cockroach-infested restaurant in Paris. You had no alternative but to stuff yourself with chick peas, beans, lentils, and then struggle to digest them, often noisily.'[13]

One day he caught a very big and rare night moth, a Death's Head, because he wanted to draw and then paint it. Its colour was amazing: black, grey, cloudy white tinged with carmine, vaguely shading off to olive-green. He regretted having to kill it, 'the beastie was so beautiful'. Butterflies were for him symbols of resurrection, so this moth-picture could be a hopeful self-portrait.

Before the end of his first month he painted one of his finest pictures, *Irises*. The close-packed flowering plants, coarsely vigorous and blooming rapturously, rhizomes buckling the ground, are rooted in a corner of the garden. It is a picture suffused with his luminous joy. A riotous southern spring is being celebrated in microcosm by this flat-waving fragment of curved petals and spears. He has left Impressionism behind and painted a Fauve piece, years ahead of his time. The lines curl and break, sharpen and twist flamily with the exuberant movement characteristic of all his future work. The colours, cold leaf-green and sky-blue, the red ground, the hazier green flecked with yellow, orange, white, are radiant but no longer paramount. The shape and motion of the forms are now the most vital things.

A new admission was disrupting the dull routine, a man in a murderous rage with everything, so worked up that he smashed the contents of his cell and yelled incessantly, tearing his shirt to shreds. He spent hours in a bath but was no calmer. In spite of the distress of this, Vincent was, he believed, steadily improving. He was not yet as active as he would have liked to be, and for this he blamed the lethargy surrounding him, that he was determined to fight off. Most of those who had been living here for years suffered from what he called 'extreme enervation'. He thought it odd that whenever he tried to establish clearly in his mind what had happened to him and why he had come here, dismay and horror stopped his thought processes from functioning. Was this a sign that his brain was definitely deranged or could it be some instinct of self-preservation, making him shy away from the memory of certain awful events?

He was soon restless indoors, anxious to make excursions and find new subjects in the vicinity. The director was amenable, but insisted on a chaperone for Vincent. Jean-François Poulet was an attendant detailed for this job. The arrangement worked well. Their outings took them into the surrounding countryside; once in the direction of the town. A painting, *The Roadmenders*, came out of this trip to Saint-Rémy.

The street being torn up was the Boulevard Victor Hugo. We are plunged forward between giant plane trees, as if the diabolical aim was to tip us headlong into the open trench dominating the foreground. Manet had depicted men at work paving, but not like this. The perspective cuts exaggeratedly across the spectator's gaze and we reel back from this slashing diagonal. The cut stone and the sand are heaped up, the massive trunks and branches heavy with foliage reach out like upended roots and are entangled. The figures are for once irrelevant, affecting nothing with their puny picks and shovels. A rage like the rage of the newly admitted man runs amok, the picture narrowly avoiding its own disintegration by a cunningly contrived harmony of colours. Warm and broken tones, green and yellow touches on doors and shutters,

and the contrasts of cold lights and darker warms rescue us somehow from the threat of total chaos.

While at Saint-Rémy he turned his attention to cypresses, a
motif he felt had been neglected by past artists. The tree was
beautiful, he commented, as an Egyptian obelisk was gravely
beautiful. Its line and proportions made it distinctive, and so did
its haughty dark green, 'a splash of black in a sunny landscape'.
The asylum was located at the foot of a small range of hills, the
Alpilles. When he looked out in that direction he saw stately
clumps of cypress trees, blackly clotted on the near horizon.

Soon he was painting cypresses unlike any found in Provence,
undulating, on fire, full of upward striving, rent by internal forces
as they struggled to uproot themselves. Traditionally associated
with graveyards, so always death symbols for him, they took on
additional meaning by exteriorising his turbulence and fears, like
discharges of black forces that had come near to breaking him.
He painted them as he had perhaps seen them under assault from
the mistral, in a torment, whipped until demented with dark
claustral suffering. And at their root, the germ of death that their
impenetrable blackness represented. Then in reaction and perhaps
revulsion from these images of storm and strain he would paint
exhausted, empty scenes of rest and sadness, presided over by
large quiet suns, or else comfort himself with sensitive studies of
small creatures as fragile as he now was, bits of life with no
power to threaten or harm him: cicadas, butterflies, rabbits, birds,
beetles.

Life in the asylum was acceptable but stupefying. Sometimes
he was simply bored to death. He was afraid he might lose
precariously stored energy. The patients around him were left to
their own devices and consequently did nothing except 'vegetate
in idleness'. Oppressed by a lack of suitable models and wanting
to break new ground, he suddenly abandoned realism, planting
a giant cypress in the foreground beneath a poetically imagined
starry sky, like a great pillar supporting his vision. *The Starry
Night* of June 1889 is a lyrical delirium without precedent.

High over the sleeping town of Saint-Rémy, birthplace of
Nostradamus, nocturnal prophecies stream through the firma-
ment. Medical opinion has settled for an epileptic fireworks display, citing the epilepsy afflicting members of the van Gogh
family. Thus two and two make four: yet this is something else,

beyond reason, shooting into heaven out of the reach of science. Here dragons of the Apocalypse spit fire, threatening the star-myth of a mother with child in the convulsed night sky. Heavenly bodies collide, copulating and sowing offspring in huge blazing spirals, a spinning St Vitus' dance out there in bodily space, in zodiacal, evangelistic space, no longer barren but brought alive and close and teeming. A torrent of strokes releases streams of star particles which are the coilings of starry beasts. It is a space wonderfully traced with paths, for our souls to follow and greet ghosts and join hands with the dead. We have to see it as inspired lunacy, by a man racing madly against time in the effort to heal himself.

Flame-like cypresses thrust the eye upward. The whole sky sizzling with volts is a great field, a playground, the land beneath it reduced and subjugated. Here is the grand attempt to merge night and day, to combine sun and orange moon in one glittering vastness. Below the writhing of eleven exploded stars creep the stiff lines and angles of a town busily complete in itself and insulated against revelations, with a thin church spire looking strangely northern as it pokes up nervously to prick the horizon.

During the time spent at Arles and Saint-Rémy Vincent had seven officially recorded attacks, four of them while at the asylum. Writing to his sister-in-law Jo in April he mentioned both *grandes crises* and fainting spells. He had spoken of dizziness and mysterious and unexplained fainting fits much earlier in his life, in Antwerp and in Nuenen. Malnutrition may have been a contributory cause. Since coming to Saint-Rémy he had refused to eat the food provided, insisting on bread and soup, but after attacks he would eat and drink enough for two, in fact 'like a hog' as he said disgustedly. After one recuperative period, when the normally stingy Peyron allowed him meat and wine to build up his strength, he said in disapproval that if he were the doctor he would forbid such a diet. It is possible that for much of his adult life he ate ascetically in order to limit his stamina, out of a fear that physical strength would fuel an inner violence. It wasn't necessary, he said, to be a Hercules in order to paint.

His attacks, which struck without warning, began with acute delirium and confusion. His mind wandered, he hallucinated, had terrifying visitations which seemed real, and people withdrew to a great distance. He ceased to recognise the most familiar faces.

251

Not only did they look different, they merged with persons recalled from the past and from elsewhere, as in dreams. Between attacks his faculties were unimpaired, although sometimes he took weeks to recover sufficiently to face others. On one occasion he shut himself in his room for two months and had to force himself to reappear, saying he was afraid of his fellow patients. His letters would remain lucid, and show him struggling bravely to come to terms with what he increasingly saw as a permanent illness. During convalescent periods he would sometimes be over-whelmed with memories of home, of his childhood, of Holland, 'until I was as sick as a lost dog.'

In a September letter he mentions reading in the *Figaro* the story of a Russian writer – could it have been Dostoevsky? – 'who suffered all his life from a nervous disease . . . which brought on terrible attacks from time to time.'[14]

Poulet, the amiable minder who kept him company for a while on his outings, taking him to Arles at least twice to visit old friends – the Reverend Salles was one, his old cleaning lady another – said in his retirement that Vincent was a good fellow, though strange and silent. He marvelled to see how the artist slaved away at his work 'with a dumb fury', to use Vincent's words, as he tried to make up for lost time and overcome his depressions. He was coming to believe in the wisdom of renunci-ation, a notion very hard for a born rebel to embrace. In the hospital at Arles, subjected to a strict regime, he found it a relief to surrender all resistance and be dominated. 'When I *have* to follow a rule, as here in the hospital, I feel at peace,' he observed.[15] He had experienced the same peace of mind when he was being treated for gonorrhea at The Hague.

Dr Peyron's regime, though a lax one, nevertheless exasperated him – perhaps for that very reason. He felt like a fool having to go up to doctors and ask permission to paint pictures. It was absurd; it put him in a bad humour. The rebel in him was sub-merged and weakened, but not dead.

He still believed in his work, and that whether he succeeded in it or not it was the best lightning conductor for his illness. One attack, however, left him so dejected that he had no desire for anything, neither work nor to see friends. Thank God, those desires stirred again and he started work on two self-portraits. One he began the day he got out of bed for the first time in a week. He was thin, pale as a ghost. He showed his head as whitish with yellow hair, on a dark violet-blue ground.

Poulet has recalled one incident which occurred as he and Vincent were coming in from a painting expedition. Vincent had gone ahead up the stairs. Suddenly he swung round and lashed out with his foot, catching Poulet a mighty kick in the belly. The young attendant, no stranger to irrational behaviour, made no comment. The next day Vincent asked to be forgiven. 'I had the Arles police after me,' he explained.[16]

There were other, more dangerous outbursts. According to Paul Signac, who visited him at Arles, he once tried to poison himself by drinking turps from a bottle. In the asylum he was prevented by Poulet from swallowing paints out of their tubes. Later he tried to steal kerosene from the boy who filled the lamps in an attempt to commit suicide. It took the combined efforts of Peyron, Poulet, and the chief attendant, Trabu, to restrain him.

When we try, assisted by Drs Lubin, Tralbaut, and many others, to determine the possible nature of Vincent's disorder, we are faced with a choice between absinthe poisoning, masked epilepsy, and schizophrenia. There is evidence to support either of the first two, or even a combination of both. As for schizophrenia, our understanding of it is far from complete.

Vincent drank a great deal of absinthe, in Antwerp, Paris, and Arles. Gauguin says it was a glass of absinthe that Vincent threw at his head in the bar at Arles. This beverage, once thought a cure for fever and brought over from Algeria by the military, was widely consumed in Provence. Banned in France in 1915, it is said to have produced epileptic-type convulsions and attacks of delirium. The absinthe plant contains Thujone, a brain toxin.[17]

Neurologists now accept that masked or latent epilepsy can produce episodic disturbances of the brain, particularly in persons susceptible to external stimuli such as powerful light or strongly vibrating colour. Such persons have been found to possess a higher than normal concentration of electrical activity in the temporal lobe of the brain. None of this, though, would have been known to Dr Rey, a locum yet to complete his degree, or Dr Peyron, an eye specialist with no training in the treatment of mental illness. Neither of them refer in their registers to the fainting spells mentioned by Vincent in his letters.

The clinical name for the malady most likely to give rise to Vincent's cluster of symptoms is toxic psychosis. Unlike manic-depressive disorders and schizophrenia, the syndrome has an organic basis. Its most common form is delirium tremens brought on by alcoholic poisoning, and manifests itself after the person has been drinking heavily over long periods and then stops. The fact that Vincent had no access to uncontrolled alcohol while at the asylum would seem to rule out abrupt withdrawal from alcohol as a cause of his disturbances.

Medical students are still being awarded doctorates for theses that set out to grapple with this impenetrable case history. The welter of medical and psychiatric opinion – a bibliography of over a hundred titles increases yearly – warns us that experts will go round in circles for ever rather than admit that no definite diagnosis is possible. The patient has got away, leaving his work to perplex doctors and rejuvenate the simple-minded.

The oils from Saint-Rémy tend to shy away from brilliant colour. It may be that Vincent feared the effect of bright contrasts on his precarious nervous system. A simpler explanation could be that the sadness of his plight, his shaming weakness, and the pathos of his circumstances had bled him, leading him to substitute a palette of broken tones and dimmed, troubled colours. He worked now in mainly minor keys, though there were striking exceptions. Yet even when he returns to the gorgeous jewelled tones of his Arles days, as in *Wheatfield with Cypresses*, vehement colour gives way to torrential brushwork and a charged leaping line.

Meyer Shapiro makes the point that there seems to be a limit of total energy, and what is subtracted from one side, in this case his colour, gets added to the other. Contour is now the insistent element, the winding and twisting lines of a bounding calligraphy that gyrates without ever coming to rest. Shapiro further notes that 'during that year at Saint-Rémy he was drawn especially to objects in strain: to landscapes, obstructed and convulsed; to a cataclysmic world of stormy movements and upheavals, nature suffering and disturbed; to sloping mountains, tumultuous hills and rocks, and fields descending like a rapid stream; to thick undergrowth, ravines and quarries.'[18] His own description of *The Ravine* bears this out, and provides clues to the symbolic meaning he was pursuing: 'the two masses of mighty solid rock . . . and at the end of the ravine a third mountain, which blocks it . . .'. In his mind the problems confronting him were truly mountainous and his attempts to find a way forward endlessly thwarted, as he struggled with forces beyond his control. His paintings were again like drawings, outlining, defining, attempts to limit, impulsive and agitated manoeuvres that mapped out his inner turmoil. The fields of force underlying one unstable world would be mastered in these forays, but always there was another waiting outside the frame.

From between the iron bars of his cell, recuperating one day, he saw the irregular ground fenced by a wall changing before his eyes. It was being reaped. Resigned now to his fate as someone wrecked, death had begun to make an ever stronger appeal, and here was 'an image of death as the great book of nature speaks of it.'[19] His painting, hitting the ecstatic high yellow note of Arles once more, was all yellow – except for a line of violet hills. He had done reapers before, but in the north his apprehension of death emerged as grim indeed. This one he saw differently, in a sense as a doppelgänger, 'fighting like a devil in the midst of the heat to get to the end of his task.' But there was nothing sad in this death, it arrived 'almost smiling', in broad daylight with 'a sun flooding everything with a light of pure gold.'[20]

The Reaper repays with interest our close study. We see that wheat and sky are the same solid gold. We observe a wildly tilted field enclosed by a long, long wall of stone. The sun, small and hot and rolling, presses its exuberant belly down on the crags and hollows of blue hills in outline.

Where, we ask, is the reaper? There is no figure in sight. Finding the reaper in the midst of life is the world's oldest enigma. Then we see him, cunningly camouflaged in yellow between the sheaves, the one clue to his presence the green smudge of his scythe. He is moving steadily across the field and not missing a stalk. We can almost hear the hiss of his blade, can almost see his yellow smile. The reaper who is never late comes closer, with his southern death.

Of the 150 oils completed at Saint-Rémy, over forty are copies after Delacroix, Rembrandt, Daumier, Millet, and others, as well as new versions of canvases he had done at Arles. One, a copy of a work accomplished in his blaze-of-noon exhilaration, is *The*

Arlésienne, a favourite among his portraits. The anonymous woman stares back at us, brazen and yet mournful, her grey elongated face against a background of pale lemon. One version he finished in an hour, so her expression could be resentment at being slashed into life without ceremony in such brutal haste. A raw Prussian blue lurking in the folds of black clothes reinforces her mood. Behind her is a ferment of lilac on a patch of wall, like a window thrown open on seas of blossom, cataracts of dawns. Indifferent, her back immovable, she leans her elbows on a green table and stubbornly exists, trapped in an armchair of yellow wood.

Not surprisingly Vincent contemplated the enclosed field beyond his window over long stretches of time, investing it with symbolic meaning. In *Landscape with Ploughed Field* the perspective, always dramatic and unexpected in his art – *the carrier of infinity*, Shapiro calls it – speeds our gaze deep into the picture and towards a goal that divides in two, mirroring the split he was so intensely aware of in himself. Furrows rush us to a source of turmoil, a clump of shapeless disturbed trees and bushes. Our path to it is blocked by the stone fence. To the right, an enormous available sun radiates lines of powerful healing. Directly beneath the sun is a cottage and its family. The mobility of the hectic furrows forces the eye towards a dark fulfilment beyond an obstacle, while the transforming power of overflowing love waits to one side.

A feeling of helplessness and a childish dependence on others that he would experience during periods of convalescence may have influenced the choice of biblical themes he painted while at Saint-Rémy. His homesickness and nostalgia at such times, when he was humbled and brought low, no doubt played a part in reviving the religious thoughts of his youth and the simple faith of his upbringing. 'Brigadier, you are right,' Gauguin would say mockingly to his companion when arguments became overheated, and then confide slyly to his friends, 'The Bible fires his Dutch brain.' Vincent, no longer a believer, carried embedded in his soul the tremendous old symbols he had absorbed as a child, of the wheeling panoply of the cosmos that was called Heaven, of martyrdom, the destruction of worldly power, the raising of the dead. They were lodged in him still. He could not deny them. It was precisely because they lived in him so vividly that he had an aversion to paintings which concocted religious figures from the artist's imagination. Far too honest to attempt any such thing himself, he objected to Bernard that 'it's an enchanted territory, old man, and one quickly finds oneself up against a wall.' Better, he thought, to turn to the sun and the stars, to the unpeopled olive groves. And yet, despite the fact that Christianity was now no more than a ruined temple, 'that does not keep me from having a terrible need of – shall I say the word – religion. Then I go out at night to paint the stars.'[21]

Gauguin had not yet come into his own, and the sickly yellowish Christs he painted in Brittany are trivial when compared with Vincent's copies after Delacroix and Rembrandt. Nervously inflamed and anxious, Vincent calmed his spirit with these awkward and intense transpositions from the masters. His *Pietà* (after Delacroix) converts the lines into his own turbulent language, widening the span of yellow and blue and pouring around the figures his Expressionist brushstrokes, sinuous dashes that were imbued with fervour, and with the throbbing ache of a love he longed to have. He gives the head and face of Christ the reddish colouring with green shadows of his own likeness in self-portraits, though nothing else is there to identify him. We need nothing else. Here for only the first or second time the mystical dark blue he used to represent eternity appears in the mother's clothes. The sky is absolute, the contours jagged. The *Mater Dolorosa* has the features of Sister Epiphany, the Mother Superior of the cloisters at Saint-Rémy. The Christ cradled in His mother's arms is as pathetic as the broken men Vincent must have seen lifted up by attendants after violent seizures.

Road with Cypress and Star, another fusion of death and heaven, consoles Vincent with the dream of doubles, as do *Pietà* and *The Good Samaritan* with its bandaged traveller. Two people walk side by side as one in the foreground, and two big cypresses, merging as one at the top, reach to the night sky between a crescent moon and a brilliant star. Other paintings from Saint-Rémy show us the solitary walking figure of the pilgrim, the subject of Vincent's English sermon. His thoughts on the heaven he was journeying towards stir us deeply, as do so many of his remarks straight from the heart: 'Why, I say to myself, should the shining dots of the sky be less accessible than the black dots on the map of France?

Just as we take the train to get to Tarascon or Rouen, we take death to reach a star.'[22]

Now, more than ever, his paintings speak to us in the language of destination. 'It seems to me not impossible that cholera, gravel, consumption may be celestial means of transport just as steam-ships, buses, railways are means of transport on this earth. To die quietly of old age would be like going on foot . . .'. Like Verkovensky in Dostoevsky's *The Possessed*, the road he trudged along on his way to the motif was 'like a man's life, a man's dream.' We have to remind ourselves also that under the triumphant materialist nineteenth century lay something ruinous, the darkly suggestive presence of future trouble, a sense of the times being out of joint. The knowledge that this was so, and the need to stand apart, stand by himself, was being mixed on his palette with increasing fury and given forms that were more to do with chaotic motion than with order, celebrating the end as much as the beginning of something. Whether these disorders, obsessions, poisons came from outside or from some torn centre of his being, the open heart of him was flung into chaos. Sometimes his fight seemed against art itself.

He paid a second visit to Arles, ostensibly to collect some of his canvases and to talk to Dr Rey. Another reason was his determination to overcome any antipathy towards him that might still remain there. After what had erupted from his unconscious, where he had been jeered at and threatened, his inferiority made public and reaffirmed, to go back again was a risky undertaking for him. Yet unless he went, he said, he would feel cowardly at the mere thought of the place, like someone nervous of a pack of mongrels that had once tried to savage him. As it was, the ugliness of the experience had turned his thoughts northwards and revived longings of home. He painted from his imagination a scene of hovels with moss-covered thatched roofs and called it *Memories of the North*.

The visit to Arles passed without incident. Two days later he was ill again. Then in July he heard that Theo's wife, Jo, was pregnant. He wrote to congratulate the sister-in-law he had yet to meet. A few days after this he was felled by his worst attack so far, when he was out in the fields some distance from the asylum.

By September he was struggling back to a semblance of normality, painting his ghostly self-portrait and a portrait of the head attendant, Trabu. Both employ the same rhythmical technique of swirling arabesques he had used to transform his cypresses. The blanched colours and the fixity of expression, common to both pictures, make them a pair. And they are paired symbolically. The grim stony Trabu, guardian of law and order, who reminded Vincent of a Spanish grandee in an etching by Legros, has vestiges of his handsome father. Trabu sits, resentfully immobilised. In his incongruously animated striped jacket he looks turned to stone, the very principle of strict negation. As if caught in the act of shaking his head, his eyes say no. He is sad but fierce. Upholding dogma is a sad but necessary task. Life-giving Roulin has been usurped by this timeless nay-sayer. The hairless bulge of his cranium overwhelms the pinched face, dwindling ever smaller as it descends in frowning lines. He tucks back his chin in disapproving grey folds, and every fold is a denial. Vincent, a transient blue shade weakly alive from the tomb, is thinned to a ghost. His cheeks are tinged green. His unwilling spirit quivers up in frail blue-green spirals, neither mortal nor immortal, hovering before us.

Feeling 'sadder and more wretched' than he could say, Vincent now began to plan his escape. While there he contained his bitterness at Peyron's indifference, only saying after he had left that the director paid no attention to his collapses, 'leaving me to vegetate with all the rest, all deeply tainted'.[23] His surroundings, that he had tried so hard to accept, now weighed on him more than ever, as is the case when one is desperate to depart, 'I need air, I feel overwhelmed with boredom and grief,' he told Theo, and asked his brother to concentrate on the old problem of where he should go next.

Unknown to him, things were stirring: the world had begun to wake up to the fact of his existence. When he was in Paris his canvases had been shown in the Restaurant la Fourche, the Cabaret du Tambourine, and at Tanguy's paint shop, and later at the exhibitions of Les Indépendants. None of it bore fruit. The twenty francs he got from Tanguy represented his total returns from these exposures.

But now a friend of Theo's, J J Isaacson, referred to him in an article on the Impressionists, in a series he was writing for an Amsterdam weekly. Vincent, immediately alarmed by what he regarded as the author's exaggeration, begged him to desist in future. Then in January 1890 a young French critic, Albert Aurier, alerted by Isaacson's piece and shown some of the work by Vincent that filled Theo's apartment to overflowing, wrote an article devoted to him in *Le Mercure de France*. In it he characterised Vincent's art as one of excess, 'excess in strength, excess in nervousness, in violence of expression. In the categorical affirmation of the character of things, in his frequently headstrong simplification of forms, in his insolence in depicting the sun face to face, he reveals a powerful being, a man bold, often brutal and sometimes ingenuously delicate.'[24] So it went on, in this highly favourable vein and at considerable length.

It was a breakthrough, and Vincent was horrified at being thus singled out. 'What sustains me in my work,' he wrote to his mother, 'is the very feeling that there are several others doing the same thing I am, so why an article on me?'[25] Why not Emile Bernard, why not Gauguin? He wrote at once to Aurier pointing out his debt to Monticelli and drawing attention to the influence of Gauguin. The recognition worried and pained him. It seemed preposterous that someone as unworthy as himself should receive praise of this kind. As soon as he heard news of the article, 'I feared at once that I should be punished for it.'[26] Indeed, punishment would have been preferable. Praise would only earn him the resentment and hatred of his fellow artists, who would see it as undeserved. Only rejection in his experience brought a measure of love.

A copy of this letter to Aurier went off to Gauguin. Gauguin's kind words at the time would be retracted later, when he came to write his memoirs. There he said that Aurier's article should have been about him. Vincent had only got into his stride as a painter after he, Gauguin, had been to Arles and put 'the sound of the bugle' into his work.

Early in January came more startling news. Aurier's article had been seen in Brussels, and a society of artists there, who had already invited *avant-garde* painters in Paris to exhibit with them, wondered whether Vincent would care to be included. They published their own journal and were proposing to reprint extracts from Aurier's feature.

Thus Vincent achieved the one bona fide sale of his career. His painting *The Red Vineyard* was brought in Brussels for 400 Belgian francs. The purchaser was Anna Boch, sister of Vincent's friend Eugene Boch, and a painter herself. Boch, it will be remembered, was the Belgian artist Vincent met shortly after arriving in Arles.

He received news of the sale and by the same post heard that Jo had given birth to a boy. Vincent had a nephew and a godson, to be named Vincent Willem in honour of him. Earlier he had objected to the suggestion, saying that if they had a son they should name him in memory of their late father. Now he set to work painting a picture to mark the occasion. What better than an image of rebirth? *The Branch of an Almond Tree in Blossom*, a tender, joyously radiant work of white petals vibrating in the exciting blue he loved, was nearly finished when he suffered the most severe of his relapses at Saint-Rémy. He lay half dead throughout the months of spring, unable to even make sense of his mail until the end of April.

Charles Mauron, who delivered a paper at the Municipal Museum at Amsterdam in March 1953 on the symbiotic relationship between the two brothers, has sought to connect Vincent's severest crises with certain key events in Theo's life. The first breakdown occurred on 23 December 1888, immediately following the news of Theo's engagement. Further attacks coincided with Theo's marriage and the birth of his child. Mauron puts forward the argument that Vincent's first unconscious premise – You are getting married, your life must now go from me to your wife and child – was followed by a second – I have been denied, I must withdraw and die, break connection, break down, so that this can be.[27]

Casting about for somewhere to live as a free man again, yet flinching at the thought of living alone, at the mercy of his bouts of melancholy and worse, he appealed to Theo for suggestions. In the same letter he asked to be shielded from any further publicity. It was more than he could bear. Gauguin, whom he had also approached – either perversely, or from a strange desire to make amends – replied with a vague mention of a shared studio in Antwerp. But this seemed a backward step. First he had to extricate himself from the asylum. He had said as much to Peyron, who made no objection. It wasn't, he explained, that he was ungrateful to the Midi. No, on the contrary it had given him a tremendous amount. Only now his face was turned to the north, he was weary, there was an ache of homesickness in him.

Pissarro, the next artist consulted, was more than willing to take him under his wing, only his wife objected, fearing for the safety of her children. Pissarro then came up with the idea of Auvers-sur-Oise, north-west of Paris, where Vincent could stay under the supervision of Pissarro's old friend and patron, Dr Gachet. Vincent cheered up, telling Theo that he thought they should fix on the offer. 'The main thing,' he wrote, 'is to know the doctor, so that in case of an attack I do not fall into the hands of the police and get carried off to an asylum by force.'[28]

So it was settled. Theo was anxious for him to be accompanied on the journey to Paris. Vincent vetoed that 'categorically'. He was not a dangerous beast. Even if he did fall ill on the train, surely they knew at every station what to do in such a case? He felt strong again – moving always made him hopeful; the last horrible attack had vanished like a thunderstorm and with luck he would give illness the slip. Placating Theo, he promised to have someone with him as far as Tarascon, or one or two stops further on. More than anything now he wanted to be there, to clasp his brother's hand and to make Jo's and the baby's acquaintance. He would like to stay with them a few days, see the old sights, and call on some friends. His head, he reported, was absolutely calm; the brush strokes came smoothly and well 'like a machine', following each other logically. Dr Peyron wrote the word 'cured' in his records.

On 16 May he caught the train, his last, for Paris, and went back the way he had come. Theo, worried to death after a disturbed night, was at the station next morning to meet him.

13

BLACK LIGHT

Johanna van Gogh, watching out for the two brothers from her apartment window, was expecting a sick man, and a man she had never met. When the open fiacre came into view she looked down at hands waving, faces smiling. Then the person she had heard so much about entered the room. 'He seems perfectly well – he looks much stronger than Theo,' was my first thought. Here was a sturdy, broad-shouldered man with a healthy colour, a smile on his face, and a very resolute appearance . . . . Apparently there had come again the puzzling change in his condition that the Reverend Salles had already observed to his great surprise at Arles.'[1]

Theo took his brother straight in to see the baby in its cradle. The infant was asleep. They stood there without saying anything, both with tears in their eyes. Jo had come in behind them. Vincent pointed to the crocheted cover on the cradle and said, smiling, 'Don't cover him with too much lace, little sister.'[2]

In the apartment *The Potato Eaters* was hanging in a place of honour over the dining room mantelpiece, his *Orchards in Bloom* in the main bedroom, and the great *Landscape from Arles* and *Night View on the Rhône* in the sitting room. The rest were in the spare room, stacked in various cupboards and jammed under the beds and sofas, 'to the great despair,' wrote Jo, 'of our *femme de ménage*'. Out they came one after another and were spread over every available surface for Vincent to examine. Next morning he was up early and walking around in his shirtsleeves studying his work, astonished by the sheer quantity of it. Later he went out to buy olives, which he liked to eat every day, he explained, urging them on his brother and sister-in-law.

He went excitedly around Paris, visiting old haunts and calling on acquaintances. He visited the annual Salon and was bewitched by 'a superb Pavis de Chavannes . . . . When one sees this picture, when one looks at it for a long time, one gets the feeling of being present at a rebirth, total but benevolent, of all the things one should have believed in, should have wished for – a strange and happy meeting of very distant antiquities and crude modernity.'³ He wrote to his sister Wil that the noise and rush of Paris scared him now, after being away so long, and was bad for his head. Theo's cough was worse, he thought, than when they had parted two years ago.

He liked Jo very much, she was 'charming and very simple and brave'. He mentioned his last days at Saint-Rémy when he had worked like a man in a frenzy on flower canvases, 'great bunches of flowers, violet irises, big bouquets of roses', all done in celebration, one imagines, of his glad rebirth into a spring he must have felt was being created yet again out of himself. What he particularly wanted was to show Wil his olive orchards against yellow, pink, and blue skies, painted he believed for the first time in this manner.

He left for Auvers on 21 May. It was hot and sunny. Arriving there, he was struck by the town's beauty, loving the thatched mossy roofs with their reminder of his childhood. The main street lies near the River Oise, the rest of the town rising in terraces up a hillside to the plains above. Strolling about in this peaceful spot beloved of artists he felt calm and normal. Dr Gachet had arranged accommodation for him at an inn for 6 francs a day. Careful as ever not to overspend Theo's allowance, he went instead to Ravoux's little café in the main street. An attic room there would cost him only 3 francs 50 centimes. The location may have also appealed to him, directly opposite the town hall, just as the vicarage had been at Zundert where he had lived as a child. Inside, the café recalled the 'Night Café' at Arles with its billiard table, iron stove, and rush-seated chairs.

It was only five minutes' walk to Dr Gachet's house. He wasted no time getting to know the medical practitioner, a middle-aged man of Flemish origin, able to talk to Vincent in his own language. Paul Gachet was an unusual combination of talents. He practised homeopathic as well as conventional medicine at his surgery in Paris, where he went three days a week. The rest of the time he spent at Auvers, painting and conversing with artists and calling on an occasional patient. He had two children, a girl of nineteen and a boy of sixteen.

Vincent was soon a close friend. Like him, Gachet was a free-thinker, utopian, an exponent of the simple life, and a socialist. The man was eccentric. In his house were eight cats and eight dogs, and in the gardens he kept chickens, peacocks, ducks, pigeons, even sheep. There was a goat called Henrietta that he took for walks on a lead. He signed his paintings with a pseudo-nym, Paul van Rysell, and was extremely knowledgeable about art. As a young man in Paris he had made lots of bohemian friends, including Murger, Courbet, and Proudhon. He special-ised in nervous diseases and was interested in the therapeutic properties of electricity. Later in life he got to know Sisley, Renoir, and Monet. Cézanne and Pissarro were his neighbours at Auvers for a while.

Vincent was fascinated with him and with the contents of his house. Canvases, framed and unframed, were everywhere, fine flower pieces by Cézanne, Pissarro landscapes – in fact all the Impressionists were represented. Gachet's house was on three storeys and overlooked the town. He had been at Auvers for twenty-five years and knew everyone, including the local artists. Vincent met several, but made no attempt to form close relation-ships with them. Next door to him at the Ravouxs' was a whole houseful of American artists, all of them members of one family. Living with him at the café was a young Dutch painter, Anton Hirschig. Once or twice he seems to have gone out with an Australian artist, Walpole Brooke. One painter who did interest him – he had lived and worked in Japan – was Louis Dumoulin (called 'Desmoulins' in Vincent's letters). Dumoulin left again for Japan on the day of Vincent's death.

One weekend Theo and Jo came out to see him, bringing the baby. Vincent carried his nephew in his arms and took him on a tour of Gachet's 'animal world'. The baby only cried when a rooster crowed under his nose and frightened him. Taking his visitors back to the station, Vincent produced a bird's nest as a present for the child.

Johanna van Gogh has said how she was struck by the

resemblance between Vincent and Dr Gachet, who had red hair, blue eyes, and a large forehead, dressed oddly, and smoked a pipe all the time. Vincent too seems to have regarded him as a mixture of father and brother. He was attracted to him and yet uncertain, seeing him as 'very queer', with a 'grief-hardened' face. Gachet had lost his wife fifteen years before, and according to Vincent was still bereft. The blazing light of his Impressionist collection contrasted weirdly with his houseful of black antiques, 'black, black, black' as Vincent reported uneasily.

What most disturbed him about the doctor was the fact that they were so much alike, 'so much do we resemble each other physically and mentally'. This was not good. If Gachet had similar weaknesses to his own, how could he help him with his? His anxiety broke out in a letter to Theo: 'I think we must not count on Dr Gachet *at all*. First of all, he is sicker than I am, I think, or shall we say just as much, so that's that. Now when one blind man leads another blind man, don't they both fall into the ditch?'[4] In short, Gachet was neurasthenic, bizarre, deeply depressed. As if to study him more intently and so find out the worst, Vincent began a portrait: the head in a white cap, the hands light-coloured, the figure in a blue frock coat, set against the ultimate blue background of cobalt that was now the keynote of his paintings, as yellow had been at Arles. In front of the doctor, who was leaning on a red table, he had placed a yellow book and a foxglove plant with purple flowers.

It is an extraordinary work, a self-portrait of his own discouraged spirit combined with the likeness of a man cursed like himself, on his face 'the heartbroken expression of our time'. For all the wearing down displayed by the doctor's drooping posture – and the droop of eyes and mouth – there is a paradoxical luxuriance to the curly coat edges, the apple-green buttons, the flooding brushstrokes like swarming molecules, and the tender bells of the foxgloves – slanting on their stalk in sympathy with the keeled-over figure – that exudes germination, growth, fertility. Dr Gachet was so 'fanatical' in his liking for it that he wanted another just like it for himself. The man was kind and generous, and Vincent was a little dismayed by the four and five course meals confronting him when he called on Sundays. He thought them bad for his digestion, and the doctor's too, but when he understood the reason for them he couldn't bring himself to protest.

Poor Gachet was recalling the old family dinners of his happier past.

There was a curious incident one day that no one has managed to explain. One of the paintings Vincent admired in Gachet's house was by Guillaumin, of a bare-breasted woman on a bed. Seeing it, Vincent reacted bitterly, according to the story told later by the doctor's son. He thought it terrible that the picture should be left unframed. Gachet agreed. He arranged with his local framer to have it done. When Vincent saw the painting again it was still unframed. He trembled, flew into a rage, and took a step towards the doctor. Gachet stared him down with a 'powerful look', just as Gauguin was supposed to have done in the street at Arles on the night of Vincent's seizure. In this case, if we can believe that it happened, there was no subsequent psychotic attack.

On 24 June he wondered what Theo would make of a portrait he had just done of a girl of sixteen, the daughter of the people with whom he was staying. This was Adeline Ravoux. He went on to paint the baby, Levert, in a delightful impromptu piece. A toddler with yellow bangs and bright pink cheeks, in blue and wearing a white bib, is clutching an orange. The child sits happily in a patch of lush green field studded with buttercups, part of nature's smiling earth. It is a cunningly 'naive' work.

Adeline Ravoux, treated with the same apparent naivety, is in fact almost impersonal, deliberate art. Placed with audacious simplicity to one side of the frame, it is a study in strict profile. The figure, wincingly shy, waits in the wings with the painful introspection of Münch's girl in *Puberty*. The drawing has a rough force, the outline stiff like an icon. All is pervaded by the sumptuous dark blue of the painting's message, flowing over the background and swamping the dress, further bleaching by contrast the tight little face, already drained to a pallor.

Always a prodigious worker, Vincent turned out 70 oils and 30 drawings in the seventy days he was at Auvers. As if anticipating the end he drove himself harder than ever. The ascending spirals, coiling lines, and curved forms of Saint-Rémy were changing, giving way to staccato broken strokes, like the jabs of a man in a frantic race to catch up. The rapturous blue of Arles was now transfigured, no longer flat and even but darkened, pulsing, and sparking around heads and above fields in expanses that were infinitely mysterious and mosaic-like, fluid entities that were never still. In the midst of this high-powered swift-moving work from stretched nerves he suddenly painted a woodland scene of absolute serenity, *Undergrowth with Two Figures*. Nothing is rushing anywhere, the pressure of time has been abolished, and we float down before the peaceful upright lines of young trees. Shapiro says it perfectly when he describes them as 'a community of friendly presences'. Colours are quiet soft harmonies of white, yellow, speckled green, and lilac. Among these tree and sapling figures move a man and a woman, perhaps lovers walking close together over the soft ground of yellow and white flowers into dense undergrowth. A succession of downward stroked verticals, falling simply like strokes of filtered rain, has brought this magical rendering of a lost domain to pass. Adam and Eve walk again in the cool of the evening.

Alas, not for long. Over the fields of poppies, fields of corn, the skies of his paintings were becoming darkly troubled. Early in July Vincent was invited to Paris to meet a gathering of old friends and have lunch with Toulouse Lautrec at Theo's apartment. It all began well. Theo was four floors up. Coming in, Lautrec got himself entangled with an undertaker's assistant who was a mute. He joked about it with Vincent.

Theo, however, was far from well. For months he had been in poor health. Vincent, always highly sensitive to his brother's worries, soon realised that things were going wrong for Theo. His son was causing anxiety, crying plaintively night after night. Jo had worn herself out looking after the child. Theo had been hinting at his financial problems in a letter to Vincent, telling him that 'those rats Boussod and Valadon are treating me as though I had just entered their business, and are keeping me on a short allowance.'[5] His employers wanted him to stop involving himself so much with the unprofitable Impressionists, so he had retaliated by threatening to resign and start up on his own unless they paid him an adequate salary. Not wishing to agitate Vincent he had sought to play all this down. Nevertheless he was on a knife-edge and it showed, as he waited tensely for a decision from 'these gentlemen (who) have not said a word about what they intend to do with me.' As soon as Vincent set eyes on him he read the whole wretched story in the other's face. Conscience-stricken once again at being a burden, he seems to have asked Theo for reassurances about his position. The atmosphere was fraught, unhappy. Vincent left sooner than expected and went back to Auvers.

Jo wrote to him in an attempt to put his mind at rest, and he thanked her for her letter's 'deliverance'. All the same he was still oppressed, he said, by the threatening storm that endangered them and him too, feeling that 'my life is also threatened at the very root, and my steps are also wavering.' When he had been with them it was as if 'you felt me to be rather a thing to be dreaded.'[6]

Theo and his family were due to leave for Holland on 15 July for Theo's usual summer vacation. Because of the difficulties Theo was in, together with his uncertain health, surely it would be better, Vincent argued, if they came instead to Auvers and recuperated in the country; after all, the journey home was arduous and expensive, the baby very small to travel so far. Their mother would understand. It was a passionate plea, developed over several days. But to no avail: Theo, Jo and the child left as planned. Eight days later Theo was back in Paris for urgent business reasons, while his wife and child divided the time between Jo's parents and Mrs van Gogh.

Vincent worked on; it was his one distraction. He had been producing vistas of pale green and blue in the blurry slants of rain, flicking them into being with Japanese touches to produce pastures that were misted, numinous, and exquisite, coming to rest before the eye like boats of light. Soon though he was absorbed in wheatfields that were 'boundless as a sea, delicate yellow, delicate soft green, the delicate violet of a dug-up and weeded piece of soil, checkered at regular intervals with the green of flowering potato plants, everything under a sky of delicate blue, white, pink, violet tones.'[7] His mother has written at the top of this letter: 'Very last letter from Auvers.' In it he said how pleased he was that his sister Wil had taken up nursing and was able to cope with her work at the hospital. He spoke of being in a mood of 'almost too much calmness'.

Crows over the Wheatfield used to be regarded as his last work, a claim since disputed. Writers inevitably interpret it as a clamorous and doom-laden portent of his imminent self-destruction.

Like so many of his paintings it has death-throes and birth pangs mingled in it. Unlike the others it depicts a great darkness lowering over the land. The sun god in the wheat, trying to rise, is being engulfed in a kind of dreadful earthquake. Centres which were split in previous perspectives, sending us towards two adjacent but separate goals, have here fallen apart. The three tracks in the field which have been made so much of by commentators begin at the bottom edge and diverge catastrophically, left, right, and the central double track aims us straight for the boiling horizon. The perspective itself has got somehow reversed and is rushing the land back at us in an upheaval, birds and torn sky with it, folding it all back on the painter. As in a horrible nightmare where one is locked in terror, unable to move or scream, the painter, helpless to advance into the world and live there, sees it toppling over him in a wave of earth and sky. Instead of painting he is being painted out; by his fate, his death. The earth has ceased warmly nurturing him like a great mother and is now a devourer, the light eclipsed, turning into black storm, a broken-up sun scattered in the wheat. The cradle of blue and gold is smashed.

Vincent's last letter to Theo was disjointed and sounded a despairing note. He badly wanted to write about the pressing need for painters to combine in a union, seeing them as 'fighting more and more with their backs to the wall,' but his hopes for some kind of cooperative endeavour had been dashed long ago.[8] Feeling he should take the initiative, he lacked the desire, he confessed.

On the evening of Sunday, 27 July, he left Ravoux's café and climbed out of the town – no one knows exactly where he went. He had borrowed a revolver from Gustave Ravoux, saying he wished to scare away the crows. He shot himself in the chest, the bullet entering level with the edge of the left ribs, close to his heart but missing it. Late for supper, Ravoux and his wife were baffled by his absence, since he had never kept them waiting and liked to be in bed by sunset. Night was falling when he stumbled in, clutching his stomach. Inside, he staggered against the billiard table, his coat wrapped round to disguise the wound. Asked what was the matter, he mumbled, 'Oh nothing, I'm wounded.' Somehow he dragged himself up the seventeen twisty stairs to his attic room. Adeline, the daughter, listening at the foot of the stairs, heard him cry out.

Gustave Ravoux went up to see what the trouble was. Vincent was lying on the iron cot with his face to the wall. 'I shot myself,' he told his landlord. 'I only hope I haven't botched it.'

The local doctor was called, but Vincent wanted his friend Gachet. Then two policemen came. They asked what he had done with the revolver. He wouldn't speak. The weapon was never found. Asked to explain his action, Vincent said calmly, 'I am free to do what I like with my own body.'

Gachet arrived with his son and Vincent asked if he might smoke. Gachet didn't object; in fact he filled his friend's pipe, lit it, and put it in Vincent's mouth. Extracting the bullet proved impossible, and Gachet asked for Theo's address. Vincent shook his head. Anton Hirschig, the young Dutch painter who lived in the café with Vincent, took a message from Gachet to Theo's gallery in Paris, and Theo rushed out to Auvers on Monday morning. Vincent, seeing his brother's distress, said, 'Don't cry, I've done it for the good of us all.'[9]

Theo and Vincent lay together on the bed. The younger man couldn't stop weeping. At one in the morning of Tuesday, 28 July, Vincent lost consciousness and died of suffocation in his brother's arms. He was thirty-seven. Moments before he had said, 'I want to go,' and then 'It's no use, misery lasts all one's life.'

As a suicide he was not entitled to a Christian burial. His funeral took place on Wednesday. Eight people came, among them Tanguy, Lucien Pissarro (whose father, Camille, was going blind), and Emile Bernard. Gachet of course was there. The coffin, draped in a white sheet, rested on the billiard table in the café. Theo and Bernard between them hung some of the Auvers paintings around the room to form 'something like a halo' around the dead man.

There was controversy after death as there was in life. The Catholic priest had forbidden the use of the town hearse for the burial of a suicide, so the neighbouring township of Méry had to provide one. At the graveside Dr Gachet tried to make a speech. No one could make it out, he wept so much. Theo said a few words of thanks. It was over.[10]

According to Otto Rank, the great artist and great work are

271

only born from the reconciliation of the two notions of deprivation and renunciation, and by the victory of a philosophy of
renunciation over an ideology of deprivation. 'How van Gogh
renounced and renounced,' wrote Rilke. He was only able to
escape his lone orphanhood when his ecstacy before nature and
the stars delivered up a painting. Deprivation returned when the
gulf that every modern artist dreads opened under his feet, the
void of no community, no love, no home, and no mother. Then
life as a living death, a servitude to be borne, came back as a
travesty of all he had tasted. 'Being friends, being brothers, love,
that is what opens the cage,' he had written once to Theo, the
one close friend of his life.[11]

He spoke of portraits as being tokens of immortality, for his
humble sitters and for himself, and it seems certain that his calm
anticipation of death in his last hours had to do with a dream of
immortality he had often nursed. Life was a trap of sorrow from
which he longed to escape. Isaac Bashevis Singer has a short story
in which an unhappy woman, who had once stopped breathing
for hours after an operation and found the sensation blissful, says
to the narrator: 'I came to tell you only one thing: that of all the
hopes a human being can have, the most splendid is death. I tasted
it, and whoever tastes this ecstasy must laugh at all the other so-
called pleasures. That which man fears from the cradle to the
grave is the highest joy.'

POSTCRIPT

An unposted letter to Theo, found on the body, had the last word of all: 'Well, my own work, I am risking my life for it and my reason has half foundered because of it – that's all right.' He urged his brother to stop floundering, in a way that invited disaster, and to make the real decision about his future. 'You can still choose your side I think, acting with humanity, but what do you want?'[1] He sensed a catastrophe ahead for Theo. His brother – as he had always maintained – was more than a simple dealer. Tussling with 'those worthy gentlemen' in business deals was beside the point, a postponement merely.

His warning came too late. Suicide devastates and accuses, and can even generate self-hatred in those brushed by it. Vincent said as much when he told Theo that the act of suicide turns one's friends into murderers. Theo, shattered by the tragedy of his brother's death, never recovered. For several weeks he was prostrated, unable to acknowledge letters of sympathy. He tried to put a memorial exhibition together and hoped to persuade Aurier to write a biography based on the letters, but none of these things was carried through. He quarrelled with his employers suddenly over a minor matter and resigned. Pissarro and Gauguin were both convinced he was unhinged. He acted erratically, sent a crazy wire to Gauguin offering to sponsor his trip to the South Seas, and then became violent at home, once attacking his wife and child. Jo took him to Holland and he was admitted to a hospital in Utrecht (the same one in which Margot Begemann had received treatment). There he sank into the kind of torpor and

273

deep sadness Vincent would experience after one of his attacks. He died on 25 January, less than six months after Vincent. He was thirty-three.

Many theories have been advanced to explain Vincent's suicide and the Shakespearean collapse of a young family that followed it. Fear of a relapse, fear of a loss of creative power, fear of success; jealousy, revenge, self-punishment; the desire to emulate Christ – the list keeps growing. In the concluding pages of his biography M E Tralbaut contributes another, one that is at least instinctive. Meeting Johanna with her baby – an irresistible combination for Vincent – would have presented him with an intolerable picture of a happiness now quite beyond him. If, says the honest Tralbaut in effect, we must have a single motive, then why not this?

Rumour has it that Marguerite Gachet, the doctor's daughter, was in love with Vincent, and that her father vehemently opposed the relationship. If true, it is a secret she carried with her to the grave. Reclusive, she never married. Vincent painted a portrait of her seated at the piano. She died in November 1949, aged seventy-eight.

Wilhelmina van Gogh, the only sister sympathetic to Vincent, developed an incapacitating psychosis and had to live in a mental hospital until she died in 1941 at the age of seventy-one. The youngest brother, Cornelius (Cor), left for South Africa, only to die there at the age of thirty-three, possibly by his own hand. Vincent's mother, Anna Cornelia, lived into vigorous old age and outlived all three sons, dying in 1907. She was eighty-six.

One contemporary of Vincent's, Friedrich Nietzsche (they were unaware of one another's existence), whose mind had given way totally in that same year of 1889, said not long before he died that one must harbour chaos within oneself to give birth to a star. Vincent had lost his faith, but not the piety that rejoiced in the night sky with its bright burning stars, reminders for him of the twinkling lights of home and the presence of the dead in heaven.

NOTES ON SOURCES

Letters addressed to Theo van Gogh in *The Complete Letters* are numbered consecutively through three volumes, as follows:

Letters 1–271   Vol I
Letters 272–517 Vol II
Letters 518–652 Vol III

Volume I also contains 'Memoir of Vincent van Gogh' by Mrs J van Gogh-Bonger, with additional notes by her son, V W van Gogh.
In Volume III are to be found letters to Anthon van Rappard, Wilhelmina van Gogh, Emile Bernard, Gauguin, and letters from Theo to his brother Vincent.

1   The Flat of the Land

1   Letter 573
2   Letter 82a
3   K H D Halen, *The Dutch in the Seventeenth Century*
4   Letter 379
5   K H D Halen, *The Dutch in the Seventeenth Century*
6   Graham Swift, *Waterland*
7   *ibid*
8   Charles Baudouin, *Psychoanalysis and Aesthetics*
9   Letter 248
10   Marc Edo Tralbaut, *Vincent van Gogh*
11   E J Hobsbawm, *The Age of Capital*
12   *ibid*
13   Anthony Wood, *Nineteenth-Century Britain*

2 The Intimate Enemy

1 Albert J Lubin, *Stranger on the Earth*
2 Letter 338
3 Marc Edo Tralbaut, *Vincent van Gogh*
4 *ibid*
5 Johanna van Gogh–Bonger, 'Memoir of Vincent van Gogh'
6 Letters 77, 248
7 Letter 341
8 A M & Renilde Hammacher, *Van Gogh: a Documentary Biography*
9 Elizabeth Huberta, *Persoonlijke Herinneringen aan Vincent van Gogh*
10 Letter 100
11 Letter 91

3 First Love

1 Letter 1
2 Letter 10
3 Letter 9
4 E J Hobsbawm, *The Age of Capital*
5 Letter 13a
6 Johanna van Gogh–Bonger, 'Memoir of Vincent van Gogh'
7 Letter 11
8 Letter 11
9 Letter 12
10 Letter 10a
11 Letter 13
12 Letter 14
13 A M & Renilde Hammacher, *Van Gogh: a Documentary Biography*
14 *ibid*
15 Johanna van Gogh–Bonger, 'Memoir of Vincent van Gogh'
16 *ibid*
17 *ibid*
18 Marc Edo Tralbaut, *Vincent van Gogh*
19 Albert J Lubin, *Stranger on the Earth*
20 Letter 26
21 Letter 82a
22 Letter 28
23 Letter 320
24 Letter to Wilhelmina J van Gogh, 10 April 1889
25 Letter 157
26 Letter to Wilhelmina J van Gogh, June–July, 1888
27 Letter 344
28 Letter 31
29 Letter 36a
30 Letter 524

31 Letter 531
32 Letter 55

4 The Soul is a Mirror

 1 Letter 60
 2 Letter 69
 3 John Keats, *Letter to G & T Keats*, 21 December, 1817
 4 William Soutar, *Diary of a Dying Man* (entry for 28 February, 1936)
 5 Albert J Lubin, *Stranger on the Earth*
 6 Letter 136
 7 Letter 69
 8 Albert J Lubin *Stranger on the Earth*
 9 See 'Vincent's Sermon' (after Letter 83, *The Complete Letters*, Vol I)
10 Marc Edo Tralbaut, *Vincent van Gogh*
11 Letter 39
12 Letter 93
13 Marc Edo Tralbaut, *Vincent van Gogh*
14 *ibid*
15 Letter 110
16 Mendes da Costa, *Het Algemeen Handelsblad*, Amsterdam
17 *ibid*
18 *ibid*
19 *ibid*
20 Letter 106
21 Letter 108
22 Letter 110
23 A M & Renilde Hammacher, *Van Gogh: a Documentary Biography*
24 Letter 116
25 Letter 118
26 Letter 252
27 Letter 106
28 Letter 347
29 Ernst Pawels, *The Nightmare of Reason*
30 Letter 100
31 Anna Cornelia van Gogh to Theo, June, 1877

5 Lowest of the Low

 1 Letter 429
 2 Letter 126
 3 Letter 542
 4 Marc Edo Tralbaut, *Vincent van Gogh*

5 *ibid*
6 Letter 126
7 Letter 129
8 *ibid*
9 Letter 143a
10 Marc Edo Tralbaut, *Vincent van Gogh*
11 *ibid*
12 *ibid*
13 Albert J Lubin, *Stranger on the Earth*
14 Marc Edo Tralbaut, *Vincent van Gogh*
15 *ibid*
16 Letter 136
17 Letter 131
18 Letter 133
19 Letter 132
20 *ibid*
21 *ibid*
22 *ibid*
23 *ibid*
24 Isaac Bashevis Singer, 'The Smuggler', *The Death of Methuselah*
25 Letter 133
26 *ibid*
27 *ibid*
28 *ibid*
29 *ibid*
30 *ibid*
31 Otto Rank, 'The Artist's Fight With Art', *Art and Artist*
32 Letter 136
33 Albert J Lubin, *Stranger on the Earth*
34 Letter 227
35 Marc Edo Tralbaut, *Vincent van Gogh*
36 Letter 138
37 Letter 140
38 Letter 138
39 Letter 139
40 Albert J Lubin, *Stranger on the Earth*
41 Leo Tolstoy, *Diary*, 5 October, 1881

6 'The Factory is in Full Swing'

1 Letter 346
2 Letter 150
3 Rainer Maria Rilke, letter to Clara Rilke, 3 October, 1902, *Letters on Cézanne*
4 Letter 149
5 *ibid*

278

6   Letter 150
7   Letter 195
8   Letter 268
9   Albert J Lubin, *Stranger on the Earth*
10 Letter 152
11 Letter 154
12 Letter 153
13 Letter 155
14 Letter 153
15 Marc Edo Tralbaut, *Vincent van Gogh*
16 Letter 154
17 Letter 158
18 Letter 161
19 Letter 159
20 Letter 155
21 Letter 154
22 *ibid*
23 *ibid*
24 Letter 158
25 Letter 161
26 Letter 159
27 Albert J Lubin, *Stranger on the Earth*
28 D H Lawrence, letter to Mrs S A Hopkin, 19 August, 1912, *The Letters of D H Lawrence*
29 Frieda Lawrence, letter to Edward Garnett, October, 1912, *The Letters of D H Lawrence*
30 D H Lawrence, 'Foreword to Sons and Lovers', *The Letters of D H Lawrence*
31 Letter 157
32 Letter 158
33 Letter 161
34 Letter 193
35 *ibid*
36 Letter 157
37 Letter 164
38 *ibid*
39 *ibid*
40 *ibid*
41 *ibid*
42 *ibid*
43 Letter 166
44 Letter 169
45 *ibid*

7 Conjugal/Maternal

1 Letter 173
2 Letter 170
3 Letter 173
4 *ibid*
5 *ibid*
6 Letter 133
7 Letter 219
8 Letter 315
9 Letter 344
10 Letter 350a
11 Letter to Anthon van Rappard, March, 1883
12 Letter 288
13 Albert J Lubin, *Stranger on the Earth*
14 Kenneth Wilkie, *The Van Gogh Assignment*
15 Letter 192
16 Marc Edo Tralbaut, *Vincent van Gogh*
17 *ibid*
18 Letter 190
19 Albert J Lubin, *Stranger on the Earth*
20 Letter 198
21 Letter 358
22 Albert J Lubin, *Stranger on the Earth*
23 Letter 262
24 Letter 180
25 Letter 189
26 Letter 242
27 John Berger, 'The Production of the World', *The White Bird*
28 Letter 238
29 Giacomo Leopardi, *Zibaldone*, 259–60 (see Berger's 'Leopardi' in *The White Bird*)
30 Letter 326
31 *ibid*
32 Letter 442
33 Letter 199
34 Letter 185
35 Letter 195
36 Letter 220
37 Letter 319
38 Letter 201
39 *ibid*
40 *ibid*
41 Letter 204
42 Letter 326
43 Letter 204
44 Letter 207

45 Letter 208
46 *ibid*
47 Letter 210
48 Letter 213
49 Letter 212
50 *ibid*
51 Letter 210
52 Letter 213
53 *ibid*
54 Albert J Lubin, *Stranger on the Earth*
55 Letter 334
56 Letter 242
57 *ibid*
58 Letter 218
59 Letter 266
60 Letter 317
61 Letter 284
62 Letter 266
63 *ibid*
64 Letter 273
65 Letter 324
66 Letter 204

8   Art of Darkness

1 Letter 325
2 Letter 411
3 Letter 328
4 Letter 334
5 Letter 331
6 Letter 328
7 Letter 339
8 Letter 333
9 *ibid*
10 Letter 343
11 Letter 339
12 Letter 340
13 *ibid*
14 *ibid*
15 Letter 427
16 Letter 345
17 Ernst Pawels, *The Nightmare of Reason*
18 Letter 379
19 Letter 362
20 Letter 345a
21 Letter 346

22 See Ernst Pawels, *The Nightmare of Reason*
23 Letter 187
24 Letter to Anthon van Rappard, April, 1884
25 Letter 418
26 Letter 377
27 *ibid*
28 Letter 375
29 Letter 378
30 Marc Edo Tralbaut, *Vincent van Gogh*
31 *ibid*
32 Ian Dunlop, *Van Gogh*
33 Albert J Lubin, *Stranger on the Earth*
34 Viktor Frankl, an article in *Phenomenology, Pure and Applied*, ed Erwin Straus, Duquesne, 1964
35 Meyer Shapiro, *Van Gogh*
36 Letter 429
37 Letter 404
38 Letter 408
39 Letter 451
40 Letter 431
41 Letter 413
42 *ibid*
43 John Berger, 'The Place of Painting', *The White Bird*

9 The Harlot's Smile

1 Letter 437
2 Letter 440
3 Letter 442
4 *ibid*
5 See Lubin, *Stranger on the Earth*
6 Letter 442
7 Marc Edo Tralbaut, *Vincent van Gogh*
8 *ibid*
9 Albert J Lubin, *Stranger on the Earth*
10 Letter 452
11 Letter 453

10 Paris is Paris

1 Letter 444
2 Letter 459
3 Ian Dunlop, *Van Gogh*
4 Albert J Lubin, *Stranger on the Earth*
5 Johanna van Gogh-Bonger, 'Memoir of Vincent van Gogh'

6 Letter to Wilhelmina van Gogh, October, 1888
7 Letter 462
8 Marc Edo Tralbaut, *Vincent van Gogh*
9 Letter 462
10 *ibid*
11 Letter 591
12 Letter to Wilhelmina van Gogh, Summer, 1887
13 Ian Dunlop, *Van Gogh*

11 Closer to the Sun

1 Letter to Wilhelmina van Gogh, Summer, 1887
2 Letter 489
3 Letter 490
4 D H Lawrence, preface to *Max Havelaar* (reprinted in *Phoenix*, Vol II)
5 J C Powys, *In Defence of Sensuality*
6 Letter 506
7 Theo to his sister Wil, 24–26 February, 1888
8 Letter to Emile Bernard, second half of May, 1888
9 Ian Dunlop, *Van Gogh*
10 Letter 470
11 Letter to Wilhelmina van Gogh, Summer, 1887
12 Letter to Emile Bernard, September, 1888
13 Letter 581
14 Letter 507
15 Letter 513
16 D H Lawrence, 'Introduction to These Paintings', *Phoenix*, Vol I
17 Letter 520
18 Meyer Shapiro, *Van Gogh*
19 *ibid*
20 Letter to Emile Bernard, second half of July, 1888
21 D H Lawrence, letter to Katherine Mansfield, 20 December, 1915
22 Letter to Emile Bernard, second half of July, 1888
23 Letter 531
24 Letter 499
25 Letter 521
26 Letter 514
27 Letter 522
28 Letter 520
29 Meyer Shapiro, *Van Gogh*
30 Letter 519
31 Rainer Maria Rilke, *Letters on Cézanne*
32 Letter to Wilhelmina van Gogh, September, 1888
33 Albert J Lubin, *Stranger on the Earth*
34 Letter 583

35 Letter to Emile Bernard, August, 1888
36 Meyer Shapiro, *Van Gogh*
37 *ibid*
38 Letter 542
39 Letter to Emile Bernard, August, 1888
40 *ibid*
41 Letter to Emile Bernard, May, 1888
42 *ibid*
43 Letter 556
44 Letter 554
45 Letter to Emile Bernard, October, 1888
46 Letter 563
47 Letter 564
48 Albert J Lubin, *Stranger on the Earth*
49 Marc Edo Tralbaut, *Vincent van Gogh*
50 Ian Dunlop, *Van Gogh*

12 Asylum

1   D H Lawrence, 'Return to Bestwood', *Phoenix*, Vol II
2   Letter 567
3   Letter 571
4   Letter 574
5   *ibid*
6   Marc Edo Tralbaut, *Vincent van Gogh*
7   Letter 579
8   *ibid*
9   Letter 581
10 Rainer Maria Rilke, *Letters on Cézanne*
11 Letter 592
12 *ibid*
13 *ibid*
14 Letter 604
15 Letter 589
16 Marc Edo Tralbaut, *Vincent van Gogh*
17 Albert J Lubin, *Stranger on the Earth*
18 Meyer Shapiro, *Van Gogh*
19 Letter 604
20 *ibid*
21 Letter 543
22 Letter 506
23 Letter 648
24 Ian Dunlop, *Van Gogh*
25 Letter 627
26 Letter 629a

27   Charles Mauron, 'Vincent et Theo', *L'Arc*, Cahiers
     Mediterranéens, No 8 (Autumn, 1959)
28   Letter 609

13 Black Light

1   Johanna van Gogh–Bonger, 'Memoir of Vincent van Gogh'
2   *ibid*
3   Letter to Wilhelmina van Gogh, June 1890
4   Letter 635
5   Theo van Gogh, letter to Vincent, 30 June, 1890
6   Letter 649
7   Letter 650
8   Letter 651
9   Marc Edo Tralbaut, *Vincent van Gogh*
10 *ibid*
11 Letter 133

POSTCRIPT

1   Letter 652

SELECT BIBLIOGRAPHY

1

Vincent van Gogh, *The Complete Letters*, London, Thames and
   Hudson, 1978
— — *The Letters of Vincent van Gogh*, selected, edited, and introduced
   by Mark Roskill, London, Collins, 1963
— — *Vincent by Himself*, edited Bruce Bernard, London, Orbis
   Publishing, 1985

2   Books about van Gogh or studies of his work

Pierre Cabanne, *Van Gogh*, London, Thames and Hudson, 1969
Ian Dunlop, *Van Gogh*, London, Weidenfeld and Nicolson, 1974
Frank Elgar, *Van Gogh*, London, Thames and Hudson, 1969
A M & Renilde Hammacher, *Van Gogh*, New York, Macmillan, 1969
Albert J Lubin, *Stranger on the Earth*, London, Paladin, 1975
W Muensterberger, *Vincent van Gogh*, London, Falcon Press, 1947
Griselda Pollock & Fred Orton, *Vincent van Gogh: Artist of his Time*,
   Oxford, Phaidon Press, 1978.
Mark Roskill, *Van Gogh, Gauguin and the Impressionist Circle*, London,
   Thames and Hudson, 1970
Meyer Shapiro, *Van Gogh*, New York, Harry Abrams, 1950
Marc Edo Tralbaut, *Vincent van Gogh*, Viking Press, New York, 1969
Bogomila Welsh-Ovcharov (ed), *Van Gogh in Perspective*, New Jersey,
   Prentice Hall, 1974
Kenneth Wilkie, *The Van Gogh Assignment*, London, Paddington Press,
   1978
Martin Bailey, *Young Vincent*, London, Allison & Busby, 1990

3   Books of general reference

John Berger, *The White Bird*, London, Hogarth Press, 1988
Leonard Baskin, *Iconologia*, London, Deutsch, 1988
Wolf-Dieter Dube, *The Expressionists*, London, Thames and Hudson, 1974
Paul Gauguin, *The Intimate Journals*, (ed) Van Wyck Brooks, Boston, Routledge and Kegan Paul, 1985
Daniel Guérin (ed), *The Writings of a Savage*, New York, Viking, 1978
Eric Hobsbawm, *The Age of Capital*, London, Weidenfeld, 1975
Michel-Claude Jalard, *Post-Impressionism*, London, Heron Books, 1968
E R Meijer, *Rembrandt*, London, Oldbourne Press, 1960
F Novotnny, *Toulouse Lautrec*, London, Phaidon Press, 1969
Yann le Pichon, *Gauguin: Life, art, inspiration*, New York, Harry Abrams, 1987
Otto Rank, *Art and Artist*, New York, Agathon Press, 1968
Herbert Read, *The Meaning of Art*, London, Faber and Faber, 1931
Rainer Maria Rilke, *Letters to Cézanne*, (ed) Clara Rilke, London, Cape, 1988
Meyer Shapiro, *Modern Art: 19th & 20th Centuries. Selected Papers*, New York, Braziller, 1978
Anthony Storr, *The Dynamics of Creation*, London, Secker and Warburg, 1972
Graham Swift, *Waterland*, London, Heinemann, 1983
Belinda Thomson, *Gauguin*, London, Thames and Hudson, 1987

Index

INDEX

INDEX

INDEX